OLD TESTAMENT FORMULAS ABOUT DEATH

by

Karl-Johan Illman

ÅBO AKADEMI
ÅBO 1979

236.1
I ℓ 6

8201186

ISBN-951-648-544-8
ISSN-0356-7109

Stiftelsens för Åbo Akademi
offset- och kopieringscentral 1979

PREFACE

One major problem I was confronted with in my dissertation *Leitwort - Tendenz - Synthese. Programm und Praxis in der Exegese Martin Bubers* was how to come to grips with the phenomenon of repetition in the Hebrew Bible. Since there are repetitions of very different types, I had no hope of being able to 'solve' the problem from any uniform perspective like that of Buber. From the outset I had to restrict myself to partial aspects regarding material as well as method. I trust, however, that entering formula criticism I have been able to tackle some important ways of repetition, which I now leave to my readers to decide.

This book evolved out of three lectures I gave as a guest at the Swedish Theological Institute in Jerusalem in October 1977. Another opportunity to present my findings came when I was invited to lecture to the Swedish Exegetical Society in Uppsala in September 1978. The discussions which followed greatly stimulated and enhanced the progress of my work, something for which I here wish to express my profound gratitude.

During my work I had the advantage and pleasure of having three students, now pastors Kari Aalto, Ralf Sandin and Ismo Seivästö, writing their degree theses on related themes. I benefited from repeated discussions with Mr. Nils Martola, assistant teacher at my institution, who also helped me in the proof reading. Mr. Christopher Grapes, lecturer in English at the Åbo Academy School of Economics, kindly took the trouble to correct the English of my typescript. I also thank the Research Institute of the Åbo Akademi Foundation for adopting my book in its series of publications and for a substantial grant connected with its preparation.

Finally I wish to thank my wife, Siw Illman, who with profound insight and great endurance has not only cared for the wellbeing of myself and our family but also persistently encouraged me in my undertaking. She and our children Mika, Hanna, Sara and Ruth have been my firm anchorage in life to make it possible to work on the theme of death.

Åbo Academy

September 1979   *Karl-Johan Illman*

CONTENTS

PREFACE 7

1. INTRODUCTION 15

2. RECOGNIZING DEATH 20
   2.1. Before Death 20
      2.1.1. *'anokî met* 20
      2.1.2. *b^{e}ṭæræm 'amût* 21
      2.1.3. *lipnê môtô* 21
      2.1.4. Related phrases 22
   2.2. Impending Death 23
      2.2.1. *qrb – yamîm lamût* 23
      2.2.2. *ḥalā – lamût* 24
   2.3. Wishing to die 25
      2.3.1. *wăyyiš'ăl 'æt năpšô lamût* 25
      2.3.2. *mî yitten mût* plus suffix 26
      2.3.3. *tamot năpšî* 26
      2.3.4. Related phrases 27
   2.4. Realizing Death 27
      2.4.1. *w^{e}hinnē met* 27
      2.4.2. *w^{e}hinnē nopel met* 28
   2.5. Recognition of Death 29
      2.5.1. *šamă' kî met* 29
      2.5.2. *ra'ā . . . kî met* 30
      2.5.3. *higgîd/bîn/yadă' . . . kî met* 31
   2.6. Repeated phrases 32
   2.7. Conclusions 34

10

3. DEATH AND BURIAL 37
  3.1. The death-burial pattern 37
    3.1.1. *wăyyamât* ... *wăyyiqqaber* 37
  3.2. Variations of the death-burial pattern 39
    3.2.1. *wăyyamât* ... *wăyyiqbᵉruhû* 39
    3.2.2. *wăyyamât* ... *wăyyiqbᵉrû ᵓotô* 40
    3.2.3. *met* ... *wăyyiqbᵉrû ᵓotô* 41
    3.2.4. Characteristics of the death-burial pattern 42
  3.3. Formulaic elements in the death-burial pattern 42
    3.3.1. *wăyyeᵛasep ᵓœl-ᶜămmâw* 43
    3.3.2. *zaqen ûśᵉbăᶜ yamîm* 45
    3.3.3. *bᵉśêbā ṭôbā* 46
    3.3.4. Summary 47
  3.4. Mourning for the dead 48
    3.4.1. Positive use of mourning phrases 48
    3.4.2. Negative use of mourning phrases 50
  3.5. Some special places of death 51
    3.5.1. *mût* ... *šam/šammā* 52
      3.5.1.1. *wăyyamât/wăttamât šam* 52
      3.5.1.2. *yamût/lamût šam/šammā* 53
    3.5.2. Death in the wilderness 55
      3.5.2.1. *met/wăyyamât bămmidbar* 55
      3.5.2.2. *lamût* etc. *bămmidbar* 56
    3.5.3. Summary 57
  3.6. Conclusions 58

4. DEATH MARKING TIME 60
  4.1. Until the death of 60
    4.1.1. *ᶜăd-môt* 60
    4.1.2. *ᶜăd-yôm môtô* 62
  4.2. At the death of 63
    4.2.1. *bᵉmôt* 63
    4.2.2. *bᵉmôtô* 64
  4.3. After the death of 66
    4.3.1. *wăyhî ᵓăhᵃrê môt* 66
    4.3.2. *wᵉᵛăhᵃrê môt* 67

4.3.3. *ăḥᵃrê môt 67
4.3.4. *ăḥᵃrê môtî 68
4.3.5. kă͓šær met 69
4.3.6. Summary 69
4.4. Succession 70
4.4.1. wăyyamàt ... wăyyimlok tăḥtăw 71
4.4.2. wăymîtehû ... wăyyimlok tăḥtăw 73
4.4.3. Summary 75
4.5. Genealogy and age 76
4.5.1. From Adam to Noah 77
4.5.2. From Terah to Job 78
4.5.3. Dying without sons 79
4.6. Conclusions 81

5. CAUSES OF DEATH 82
5.1. Why should you die? 82
5.2. Death because of sin 83
5.2.1. mût baᵉᵈwôn(ô) /bᵉᶜᵈwlô 84
5.2.2. bᵉḥæ·*ô / baᵉᵈwôn(ô) /bᵉᶜăwlô 85
5.2.3. ḥeṭ*/mišpăṭ mawæt 86
5.2.4. Function and Sitz im Leben 88
5.3. Ways of Death 88
5.3.1. mût/mawæt (băm)milḥamā 89
5.3.2. mût băḥæræb 89
5.3.3. mût/hemît barᵈᶜab/băṣṣama*/băddæbær 92
5.3.4. mût băḥæræb – baraᶜab 93
5.3.5. mût băḥæræb – baraᵃab – băddæbær 94
5.4. Conclusions 97

6. DEATH AS CONSEQUENCE. 98
6.1. The qal perfect consecutive 99
6.2. The qal imperfect 103
6.2.1. ... wᵉyamot. 103
6.2.2. môt tamût 104
6.2.3. môt yamût(û) 105
6.2.4. môt namût 106
6.2.5. Conclusions 107
6.3. The negated qal imperfect 107

12

6.3.1. $(w^e)lo^{\scriptsize o}/pæn \ {}^{\flat}amût$ 107

6.3.2. $(w^e)lo^{\scriptsize o} \ tamût$ 108

6.3.3. $(w^e)lo^{\scriptsize o}/pæn/w^{\breve{e}_{\flat}}\breve{a}l \ yamût$ 110

6.3.4. $w^e lo^{\scriptsize o}/pæn/w^{\breve{e}_{\flat}}\breve{a}l \ namût$ 112

6.3.5. $w^e lo^{\scriptsize o}/ (w^e)pæn \ tamûtû/ \ t^e mutûn$ 113

6.3.6. $(w^e)lo^{\scriptsize o} \ yamûtû$ 114

6.3.7. Conclusions 115

6.4. The hif'il perfect consecutive 116

6.5. The hif'il imperfect 117

6.6. The hof'al imperfect 119

6.6.1. $yûm\breve{a}t$ etc. 120

6.6.2. $lo^{\scriptsize o} \ yûm^e tû$ 122

6.6.3. $môt \ yûmat/yûm^e tû$. 122

6.6.4. Conclusions 126

6.7. Threats and laws with $mawæt$ 127

6.8. 'Fall' and 'die' 128

6.9. Trying and denying 129

6.10. Slaying 131

6.10.1. $hikk\bar{a} \ldots mût$ 131

6.10.2. $hikk\bar{a} \ldots hem\hat{i}t$ 132

6.11. Repeated expressions 133

6.12. Summary 137

7. DEATH AND THE NETHER WORLD. 140

7.1. Delivery and rescue 140

7.2. The dead 141

7.2.1. Parallels to met 141

7.2.2. Touching the dead 143

7.2.3. Excursus: 'the dead dog' 145

7.3. The Nether World 145

7.3.1. The gates of death 146

7.3.2. The snares and the toils of death 146

7.3.3. Word pairs with $mawæt$ 149

7.4. The transience of life 151

7.5. Conclusions 152

8. DEATH AND LIFE 154

8.1. "Live and not die" 154

8.2. 'Live' or 'die' 156
8.3. "The living and the dead" 160
8.4. 'Kill' and 'make'/'keep alive' 164
8.5. Choose between 'life' and 'death' 168
8.6. The spheres of 'life' and 'death' 171
8.7. "In life and death"............................... 173
8.8. Two additional notes 175
8.9. Summary 176

9. SUMMARY 178

NOTES 183

ABBREVIATIONS 208

BIBLIOGRAPHY.................................... 209

INDEX OF BIBLICAL REFERENCES 218

OLD TESTAMENT FORMULAS ABOUT DEATH

1. INTRODUCTION

Although there is no lack of scholarly books about the conceptions of death in the Old Testament,[1] L. Wächter may be right in his assertion that this theme in its entirety has not yet been the subject of a comprehensive study.[2] At different times various aspects have aroused the interest of biblical scholarship.[3] However, N.J. Tromp is right, too, when he declares that "a new approach is imperative to justify another study of our theme".[4] For as long as one is not content with putting together, if that were possible, everything that has emerged from, say, a hundred years of biblical scholarship, one has really to point out what perhaps may still be missing or insufficiently understood.

A general characteristic of most of what has been written about death in Old Testament has been, as far as I know, that the interpreter has proceeded rather swiftly to the conceptions, and has not paid much attention to the form or the mode of expression. Here one should not generalize too much of course: there is some discussion about certain formulas in Wächter's standard work, and Tromp starts from the linguistic expressions in his comparative study of Ugaritic and Old Testament conceptions. H. Schultz[5] and H. Schüngel-Straumann[6] have paid considerable attention to the formulations of the pentateuchal laws about capital punishment. But on the whole it seems to be the 'theme', the 'conceptions' and their eternal actuality which so preoccupy scholars that they can hardly afford to dwell on the seemingly trivial matter of form and formulas. This is somewhat astonishing, too, because the general direction in biblical scholarship has for years now been to pay more and more attention to matters of form and modes of expression. However, one has to look in lexical articles and not in monographs in order to read about such things as that the stem *mût* with its derivations occurs a total of a thousand times in the Hebrew Bible[7] and how the pair of opposites, *mût* and *ḥyh,* are combined there.[8] These and other similar observations, however, are more important for the purpose of this study than the often very sweeping formulations about "Death in the Old Testament" found in the more comprehensive works on this subject or in the "Theologies of the Old Testament".[9]

Even a brief look in a concordance shows that the stem *mût* is used in a great many stereotype expressions, repeated phrases or whatever you may prefer to call the phenomenon. This, I should hasten to add, is not an optical error due to the way in which concordances list together identical or similar forms of a stem. The similarities are by no means restricted to the word level but rather extended to the phrase or sentence level and sometimes even to the wider context. I readily admit that it was James Barr's[10] well known battle cry against certain types of word studies, which has guided me on this point. But his book does not prescribe the cure. You could make a *semantic study* of the fields 'die', 'kill', etc. in the manner of Barr and his followers: such are very useful indeed. When, however, I choose instead to ask what the so called *formula criticism* might have to contribute in this particular case, I refer in the first instance to the above mentioned elementary observation about the occurrence of repeated, stereotype expressions. Another reason for looking at the material from this point of view I have found in the present state of affairs within formula criticism as a methodological tool.

Formulas and formulaic phrases have been well known phenomena not only in classical but also in biblical studies for a long time. Attempts to formulate a theory of formula, however, are comparatively recent. The most influential theory is that of M. Parry,[11] which was later developed by A.B. Lord[12] and applied to biblical poetry by R.C. Culley.[13] One should not, however, forget I. Landes' dissertation regarding the formulas within "ordinary speech" in the Old Testament. According to her definition the essence of a formula is what[14] "einer häufig vorkommenden Situation den ihr gemässen Ausdruck verleiht, und — entsprechend häufig angewendet — zum stehenden Ausdruck wird". According to her a formula can be a word group or a single word. She supposes that most of the formulas have been coined in what she calls "ordinary speech" ('Umgangssprache') and have found their way from there into poetry, cultic language, narrative and historical works. She does not exclude the possibility, however, that formulas can have been created within these literary genres. Another general definition of formula can be found in W. Richter's programmatic study *Exegese als Literaturwissenschaft.* Formulas are here "formal gleichgebaute Wortverbindungen oder Wortgruppen". Richter makes a distinction between "geprägte Wendung", when such a word combination is contained in only *one* literary work, and a "Formel", which can be found in *several* independent works or sources.[15]

While Lande and Richter thus have given rather general and wide definitions of formulas, Culley works with a far more special and narrow definition. Following Parry and Lord he applies his definition to "oral poetry", his definition running as follows: "A formula in oral poetry is a repeated group of words the length of which corresponds to the divisions in the poetic structure ...".[16]

One difficulty with this definition, apart from the fact that it is restricted to poetry only, is that there is no fixed metrical system in the Hebrew Bible. In this respect the situation in, say, Homerical studies is quite different. Thus J.B. Hainsworth has been able to establish quite precise criteria for the flexibility of a Homeric formula. An important factor from our point of view, however, is that he admits that it is necessary to start from a very general definition, if you wish to use the term 'formula' in various fields of literature:

> In any field the essence of a formula is repetition. In literature, as opposed to the sciences, the repetition is normally of the matter and not of its arrangement. This is a convenient practice, for it permits the application of the term 'formula' to be confined to the poet's diction with the least departure from normal usage, and leaves the terms 'pattern' and 'theme' free to be used for repetitions respectively in the arrangement of the words and the subject-matter of the poems. The genus of formula is thus a 'repeated word-group'.[17]

Now there is another type of word combination which may also be regarded as a formula, namely the word pair.[18] Such have been traced in Northwest Semitic texts by H.L. Ginsberg, U. Cassuto and others and in biblical texts by W. Whallon[19] and W. Watters.[20] The word pairs found in poetical texts play a decisive role in forming parallel lines (hemistichs), and Whallon, although aware of the fact that word pairs do occur in prose,[21] tends to restrict the term only to their use in poetry. In this respect he is followed by Watters, who wholly disregards the occurrence of word pairs in prose.[22] The primary reason for this may be that he regards such pairs, where one word follows immediately after the other, as formulaic phrases. For him the use of word pairs in parallel lines is the main criterion for what should be called poetry in the Hebrew Bible.[23]

The restriction of formulas to poetry by Culley, Whallon and Watters, on the one hand, and the concentration on prose by Richter and others have led to the present situation, where a synthesis within formula criticism is urgently called for. What we need is a definition of the term formula, which can be used in all the different genres of prose and poetry in the Old Testament. The first step should then obviously be to return to the general definitions of Richter and Hainsworth: *a formula is a repeated word group or a repeated word combination.*

Such a general definition, however, is beset with severe difficulties. Since it is obvious that the repetition of formulas does not occur in exactly the same form, how great flexibility can then be tolerated? Culley and, following him, Watters allow for the following variations: "The addition or omission of the definite article and other elements such as the final pronominal suffixes and the $(-\bar{a})$ ending on the imperative and the first person of the imperfect..., changes of aspect, person, gender, and number". He uses the term *"formulaic phrase"* only about "phrases in which substitution in some major lexical item occurs".[24] These restrictions seem to me not only acceptable but also rather useful. I shall also adopt the distinction made by Richter, using the term formula only for repeated phrases or word pairs in works independent of each other, as far as such an independence can be established or assumed; when the repetition occurs within the same work I shall speak about a *repeated phrase,* when it can be considered as a borrowing, quotation or imitation from another I shall speak about a *coined phrase.*

But still one could ask whether these criteria suffice in determining the formula. It is easy to imagine a repetition which is due simply to the fact that it is an idiomatic expression for something. It would be a misuse of the term formula if this were to cover every idiomatic expression which happens to be repeated in the Hebrew Bible, something that inevitably would follow from a very general definition like that of Richter. He certainly assumes[25] that formulas also have functions but this is not a prerequisite for the identification of them, which is done on formal grounds only. Sometimes it is obvious that a formula belongs to a certain genre.[26] On the other hand it seems impossible to make it a general criterion, that a formula should have a distinct function within a given genre. I shall therefore introduce what I shall regard as a tentative definition: *a formula has a distinct function within the larger context.* Repeated phrases which do not have such a function I shall regard as idioms or as formulas which have lost their original function.[27]

Now I shall finally return to the material chosen for this treatise. I shall follow the stem *mût* with its various derivations in the various word combinations where it occurs. This stem is the constant element in all the repeated phrases I shall discuss. It has one big advantage: it is distributed rather evenly throughout the entire Hebrew Bible, i.e., it is represented in all the main genres of Old Testament literature. Looking for formulas in this way does, however, impose rather strict limitations in other respects: I shall not deal with all kinds of formulas occurring within a certain context, nor shall I discuss the occurrence of formulas in certain genres or types of literature. This has, in my opinion, already been done to a fairly large extent by some of the scholars mentioned above. What I shall try to do is to make a cross examination from the horizon of one particular stem. What kind of formulas or repeated phrases does this stem form in the context where it occurs? If this should contribute to an understanding of the characteristics of the Hebrew formula, such as it is found in the Bible, one of my aims will have been achieved. Since there are many books on the conceptions of death, I shall concentrate on the mode of expression, that is *how* the Old Testament speaks about death. But since form and content, expression and conception cannot easily be separated from each other in any field of literature, I expect that this study will shed some light upon the meaning of the stem *mût* in its various derivations and uses. If so the other aim of my investigation will have been reached, too.

2. RECOGNIZING DEATH

In this chapter I intend to deal with expressions about impending death, on the one hand, but also about the realization that death has already occurred, on the other. Formally we have a series of more or less similar expressions, but in some cases with quite different phrases, too.

2.1. Before Death

I shall begin with some phrases found chiefly in the patriarchal narratives, which have in common that they introduce the last wish or the will of the dying person. Here I shall deal with three formally distinct phrases.

2.1.1. *ʾanokî̂ met*

This expression is a nominal clause consisting of the personal pronoun *ʾanokî̂* as a subject and the qal active participle as its predicate. It occurs in this short form in Gen 50,24 in the mouth of Joseph. In Gen 48,21 and 50,5 the same expression in the mouth of Jacob is preceded by *hinnē*, "look" and in Deut 4,22 in the mouth of Moses preceded by *kî̂*, "for".[28] The common element in all instances is thus *anokî̂ met*, a phrase distinct in form and content, although in three cases extended by the initial *hinnē* or *kî̂*. Three instances fall within the JE stratum of the patriarchal narrative, whereas the fourth belongs to D.[29]

   The function of this phrase seems to be clear enough: it marks the departure of the head of the family or the leader and introduces his last wish or will: that God bring the Israelites back to the promised land (Gen 48,21), that the body of the deceased be buried in the family grave (Gen 50,5.24);

and that the Israelites proceed to enter Canaan (Deut 4,22). Although the speech of Moses is not of the same genre as those of the patriarchs, it too contains a testament with exhortations to do what should be done after the death of the leader. It could therefore be said to introduce what has been called "testamentarische Verfügungen".[30]

2.1.2. $b^e t \alpha r \alpha m$ 'amût

This phrase, consisting of the adverbial $b^e t \alpha r \alpha m$ and the qal imperfect 1st person sing form of mût, occurs three times in the Hebrew Bible. In Gen 27,4 it marks the time when Isaac wishes to give his blessing to his elder son. It is used again by Jacob, when he expresses his intention to go down to Egypt to see Joseph (Gen 45,28). Finally it occurs in Prov 30,7, where two things are asked for, these are then mentioned in the following verse: "Put fraud and lying far from me; give me neither poverty nor wealth . . .".[31]

Two of the three instances occur within the patriarchal narratives, which corresponds to the distribution of the phrase ᵃ ᵃnokî met discussed above. However, the testamental connection does not seem to be the same here. It is true, that the blessing of Gen 27,4 is rather close to the last will of Gen 48,21, for example. But in Gen 45,28 the phrase does not have a testamental connection at all. Instead the phrase is connected with ᶜôd-yôsep b^enî hay, "my son Joseph is still alive (cf. below 8.3.). Jacob's journey can be viewed as a preliminary move which precedes his final departure, to which his blessings and last will belong. In Prov 30,7 we have the wish of the wise man to get his share of a life without things he regards as evil. We can conclude, therefore, that although ᵃnokî met and $b^e t \alpha r \alpha m$ ᵃamût are used in the patriarchal narratives in similar ways, the latter phrase seems to be connected with the last wish of the dying person himself rather than with his last will concerning those left behind.

2.1.3. lipnê môtô

When Rebecca retells Isaac's wish to bless his firstborn, she uses the expression lipnê môtî (Gen 27,7) instead of $b^e t \alpha r \alpha m$ ᵃamût (v. 4, cf. above). When she then goes on to instruct Jacob, she refers to the same wish in the form *lipnê môtô* (v. 10). Now *môtî/môtô* are forms of the substantive *mawœt* with the appropriate suffixes, and *lipnê môtî* is apparently equivalent to *bᵉtœrœm ᵓamût*. *lipnê môtô,* on the other hand, occurs again in reference to Jacob's death in Gen 50,16 – which in fact had happened by this time –, to Moses' death in Deut 33,1 and finally to David's death in 1 Chron 22,5. Two out of four instances belong to the patriarchal narratives.[32]

As to its function Gen 27,10 again refers to Isaac's blessing, while Jacob's wish that Joseph may forgive his brothers is expressed in Gen 50,16. In Deut 33,1 the so called blessing of Moses over the tribes is introduced. In 1 Chron 22,5 we are told that David had to make preparations for the building of the temple, since Solomon was still a young man.[31] It follows, then, that the phrase in question twice introduces or refers to a blessing, whereas in Gen 50,16 it has to do with a kind of last will[33] and in 1 Chron 22,5 with the last measures before death. Although the phrase in these two last instances refers to death already being a fact, this does not seem to affect its function. When formulated in the 3rd person the phrase can easily be used about the past, and is not to be restricted in the same way as in the 1st person. So it is perhaps no coincidence that *lipnê môtî* occurs only once.

2.1.4. Related phrases

There are some phrases which are similarly constructed as the above but which do not meet with the qualifications of formulas: either they are not repeated, or they do not employ the stem *mût*, or they do not have a distinct function. They may nevertheless serve as a background of those discussed above. Thus we have threats like *hinnᵉka met* (Gen 20,3) and *ᵓăttā met* (Jer 28,16), both meaning "You shall die". A collective fear of dying is expressed by *kullanû metîm,* "we shall be dead" (Ex 12,33), whereas *wᵉkullanû hăyyôm metîm,* "and all of us dead" (2 Sam 19,7) is an unreal supposition. In 1 Sam 14,43 Jonathan declares his readiness to receive the punishment for his transgression of the king's order: *hinnî ᵓamût.*

In testamental contexts we have some figurative expressions[34] of impending death like: *wᵉšakăbtî ᶜim-ᵃbotăy,* "when I lie down with my fathers" (Gen 47,30 J) and *ᵃnî nœᵃœsap ᵓœlᶜămmî,* "I am about to be gathered to my kin"

(Gen 49,29 P). In Jos 23,14 and 1 Kings 2,2 we meet what is probably a deuteronomistic phrase: $^{3a}nok\hat{\imath}$ $holek$ $b^e d\alpha r\alpha k$ $k\hat{a}l$-$ha^{\gamma}ar\alpha s$, "I am going the way of all the earth".[35] This again can be compared with $b^e t\alpha r\alpha m$ $^{\gamma}elek$ $w^{e \gamma}en\alpha nn\hat{\imath}$, "before I go away and cease to be" (Ps 39,14) and $b^e t\alpha r\alpha m$ $^{\gamma}elek$ $w^e lo^{\gamma \gamma}a\check{s}\hat{u}b$, "before I depart not to return" (Job 10,21). Here, however, we do not have the testamental connection. They are expressions of the universal fate[36] of man. We have a concrete but non-testamental situation in Jer 38,10: $b^e t\alpha r\alpha m$ $yam\hat{u}t$, "before he dies".

It would seem, then, that none of these expressions or phrases can be viewed as formulas in the way as $^{\gamma}anok\hat{\imath}$ met (2.1.1), $b^e t\alpha r\alpha m$ $^{\gamma}am\hat{u}t$ (2.1.2) and $lipn\hat{e}$ $m\hat{o}t\hat{o}$ (2.1.3). These, however, do meet with the required criteria. Their function is to introduce final words or to anticipate them or refer to them in retrospective.

2.2. Impending Death

I shall here discuss another group of two phrases, which are built on the infinitive $lam\hat{u}t$ preceded by a finite form of another verb. They too point to the future.

2.2.1. qrb – $yam\hat{\imath}m$ – $lam\hat{u}t$

This phrase occurs three times, in two of which it has quite the same form apart from the personal name of the subject: $w\check{a}yyiqr^e b\hat{u}$ $y^e m\hat{e}$-$yi\acute{s}ra^{\gamma}el$ $lam\hat{u}t$, "The time for Israel's death drew near" (Gen 47,29), whereas the dying person in 1 Kings 2,1 is David. The third example differs from these regarding the person, who is not mentioned in the statement, but instead addressed in the 2nd person. The verb qrb is not in ipf consecutivum but in perf: $qar^e b\hat{u}$ $yam\check{e}ka$ $lam\hat{u}t$, "the time of your death is drawing near" (Deut 31,14), the person addressed being Moses. Now I consider this deviation a minor one in comparison with, for example, $^{\gamma}anok\hat{\imath}$ $holek$ $lam\hat{u}t$, "I am at the point of death" (Gen 25,32), which otherwise seems to be the closest in meaning to qrb - $yam\hat{\imath}m$ - $lam\hat{u}t$ and $^{\gamma}anok\hat{\imath}$ met (2.1.1.). Therefore I think we are justified in speaking of a formula consisting of the three common elements: *qrb*, *yamîm* and *lamût*.

Looking at the function of the formulas, we can recognize a certain similarity between Gen 47,29 and 1 Kings 2,1: Jacob calls for Joseph and extracts an oath from him to bury him in the cave of Machpelah and David summons Solomon and obliges him to follow the commandments of God. In Deut 31,14, however, it is the dying Moses who is being commanded by God to summon Joshua to the Tent of Meeting, and then to assemble the people to listen to the law. It is, if not quite the same function, in all cases however a highly similar one: the closest son or the follower is summoned to the presence of the dying head of the family or the leader for his final instructions or his will. Thus the function is much the same as in the formulas discussed above.[37]

2.2.2. *ḥalā – lamût*

The phrase about "mortal illness" is used three times about King Hezekiah (2 Kings 20,1 = Is 38,1 and 2 Chron 32,24). They are identical in formulation apart from the third instance, where we have an addition of the preposition *ʿad* before the infinitive *lamût*. Each time we have the initial time marking expression *bayyamîm hahem*, "in those days". It seems clear that Is 38 is to be considered a slightly shortened version[38] of 2 Kings 20, whereas 2 Chron 32 uses the latter as a source and thereby heavily depends upon its formulation.[39] This would mean, then, that we do not have a formula proper here, but rather a "coined phrase" ("geprägte Wendung"). In 2 Kings 13,14, however, we have an independent formulation regarding the prophet Elisha: *ḥalā ʾæt ḥālyô ʾašær yamût bô*, " . . . fell ill and lay on his death bed". Here the deviations are far too great in form as well as in content — Elisha's illness was in fact fatal — for it to be counted as the same phrase.

The phrase about Hezekiah's illness can be said to have a compositional function: it introduces a chapter about his sickness, his prayer to God (v. 3), the prophet's transmission of God's answer (v. 4-8), the psalm ascribed to King Hezekiah (v. 9-20), and the concluding words by the king and the prophet. If we take in account that the chapter is not uniform, this introductory phrase can be said to play an important role in the composition.[40]

In the case of Elisha the illness marks the end of his activity, but, while Hezekiah had wept over his own impending death (*wăyyebk*, 2 Kings 20,3), it is King Joash, who weeps at the death bed of the prophet Elisha (*wăyyebk*, 2 Kings 13,14). Hezekiah's illness was not "unto death": it was a warning, that he was mortal and on his way to death. When Elisha's death occurs, we have the finite form *yamût* instead of the infinitive *lamût*, and then *wăyyamât* (v. 20).

2.3. Wishing to die

In this section I shall discuss some phrases expressing the *wish to die*. They are formally quite different.

2.3.1. *wăyyiš'ăl 'æt năpšô lamût*

This phrase occurs twice in exactly the same form (1 Kings 19,4 and Jon 4,8). Now there are in the respective contexts other similar expressions about Eliah and Jonah. Having withdrawn from their place of activity, both 'sat down' (*wăyyešœb*), Eliah in the shade of a bush, Jonah at a place, where God then caused a bush to grow up and give him shade. Both ask for the same thing, namely that God take their lives: *'attā yhwh qăh năpšî* (1 Kings 19,4) and *wᵉ'attā qăh-na' 'æt-năpšî* (Jon 4,3). The reasons given for this have a certain similarity of form, although they are quite different in meaning: *kî-lo'-ṭôb 'anokî meᵃbotay*, "for I am not better than my fathers" (Eliah), and *kî ṭôb môtî mehăyyay*, "for I should be better death than alive" v. 3 repeated in v. 8 without *kî*.[41] The real, underlying reasons for both prophets' depression are almost the opposite: while Eliah was unsuccessful in his fight against Ahab and Jezebel and had to flee from them, Jonah was in his own mind too successful, having made Niniveh repent and thus saving the city from God's punishment. It is in any case not easy to escape the impression that one of the stories is dependent upon the other, and there should be no doubt about the originality of the Eliah version. The author of the book of Jonah has therefore used it to depict a rather artificial situation with a totally different meaning.[42] Accordingly we do not have a formula proper here but again a coined phrase, which the author of Jonah has borrowed from the story about Eliah. This holds true for the other repetitions and similarities, too. The phrase asking God to take the prophet's life is actually another coined phrase related to the first one, although not containing the stem *mût*, but instead *lqḥ* with God as the subject.[43]

2.3.2. *mî yitten mût* plus suffix

The phrase *mî yitten* is already a formula itself, namely what Lande calls "the unreal wish phrase".[44] Combined with forms of *mût* it occurs twice: *mî yitten mûtenû b^eyád yhwh b^eꜣæræṣ miṣráyim*, "if only we had died by the hand of the Lord in Egypt" (Ex 16,3) and *mî yitten mûtî ꜣᵃnî tăḥtǽka*, "if only I had died instead of you" (2 Sam 19,1). Although the situations are quite different – the Israelites complaining in the wilderness of Sin and King David bewailing his son, Absalom – we could speak of laments as a common denominator in both instances. One should therefore not hesitate to regard this extended phrase as a formula expressing, as it does, an unreal wish to die.

2.3.3. *tamot nǎpšî*

Here we have another two instances where the contexts again differ quite strongly from each other. Numb 23,10 reads *tamot nǎpšî môt y^ešarîm*, "may I die the death of the upright" at the end of Balaam's first *mašal* on Israel.[45] Judg 16,30 cites Samson's last words: *tamôt nǎpšî ꜥim-p^elištîm*, "let me die with the Philistines". This is not a wish concerning his death in a distant future, but an expression of his intention to take his enemies with him in his death,[46] which he himself immediately brings about. It could reasonably be asked, whether *tamôt nǎpšî* should be regarded a formula then, because it can be used in such different connections. Is it not rather an idiom expressing the wish to die quite apart from any specific situation and without any specific function? On the other hand, we have here just as in the other cases too small a number of cases to allow any far reaching distinctions about function and meaning. However, we can count it among three different repeated phrases expressing the wish to die.

2.3.4. Related phrases

There are a few phrases which contain the combination *năpšô lamût* as an element common to the foregoing phrases. It is preceded by different verbs:

Judg 5,18 . . . *herep năpšô lamût* "(the people of Zebulun) risked their lives";

Judg 16,16 *wăttiqṣár năpšô lamût,* "she wearied him to death"; cf.

Is 53,12 *hœˁᵃrā lămmawœt năpšô,* "for he exposed himself to death";

It is obvious that Is 53,12 although different in form, is closer in meaning to Judg 5,18 than Judg 16,16 is: here the subject is not identical with the object as in the two other cases. It is also clear that we cannot regard these phrases as formulaic by virtue of the substitution of one major element in otherwise similar phrases. This does not pertain to Judg 5,18 and Is 53,12 either, although they come close to this definition. The only thing than can be positively stated is that the word combination is connected in different ways with different verbs, thus forming phrases with quite different meanings.

2.4. Realizing Death

Now I shall proceed to phrases which express a recognition that death has already occurred. They have in common the qal perf form *met* or, in some cases the participle *met*. The qal form is of course used about many different persons identified by name or otherwise. But I would not regard such expressions as formulaic, since they are the simplest way of telling that someone has died. Whether phrases where this same *met* is preceded by *hinnē* or *kî* and a cognitive verb should be regarded as formulaic, is a question to which I shall return below.

2.4.1. *wᵉhinnē met* . . .

In 2 Sam 4,10 David tells how in Ziklag he had killed the man who told him (*hămmăggîd lî leʾmor*) that Saul was dead (*hinnē-met šaʾûl*). The information is thus expressed through two cognitive verbs, whereupon the formula follows as direct discourse. In 1 Kings 3,21, however, the formula occurs within a longer discourse without the corresponding verbs. The woman whose child had been exchanged recognizes that the child she had got instead was dead (*wᵉhinnē met*).

In 2 Kings 4,32 the prophet Elisha upon returning to Shunem recognizes that the boy whose birth he had foretold (v. 16-17) had now died: *wᵉhinnē hănnă'ɐr met* . . . When we finally turn to Ez 18,18, we meet the phrase once more with an explanation of the possible cause of death: ". . . has died because of his iniquity" (*bă'ᵃwônô*).

The phrase is common to all these instances and is used each time about a person whose death is recognized but each time in different contexts: in 2 Sam 4,10 in direct discourse within another quotation, in 1 Kings 3,21 within a simple quotation, in 2 Kings 4,32 as a narrated event and in Ez 18,18 in a long didactic discourse.[47] This difference does not, however, mean that the phrase as such has a different meaning each time. It expresses the recognition that death in certain cases has taken place: once stated by someone other than the speaker, once by the speaker himself, once recognized by the hero of the story, and once referred to in a hypothetical question as to the cause of death. It is obviously an idiom, whether it should be regarded as formula depends again on the requirements of function. Here there does not seem to be such a distinct function within a certain context.

2.4.2. *wᵉhinnē nopel met*

In Judg 3,25 and 4,22 we have a combination of the two participles *nopel* and *met* preceded by *wᵉhinnē*. King Eglon of Moab after he had been assassinated by Ehud was found dead by his servants: "and there was their master lying dead on the floor" (Judg 3,25). The same phrase is used about Sisera, who was killed by Jael and found dead by Barak: "and there was Sisera lying dead" (Judg 4,22). Since the phrase is used both times about a foreign ruler who was assassinated by the Israelites, it is highly probable that it was formulated by the same author or redactor.[48] This would mean that we do not have a formula proper here but rather a coined phrase or a simple repetition. Compared with the phrase *wᵉhinnē met* above, what seems to be stressed here is not the fact that death has occurred (perf), but rather the 'lying dead' (part). The persons in question were actually found dead shortly after they had been killed. There is a moment of surprise too: Eglon and Sisera were surely looked for, but those who found them did not know about their fate and thus did not expect to find them dead. But, according to the finders' status as servants or enemy, this surprise was in the first case a disaster, in the other a happy event.

2.5. Recognition of Death

Here I shall turn to the phrase *kî̂ met* in subordinate clauses. We have the word combination in some main clauses too, but there are often one or several other words inserted between *kî̂*, 'for', and the perfect *met*. There does not seem to be any formulaic use of this word combination, and its meaning is altogether different from those found in subordinate clauses.[49] As for these again, there are several different verbs in the respective guiding clauses, but they have in common that they are cognitive: *ra'ā*, 'see', *šamā̆ᶜ*, 'hear', and a few instances with *higgîd*, 'tell', *bîn*, 'realize' and *yadā̆ᶜ*, 'know'. I shall divide the material according to these verbs.

2.5.1. *šamā̆ᶜ ... kî̂ met ...*

In Sam 25,39 we have the simple sentence *wăyyišmă̂ dawid kî̂ met nabal*, "David heard that Nabal was dead". Turning to 2 Sam 4,1 the name of the subject of *wăyyišmă̂ᶜ* should read "Saul's son, Ishboseth"[50] and its object being Abner, the sentence is, however, otherwise quite similarly constructed. In 2 Sam 11,26 we read *wăttišmă̂ᶜ 'ešæt 'ûriyyā kî̂-met 'ûriyyā 'îšah*, "When Uriah's wife heard that her husband was dead . . .". Apart from the repetitive style this sentence, too, is quite simple: as in the other examples the name of the dead person follows immediately after the phrase. As to the subject of the cognitive *šamă̆ᶜ* it is here not mentioned by its proper name (Bathsheba). In 1 Kings 11,21 the Edomite adversary of David, Hadad, "heard in Egypt that David rested with his forefathers and that his commander-in-chief Joab was also dead" (*wᵉkî̂-met yô'ab šăr-hăṣṣaba'*). Here the information about Davids death is expressed by a phrase to be discussed in another connection (below 3.1.1.) whereas Joab's death is reported by means of the present phrase paratactically connected with the former. Finally, in 1 Kings 21,16, we read about Naboth's death: *wǎyhî kišmoáʿ ʾǎhʾab kî met nabôt,* "When Ahab heard about Naboth's death . . .". The guiding clause is constructed differently, but the phrase is again followed by the proper name of the dead person. This, then, is a common feature of all five instances discussed here.

Considering the function of the phrase together with the guiding clause, we can view them as introducing a *reaction* upon the death thus reported. Although the death is murder in all cases except 1 Sam 25,39, this fact is not explicitly stated. It is only the fact of death that is reported. The sentences do not rest in themselves either, but are rather introductory; all of them can be translated: "When . . . heard . . . that . . . was dead . . . he/she . . .". This is easily seen in 1 Kings 21,16, but it also holds true in the other cases, where we have ipf consecutivum or perf of the guiding verb *šamǎʿ.* Thus the death reported leads to further action of the hearer, who – except for Uriah's wife – is an adversary to the dead, and for whom the death accordingly is welcome.

2.5.2. *ra•ā . . . kî met . . .*

If we follow the masoretic text of Gen 50,15 Joseph's brothers "saw (*wǎyyir•û*) that their father was dead".[51] A similar phrase is used about Abimelech in Judg 9,55. The subject of the recognition (*wǎyyir•û*) is here the collective *ʾîš yiśra•el,* "the Israelites". Interestingly enough both these statements are followed by similar sentences: *wᵉhašeb yašîb lanû •et kāl-hara·ā •ašœr gamǎlnû •otô* (Gen 50,15b); *wǎyyašœb ·ᵉlohîm •et ra·ǎt •ᵃbîmœlœk •ašœr ·asā lᵉ·abîw* (Judg 9,56).

It is a question of revenge: in Gen 50,15 Joseph's brothers fear the revenge that Joseph may take after their father's death, whereas in Judg 9,56 it is said, that God thus took revenge for what Abimelech had done to his father Gideon. It may be pure coincidence that recognizing death in both instances is followed by these statements about revenge. And they are in fact quite different. In the first[52] instance we have the fear of revenge expressed, in the second[53] death itself was considered to be revenge.

If we turn to 1 Sam 17,51 it is the Philistines who saw (*wǎyyir'û*) that their hero Goliath was dead, whereupon they fled and were persecuted by the Israelites. This is not strictly speaking revenge, but rather the natural outcome of the duel between David and Goliath. In 1 Sam 31,5 (= 1 Chron 10,5) Saul's armour-bearer realizes (*wǎyyǎr'*) that Saul is dead, and thereupon takes his own life. The recognition of the fate of Saul and his sons is expressed in plur in 1 Sam 31,7 (= 1 Chron 10,7): *wǎyyir'û . . . w^e kî metû . . .* But here we do not have the same strictly formulated expression any more. To this phraseological complex we have to add 2 Kings 11,1 (= 2 Chron 22,10), where queen Athaljah realizes that her son Ahazjah has been murdered (*ra'^a tā kî met b^e nah*) and proceeds to exterminate the whole royal family except her grandson Joash, who is rescued. This act of violence and usurpation of the throne is not to be considered as revenge either.

The phrases about seeing that one person is dead occur — with the exception of Jacob's death — in contexts of war and violence. The theme of revenge is restricted to two of them. But in neither case does death produce further violence: the reconciliation between Jacob's sons prevails and the Israelites return home after the death of Abimelech. In the other cases, however, the deaths are signals for or parts of further violence: Goliath's death results in a veritable massacre of the Philistines; Saul's suicide follows the fall of his sons and is followed by that of his armour-bearer. The murder of king Ahazjah of Judah is a preamble to the great slaughter of the Judean royal house by the queen mother, herself princess of Samaria and daughter of Ahab and Jezebel.

2.5.3. *higgîd/bîn/yadǎ' . . . kî met*

There are a few cases where the phrase *kî met* is syntactically guided by a cognitive verb other than *šamǎ'* and *ra'ā*. In 2 Sam 4,10 we have already met *higgîd*, but here it was connected with *hinnē met*. In 2 Sam 12,18, however, we have a clear case: the servants of David were afraid "to tell him that the boy was dead" (*l^e hǎggîd lô kî-met hǎyyælœd*). In the following verse we read, that — from their whispering — "David understood that the boy was dead" (*wǎyyabœn dawid kî met hǎyyœlœd*).[54] Finally, in 2 Sam 1,5, David asks the messenger: "How do you know that Saul and Jonathan his son are dead?" (*'êk yadǎ'ta kî-met ša'ûl wîhônatan b^e nô*). The messenger is called *hămmăggîd lô*, "the one who told him". From these examples we can conclude that the phrase *kî met* is syntactically linked to *higgîd, bîn* and *yădắᶜ*. These combinations are not repeated as such,[55] but they can be viewed as variations of the phrases discussed above, where the guiding verb was *šamăᵛ-* or *raᵓā*. In addition there is the fact that the participle *hămmăggîd* plus *lî/lô* is indirectly combined with *hinnē met* (2 Sam 4,10) and *kî met* (2 Sam 1,5). All these phrases are found in 2 Sam, and it is questionable whether they should be regarded as 'formulaic' because of their similarities with the phrases guided by *šamăᵛᶜ* and *raᵓā*. Although many of these have an introductory function and occur in contexts of war and violence, it is not possible to establish one common function for all of them. It might also be asked whether they are not in reality the simplest way of telling that someone has died, and thus to be regarded as 'idiomatic' rather than 'formulaic' phrases. Here the lack of a common function indeed seems to support this interpretation.

2.6. Repeated phrases

Certain repeated phrases occur within the same context and can therefore be regarded not as formulas or coined phrases but repetitions due to the style of the narrator, if not to the composition of material from two 'sources' about the same event.[56] I shall here briefly discuss some such cases:

Gen 42,38 *kî-ᵓahîw met wᵉhûᵓ lᵉbăddô nišᵓar,*	"for his brother is
Gen 44,20 *wᵉᵓahîw met wăyyiwwater hûᵓ lᵉbăddô*	dead and he alone is
lᵉᵓimmô	left / of his mother /"

Whereas Gen 44,20 is generally attributed to 'J', there are different opinions about 42,38, whether it should be regarded as the conclusion of an 'E' account (Speiser) or the inception of the following 'J' narrative (Eissfeldt and others). Be that as it may, it is hardly two independent formulations to be found here, but obviously two variations of the same phrase.

Ex 9,4 *wᵉloᵓ yamût mikkăl-libnê yiśraᵓel dabar,*	"so that nothing shall die of all that belongs to
9,6 *ûmmiqnê bᵉnê yiśraᵓel loᵓ-met ᵓæhad*	the Israelites" / "but of
9,7 *loᵓ-met mimmiqnê yiśraᵓel ᶜăd-œhad*	the livestock of Israel not a beast had died"

Ex 9,4 foretells what 9,6-7 then confirms: the two latter formulations come closer to each other in wording, but all three illustrate the repetitiveness of the narrator's ('J') style.

Lev 10,2 *wăyyamutû lipnê yhwh,* "thus they died at the instance of the Lord" (NJV) "in the presence of the Lord" (NEB)

Lev 16,1 *bᵉqårbatam lipnê-yhwh wăyyamutû* "who died when they drew close to the presence of the Lord" (NJV)

Lev 10,1 also has the phrase *wăyyăqrîbû lipnê yhwh ʾeš zarā,* "and they offered before the Lord alien fire", giving the cause of Nadab's and Abihu's death. Lev 16,1b can be said to give a short summary of Lev 10,1-2 using three of the key words: *qrb, lipnê-yhwh* and *wăyyamutû.* Again there is no reason to think of two distinct authors, but one and the same, who refers the earlier event.

1 Sam 4,11 *ûšᵉnê bᵉnê- eĺ metû ḥåpnî ûpînᵉḥas,* "and Eli's two sons,

4,17 *wᵉgăm-šᵉnê banêka metû ḥåpnî ûpînᵉḥas* Hophni and Pinehas, died" / your two sons/

First the death of Eli's sons is stated in the context of the disastrous battle against the Philistines, and then it is reported in almost the same words by the messenger to their father. If the names of the sons are regarded as an addition in v. 17, the similarity is not so extensive, as MT would suggest, but the repetition of the expression is nevertheless quite obvious.

If we consider the above examples as instances of 'repeated phrases', then one may ask, what is the difference between them and the 'coined phrases'? Strictly speaking a coined phrase is a phrase coined by one author, and then cited or used by one or several other authors. If the same author uses it again in the same context or later in his work, or in his redactional work, it would be a kind of repetition. Richter, however, uses the term "geprägte Wendung" for all those kinds of repetition, and my distinction here would be an attempt to discriminate between quotations and borrowings on the one hand and repetitions on the other. This presupposes, of course, that one is able to determine whether a repetition is made by the same author or borrowed or reused by another. But this is the problem with the distinction between formulas and other repetitions, too. How do we know, whether a phrase is used independently by two or several authors? It would seem, then, that we are right in making these distinctions theoretically, but the biblical material does not always allow, or only occasionally allows, us to demonstrate this in practice.

2.7. Conclusions

I shall here, in retrospect, sum up the findings in this chapter. First we have a group consisting of four formulas:

2.1.1. *ʾanokî met*: Gen 48,21; 50,5.24; Deut 4,22;

2.1.2. *bᵉṭœrœm ʾamût*: Gen 27,4; 45,28; Prov 30,7;

2.1.3. *lipnê môtô/î*: Gen 27,10; 50,16; Deut 33,1; 1 Chron 22,5;

2.2.1. *qrb - yamîm - lamût*: Gen 47,29; Deut 31,14; 1 Kings 2,1.

Out of a total of 14 instances 8 belong to Gen, 3 to Deut and 1 to Prov, 1 Kings and 1 Chron. Although the total number is admittedly a small one, we can speak of a clear concentration to the patriarchal narratives in Gen. More significant, however, is the fact that they all in some degree have to do with what has been called "testamentarische Verfügungen": blessings, last wills or wishes, last deeds. They are used to introduce or announce such last words of Isaac, Jacob, Joseph and Moses, or the last measures of David. These again are mainly concerned with the 'hereafter' of those left behind, except for the cases when burial instructions are given. But sometimes the burial instructions are part of a will to which also reassurances about the survivors' future belong (Gen 50,24f.). Once the formula is used as a motive for making a journey to see the lost son. Nowhere there is a hint of concern about the dying person's own 'after-life', again of course provided that we do not interpret the burial instructions in this manner. But we shall have an opportunity to return to this question below.

Then we have some phrases expressing the wish to die. Whereas *wăyyiš•ăl ʾœt năpšô lamût* (2.3.1.) was considered a coined phrase like *ḥalā lamût* (2.2.2.), there is at least one formula expressing the wish to die, namely *mî yitten mût* plus suffix (2.3.2.). *tamot nǎpšî* (2.3.3.) was regarded as another possibility but here the two occurrences found were not regarded sufficient for deciding whether the phrase belongs to the one category or the other.

In this chapter I have also dealt with some other phrases about *recognition of the fact of death.* They are:

2.4.1. w^e *hinnē met* (perf.): 2 Sam 4,10; 1 Kings 3,21; 2 Kings 4,32;   cf.
Ez 18,18 (cause of death)

2.4.2. w^e *hinnē nopel met* (part.): Judg 3,25 and 4,22;

2.5.1. *šamǎᶜ. . . kî met* (perf.): 1 Sam 25,39; 2 Sam 4,1; 11,26; 1 Kings
11,21; 21,16;

2.5.2. *raᵓā . . . kî met* (perf.): Gen 50,15; Judg 9,55; 1 Sam 17,51 =
1 Chron 10,5; 2 Kings 11,1 = 2 Chron
22,10;

2.5.3. *higgîd/bîn/yadǎᶜ. . . kî met*: 2 Sam 12,18-19; 2 Sam 1,5.

While 2.4.1. could be considered a formula proper, 2.4.2. can be viewed either as a repeated phrase (used by the same author both times) or as a coined phrase (borrowed by another once). It is not easy to choose between these two possibilities but the first alternative seems more probable. As for the remaining cases, 2.5.1. shows the characteristics of a formula and so too, to a lesser degree, does 2.5.2. Here the variations in wording are greater, and the function less tangible. 2.5.3. could be viewed as formulaic phrases, since there are different guiding verbs. Whereas the meaning is always the recognition of someone's death, the ways of death, causes of death, reactions and so on are secondary. Such things are usually expressed by other formulas to be discussed below. As to the functions, we can point to the introductory character in many instances: the recognition of the fact does not exist in isolation, but leads immediately to other actions. But this, to be sure, is a very general characteristic, and there does not seem to be any uniform function. The phrases are idioms used rather freely in a variety of contexts, although in most cases about violent deaths in war or through murder.

Finally I have dealt with some 'related phrases' (2.3.4.) and 'repeated phrases' (2.6.). In the first category I have included some phrases which have certain major lexical items in common with those discussed   immediately before, but nevertheless differed from them quite substantially in form and meaning, and from each other too. To the second category I have assigned phrases which were repeated within a short distance and presumably by the same author. Although they formally meet the criterion for 'coined phrases' in the sense of Richter, I would prefer to call them 'repeated phrases' and reserve the term 'coined phrases' for cases, where one can assume that they are being borrowed by another author and redactor, and the repetition does not occur in the immediate context.

One major difficulty in this chapter has been the scarcity of the occurrences of each phrase. This being the case, it is extremely difficult to decide whether a certain phrase should be assigned to one category or another. Thus the categorization is largely tentative, and caution is called for throughout.

3. DEATH AND BURIAL

Phrases about death often include some data about the place of death and burial, sometimes about ritual mourning, too. This holds true not only when death occurs in a normal way, but also when it occurs under extraordinary circumstances. Such elementary data can be found even when death has not yet occurred, but is predicted in the form of a threat. Not all these data are present in every case, of course, but at least those about 'death' and 'burial' seem to be very tenacious, which I should like to indicate by the heading of this chapter.

3.1. The death – burial pattern

In this section I shall deal with what I shall call the death – burial pattern. It consists of a syntactic combination of two finite forms of the verbs *mût* and *qbr*. Sometimes the second follows immediately efter the first, but usually there are one or several expressions or phrases between them. In some instances they are constructed in the same form, but often they differ from each other formally. According to such similarities and deviations I shall divide my treatment in paragraphs.

3.1.1. *wǎyyamåt ... wǎyyiqqaber*

I shall here deal with the instances where both verbs take the qal impf cons form. In Judg 10,1-5 and 12,7-15 we have two lists about the so called minor judges. They are composed in a highly formulaic language and it is therefore not surprising that death and burial of these judges should be expressed in almost the same way. In five[57] out of six instances the name of the judge follows immediately after *wǎyyamåt* and in all six *wǎyyiqqaber* is followed by mention of the burial place, which is the same as the ancestral home, be it the town or region or both.[58] In three instances we have appositions to the name of the judge also indicating his geographical origins, which thus results in a paronomasia.[59] In only one instance do we have a second apposition giving the family name.[60] We can conclude from this that only both verbs together are to be considered formulaic, whereas mention of the name of the deceased and the burial place and possibly other determinations can be said to belong to the pattern but since they vary as such they do not constitute formulaic elements. Since both lists presumably stem from the same source we have to look for occurrences of the sequence *wǎyyamåt* ... *wǎyyiqqaber* elsewhere before we can speak of a formula proper.

I shall next discuss five instances which are very similar to those found in Judg 10 and 12. First we have 2 Sam 17,23 where we learn about Ahithophel's suicide with the closing phrase "so he died and was buried in his father's grave" (*wǎyyamåt wǎyyiqqaber bᵉqœbœr ᵓabîw*). The burial place is not mentioned by name, but "his father's grave" indicates that it is his ancestral home. In Judg 8,32 the pattern is completed with another phrase to be discussed below.[61] The grave place is mentioned in a fuller but textually uncertain expression: ". . . and was buried in Joash's, his father's grave at Ophra of the Abiezrites".[62] In the following three examples we meet the two verbs in the corresponding feminine forms *wǎttamåt* ... *wǎttiqqaber*, a variation that does not constitute different formulaic elements, since it is only due to the fact that the dead persons happen to be women. Their names are — like the name of Gideon — each time given after the first verb: Deborah (Gen 35,8), Rachel (Gen 35,19) and Miriam (Numb 20,1). The grave place is in the two first instances a certain station "on the way" of their wanderings (Bethel and Bethlehem). The twice repeated *šam* in Numb 20,1 is a reference to Qadesh in the same verse.[63] In Gen 35,8 the grave place has an additional etiological explanation.[64] We can therefore conclude that the pattern observed in Judg 10 and 12 is followed here too: the name of the deceased is given immediately after the first verb except when it is mentioned shortly before (2 Sam 17,23) or divided from the verb through a short word (*šam* in Numb 20,1) and the burial place is indicated if not expressly mentioned by name — which is the case only in Judg 8,32. In the case of the three women death occurs not at home but during wanderings and burial accordingly takes place not at the ancestral home as was the case with the judges and Ahithophel. In all cases the pattern does not seem to stem from a redactor but rather to belong to the narrative itself.[65]

3.2. Variations of the death − burial pattern

I shall here discuss three types of variations of the pattern. They all have in common the qal ipf cons 3rd person plur form of the second verb *qbr*. To this we have the object expressed either through suffix or nota accusativi plus suffix, which assumes the 3rd person sing masc form. The verb *mût* is in two cases constructed as qal ipf cons and in one case as qal perf. These deviations are relatively small in form and few in number, and can thus be regarded as variations within the same pattern, which was discussed above (3.1.).

3.2.1. *wǎyyamât . . . wǎyyiqbᵉruhû*

The shortest of the three examples of this variation is to be found in 2 Kings 13,20: *wǎyyamât ᵊᶜlîša° wǎyyiqbᵉruhû,* "Then Elisha died and they buried him". The striking shortness of this note is obviously due to the fact that the prophet's illness had already been reported (cf. above 2.2.3.) in v. 14 and so was the remarkable visit of King Joash at his deathbed. The pattern usually has a note of where the burial takes place. This is omitted here, nor is there in the context any indication other than that the king left Jerusalem to visit him (v. 14).[66]

When we turn to 1 Sam 25,1 we have by contrast a very full description of Samuel's death: in addition to the common elements we have the phrase "and all Israel came together to mourn for him" between the two key verbs *mût . . . qbr.* The name of Samuel is given as well as the place of burial "in his house in Ramah". We will return to the mourning phrase below (3.4.1.).[67] The third example found in 2 Chron 24,15-16 has a phrase about the good age of the high priest Jehojadah (cf. below 3.3.2.), which however precedes the first verb. Then there follows a note about his actual age (cf. below 4.2.2.) and finally after *wǎyyiqbᵉruhû* the place of burial: "in the city of David with the kings of Israel".[68] The reason for his burial in the royal tombs is given too: "because he had done good in Israel and served God and his house" (v. 16). None of these examples is quite similar, but we shall return to a more detailed comparison after having discussed the two other types of variations first.

3.2.2. *wăyyamåt . . . wăyyiqb^erû ᵓotô*

In Jos 24,29-30 the death of Joshua is formulated within the pattern. To the name Joshua are added two determinations: "son of Nun" about his family and "the servant of the Lord" (*ᶜæbæd yhwh*) about his special relationship to God. Then follows a note about his age as was the case with Jehojadah (3.2.1.). His grave place is somewhat exceptional because coming from the desert he had no ancestral home but rather a conquered patrimony: "within the border of his own patrimony in Timnat-serah . . ." (v. 30). Deut 34,5-6 follows the pattern too, but Moses' death and burial are quite exceptional. In common with Joshua he has the epitet *ᶜæbæd yhwh,* but then follow two notes, one indicating the place of death (*b^eᵓæræṣ mô᾽ab*) and the other the cause of death, "at the command of the Lord" (*ᶜäl-pî yhwh*). The formulation of his burial phrase is in keeping with this strange situation: "he buried him in the valley in the land of Moab near Beth-peor . . .". *wăyyiqbor* (sing) indicates that the Lord himself took care of the burial of His servant. The grave place is a little more specified compared with what was said about his death: "in the valley" (*băggăy*) and "near Beth-peor" (*mûl bêt p^eᶜôr*). But then of course we have the famous statement "but to this day no one knows his burial place".[69]

Two more extensive statements about the death of Abraham and Isaac also fall into this pattern. They are both preceded by notes about the actual age (Abraham 175 years, Gen 25,7; Isaac 180 years, Gen 35,28). Then follow the statements themselves in Gen 25,8-9 and 35,29. In both cases *wăyyamåt* is preceded by another qal ipf cons *wăyyigwăᶜ,* "(he) breathed his last".[70]

Between *mût* and *qbr* we have the phrases about the "good age" and about being "gathered to his kin", to which we shall direct our attention below (3.3.1., 3.3.2. and 3.3.3.). What is new and again unique to both is that those who undertook the burial are mentioned by name and are in both cases the not so friendly pairs of brothers Isaac – Ishmael and Esau – Jacob, who here however come together to bury their fathers. Only in the case of Abraham is the grave place expressly mentioned: "the cave of Machpelah ...". Characteristic of all four statements discussed here is their considerable length, which is due to the various determinations of the name of the deceased, of the place of the grave or of those who undertook the burial.

3.2.3. met ... wăyyiqb^e rû ʾotô

Whereas the burial phrase here is the same as above (3.2.2.) the expression of dying is the simple qal perf, which, however, has the same meaning as the qal impf cons used in the other instances. Here we have only two examples: Jos 24,33 about Aaron's son Eleazar and 1 Sam 28,3 about Samuel. In the case of Eleazar the father's name is given, as was the case with Aaron himself (cf. above 3.2.2.). In the case of Samuel, we have a phrase about the gathering of all Israel to mourn for him in an only slightly different wording from that in 1 Sam 25,1. Concerning the burial place we have in Jos 24,33 a longer description: "in the hill which had been given to Pinehas his son in the hill country of Ephraim". This is again exceptional of course; the father is buried on the property of his son. According to 1 Sam 28,3 Samuel was buried "in Rama, his own city", that is ûb^{e}c îrô instead of b^e bêtô in 1 Sam 25,1. In spite of the differences we can view both these statements about Samuel's death as mere variations of the same statement.[71] Gen 48,7 can be viewed as a variation and combination of 3.2.1. and 3.2.3.; here Jacob refers to Rachel's death (cf. 35,19 and 3.1.1.) with the phrase metā ʿalăy rahel ... waʾæqb^e ræha, "Rachel died, to my sorrow,[72] ... and I buried her ...". Here too, as in Gen 35 the burial place is carefully noted: it was en route to Ephrath, that is Bethlehem. According to Speiser[73] this reference in Gen 48,7 belongs to 'P', whereas Gen 35,19 is regarded as belonging to 'E'. This being as it may, we have here clearly still another variation of the death – burial pattern.

3.2.4. Characteristics of the death-burial pattern

Summing up the characteristics of the pattern we can discern the following essential elements: *mût* in qal ipf cons/ qal perf + name of the deceased + *qbr* in nif ipf cons/ qal ipf cons with object suffix or *nota accusativi* with suffix + burial place.

Now if this is to be considered the broad framework of the pattern, there were alternatives of different kinds: a) the name of the deceased was left out, when it had been mentioned earlier in the context; b) the name of the burial place although in most cases given and meaning the ancestral home, is sometimes left out or hinted at by means of a *šam* when previously mentioned; c) alternative forms of the verbs such as the imperative *mût* directed to Moses and the 3rd person sing *wăyyiqbor* with God as subject at the burial of Moses. In addition to these alternatives there are different determinations to the names of the deceased and the burial places. Some of these are formulaic, some are not (cf. below 3.3.).

It should be pointed out, however, that there are a number of combinations of *mût* and *qbr* which do not form a pattern of the kind discussed above or cannot even be considered formulaic.[74] A quite special case are the combinations in Gen 23, which since they occur only within one chapter stemming from one author, should not be regarded as formulas but repeated phrases due to the repetitive style of the chapter in question.[75] We have no less than 9 occurrences of the stem *mût* and 12 of the stem *qbr*. Since we have an extended dialogue between Abraham and the Hittites, it is no surprise that the same expressions should be employed again and again. And since the whole chapter deals with the important act of buying a piece of land as a family property, it is only natural that this fact should be stressed in this way. It is a one-off transaction and the situation is quite unique. Thus the expressions are repeated only here and not found outside this chapter.

3.3. Formulaic elements in the death – burial pattern

Among the various determinations which follow the name of the deceased I shall here deal only with those which I regard as formulaic. Although they occur only in a few cases in the pattern, there are some additional occurrences without the pattern which I shall take in consideration, too.

3.3.1. *wăyye²asep ²æl-ᶜắmmâw*

This phrase is used about Abraham (Gen 25,8) and Isaac (Gen 35,29) within the pattern, and about Ishmael (Gen 25,17) without the *qbr* element. Each time *wăyyamât* is preceded by *wăyyigwă͏ᶜ* (cf. above 3.2.2. and n. 70). There are, however, in addition to this some other combinations, which are of particular interest here:

Gen 49,29   *²ᵃnî nœ²ᵃᵉsap ²æl-ᶜắmmî qibrû ²otî ²æl²ᵃbotăy* (Jacob)
Gen 49,33   *wăyyigwăᶜ wăyye²asep ²æl-ᶜắmmâw* (Jacob)
Numb 20,24   *ye²asep ²ăhᵃron ²æl-ᶜắmmâw* (Aaron)
Numb 20,26   *wᵉ²ăhᵃron ye²asep ûmet šam* (Aaron)
Numb 27,13   *wᵉnœ²ᵃᵉsăpta ²æl-ᶜắmmæ̂ka găm-²attā* (Moses)
           kă²ᵃšœr nœ²ᵃᵉsăp ²ăhᵃron ²ahîka (Aaron)
Numb 31,2   *²ăhăr te²asep ²æl-ᶜắmmæ̂ka* (Moses)
Deut 32,50   *ûmut bahar ... wᵉhe²asep ²æl-ᶜắmmæ̂ka* (Moses)
           kă²ᵃšœr-met ²ăhᵃron ²ahîka ... wăyye²asep ²æl-ᶜắmmâw
                                        (Aaron)

Although it is obvious that we are dealing here with the same phrase, it takes different forms and is used in a different way in these examples. Thus it is combined with forms of *mût* only in Numb 20,26 and in Deut 32,50. In Gen 49,29 it is used *instead* of *mût* and is here also combined with a form of *qbr*. This case, together with v. 33, can thus be seen as a counterpart to phrases about the other patriarchs. About Moses and Aaron it is used quite independently (Numb 20,24; 27,13; 31,2). The forms are varied, too, according to the various contexts.

For an interpretation of the formula, we may observe the following points made by Alfrink, Driver and Tromp:

a) it is used exclusively in the Pentateuch ("in priestly tradition") – although we have an alternative form of it in Judg 2,10 and 2 Kings 22,20 (= 2 Chron 34,28);[76]

b) it is used in 3rd person about the patriarchs, except for Gen 49,29, where it is in 1st person in the mouth of Jacob "probably for solemnity's sake"[77] and then in the mouth of God about, or directed to, Aaron and

Moses, which may be due to its "archaic ring". Later, however, it is used also about women and non-Israelites (Sir);[78]

    c) in its oldest use it is distinguished from death as well as from burial, cf. Gen 25,8-9; 35,9 and 49,33, where the verbs are in narrative forms;[79]

    d) it does not apply to the family grave, since this is ruled out, at least in the cases of Aaron and Moses;[80]

    e) there is a development of the formula to be seen in Judg 2,10, where ⁽ammâw is replaced by ᵃbotâw, cf. also 2 Kings 22,20, where we have qibrotêka. The verb næᵃsãp takes the meaning of simply 'die' in Ps 26,9 and Is 57,1. Finally the verb is applied to the 'bones' in 2 Sam 21,13; Jer 8,2 etc.[81]

According to Alfrink, Driver and Tromp, the formula refers to the union of the deceased with his forefathers in Sheol.[82] It is viewed as clearly distinct from another formula, šakãb ⁽im-ᵃbotâw, "sleep with one's fathers".[83] This may originally have meant burial in the family grave, but in biblical use it refers mainly to the death of kings, and among them only those who died a customary, usual death. When a king fell in battle or was murdered the verb mût is used. According to Tromp, this formula has become a *testimonium pietatis*.[84]

On the other hand it has been pointed out that, since both formulas are used about Jacob (Gen 47,30 and 49,29, cf. v. 33), we could infer, that they originally had the same meaning. Furthermore, since wᵉšakãbti ⁽im-ᵃbotãy ('J') ostensibly has the meaning of burial in the family grave, this would hold true for næᵃsãp ᵓæl-⁽ammâw, too.[85] In the patriarchal narratives, however, this formula being used only in priestly and, according to Wächter, late traditions is already a "festgeprägte Redewendung" referring to death and burial.[86] We have such a secondary use of the other formula, too, namely in the Deuteronomistic redactions of Kings and following them in Chronicles.[87] Thus Wächter is opposed to Alfrink, Driver and Tromp in his interpretation of the original meaning of næᵃsãp ᵓæl- ammâw, whereas he comes rather close regarding šakãb ⁽ im-ᵃbotâw. The reference to the family grave in the first formula is supposed to be the original meaning also by Quell[88] and Dürr.[89]

But one may ask whether these two lines of interpretation really are irreconcilable. E.M. Meyers has come forward with an explanation built upon the archaeological evidence of what he calls "secondary burials" in ancient

Palestine. "Such a practice is characterized by the collection of skeletized remains at some point after the flesh had wasted away and by their deposition in a new place of repose".[90] From Middle Bronze I we have evidence of such secondary burials and in Iron Age tombs there is often a "communal ossuary or respository which was adopted to insure the safekeeping of the bones of former burials".[91] From this Meyers concludes that the formula *næ⁾ᵆsăp ⁾æl-⁽ămmâw*, while meaning "to die and to descend to Sheol where the family of all Israel was assembled", at the same time "may reflect rather literally the MB I tombs discussed . . . it would elucidate Abraham's preoccupation with proper burial and it would explain the Iron Age innovation of the communal ossuary, the actual means by which one was joined to the common soul of his ancestors".[92]

If Meyers is right, we would not have to choose between two interpretations of the formula *næ⁾ᵆsăp ⁾æl-⁽ămmâw*. Its meaning is "to die and descend to Sheol", but the expression reflects at the same time the specific custom of secondary burial and the function of the ossuaries. This being the original content of the phrase it has undoubtely undergone developments and to some extent been confused with the other formula, namely *šakăb ⁽im-⁾ᵃbotâw*. This formula does not occur within the death - burial pattern at all: it substitutes it in the Deuteronomistic conclusions about most of the kings. Moreover, the first formula is integrated in the pattern, strictly speaking, only in Gen 25,8 and 35,29. In all the above listed cases, however, and Gen 25,17, either *mût* or *qbr* or both are lacking. This means that it is used also in the Pentateuch instead of one or both of the verbs which constitute the pattern itself. If it is to be considered an euphemism is another question altogether. In the light of the formula's originally quite distinct meaning, I would deny this. But when the original meaning was lost, it is easy to imagine such an euphemistic use. Exactly at which point this change could be assumed to have taken place is not easy to say.

3.3.2. *zaqen ûśᵉbă⁽ yamîm*

In this form the formula occurs in Gen 25,8 (Abraham); Gen 35,29 (Isaac); Job 42,17 (Job) and 1 Chron 23,1 (David). Only in the two first cases does it occur within the pattern; in Job 42,17 the burial element is missing, and in

1 Chron 23,1 it is not yet about David's death. Now we have some varied forms: $š^eb\ddot{a}^c$ yamîm only in 1 Chron 29,28 about David within the pattern, and $w\breve{a}yyizq\breve{a}n$ $y^eh\hat{o}yad\bar{a}$ $w\breve{a}yyi\acute{s}ba^c$ yamîm in 2 Chron 24,15 about the High Priest Jehojadah, also within the pattern.[93]

Although all instances occur in relatively late texts, it has been pointed out that they have their counterparts in Ackadian and Egyptian texts.[94] Also, although the formula is restricted to a few persons only, we may inquire whether it refers to something more than merely "old age". Wächter[95] regards the Chronicler's use of the phrase as "Tugenderweis" and turns to Job 42,17. Here it is clearly the blessing to live to see several generations of descendants (v. 16) that counts. This is also the case in Gen 35,22b-29, where we have a list of the sons of Jacob, a note about Isaac's return to Mamre, his old age (180 years) and the burial by both his sons. Finally, Abraham too was blessed with great age, burial in the family grave, and many descendants, although not all of them remained in the patrimony. Although the formula is late, the motif can be found in older 'sources'. It is elaborated in great detail in the account of the late years of Jacob (Gen 47,28-50,41) and Joseph too is characterized in the same manner (Gen 50,22-26). We have to take in account the possibility that the Ackadian and especially the Egyptian equivalents has contributed to the late 'P' formula of the considerable older motif.[96] However, the formula means "great age", but this includes the specific blessings of many descendants and burial in the family grave.[97]

3.3.3. $b^e\acute{s}\hat{e}b\bar{a}$ $\d{t}\hat{o}b\bar{a}$

This formula is used about Abraham (Gen 15,15; 25,8), Gideon (Judg 8,32) and David (1 Chron 29,28). In Gen 25,8 and Judg 8,32 it falls within the death-burial pattern. In Gen 15,15 we have a variation: w^eʾattā $tab\hat{o}$ʾ ʾel-ʾ^{a}botêka $b^e\check{s}al\hat{o}m$ tiqqaber $b^e\acute{s}\hat{e}b\bar{a}$ $\d{t}\hat{o}b\bar{a}$. The phrase $b\hat{o}$ʾʾ$æl$-ʾ^{a}botêka can be considered a variation, and partly a contamination of $\acute{s}ak\breve{a}b$ ^cim-ʾ^{a}botâw and $n\ae$ʾ$^{ae}s\breve{a}p$ ʾ$æl$- $\breve{a}mm\hat{a}w$ discussed above whereas $b^e\acute{s}al\hat{o}m$ corresponds to $b^e\acute{s}\hat{e}b\bar{a}$ $\d{t}\hat{o}b\bar{a}$ and both obviously have the same meaning. Turning to 1 Chron 29,28 we have another pattern, namely the *succession* pattern to be discussed below: $w\breve{a}yyam\^at$ $b^e\acute{s}\hat{e}b\bar{a}$ $\d{t}\hat{o}b\bar{a}$ $\acute{s}^eba^c$ yamîm $^co\acute{s}ær$ $w^ekab\hat{o}d$ $w\breve{a}yyimlok$ $š^elom\ddot{o}$ʾ $b^en\hat{o}$ $t\breve{a}\d{h}t\^aw$, "he died in ripe old age, full of years, wealth and honour; and

Solomon his son ruled in his place". Here $b^e\check{s}\hat{e}b\bar{a}$ $\underline{t}\hat{o}b\bar{a}$ is complemented by the somewhat different and extended phrase 3.3.2. in a similar way to that in Gen 25,8. From this one may conclude that both expressions have the same meaning: death at a great age and in a state of fullfilment.[98] Both are restricted to a few persons of stature. This does not mean that their deaths are unusual, exceptional, but rather that the persons of whom these formulas are used are exceptional.[99]

3.3.4. Summary

All the three formulas discussed above are used about Abraham (Gen 25,8), two of them about Isaac (Gen 35,29) and about David (1 Chron 29,28). These cumulations of phrases are built into the death-burial pattern (Gen: P) and the succession pattern (Chron) respectively and as such are relatively late. Elsewhere we found the phrases used separately, sometimes instead of the verbs *mût* and *qbr* as was the case with *næᵓᵆsăp ᵓæl-ᵊbotâw*. As for the meaning of the various expressions according to Driver, we would have to distinguish between *gwˤ*, 'breathing one's last breath', *mût*, 'dying', *næᵓᵆsăp ᵓæl-ˤămmâw*, 'being gathered to one's ancestors or one's people' and *qbr*, 'being buried in the grave'.[100] There may indeed have been such distinct meanings, but when we reach the actual cumulations of such expressions in 'P' and Chron, we may doubt whether they are so distinct any more. They have already become formulaic and the use of such cumulative formulaic elements is due to the importance of the persons rather than a wish to be precise.

As for the meaning of the phrases of "fulfilment of life" I quote von Rad: "The expression 'old man and full of years' shows that in ancient Israel one accepted life not with a defiant claim to endlessness but from the start in resignation, as something limited, something assigned to man, in which then the state of satiation was to be reached . . . The expression reveals that one felt only an early or an 'evil' death as a judgement from God. 'Old and full of years' is the fulfilment of what was planned by God for the life in question and a death without fear concludes such a fulfilled life".[101]

I agree with von Rad that life in Ancient Israel was accepted as something limited, and that death in due time was not a tragic fate but a quite natural fact. However, I think he is overstating his case, when he speaks about "the fullfilment of what was planned by God for the life in question". Regarding these formulas we are not told of anything God had planned. Abraham, Isaac and Jacob were thought of as actors in God's plans to be sure, but the statement about their deaths do not even mention the name of God. This is generally the case, when we consider the death-burial pattern. Exceptions from this rule are the statements about Aaron and Moses, but as we saw, their way of death was quite exceptional, too. We don't know anything about "a death without fear", either. Surely, the lives of these persons were thought of as 'fulfilled' and they had indeed reached a "state of satiation". But there is no hint of fear or absence of fear. Arguments *e silentio* should not be introduced here because formulaic speech does not permit such interpretations and therefore we have to be content with what is really said and how it should be interpreted.

3.4. Mourning for the dead

I shall here briefly consider some phrases about mourning in connection with death and burial. The main verb expressing mourning rites is *spd*, while others like *bkh* and *nhm* although quite usual themselves are used in only a few instances in this connection. Then there are special expressions for these rites which form various series and our question will be if there is possibly a "mourning pattern" to be detected in these series of expressions.

3.4.1. Positive use of mourning phrases

Within the death-burial pattern we have a slightly different phrase about the death of Samuel (cf. above 3.2.1.). In 1 Sam 25,1 we read *wǎyyiqqabᵉṣû kǎl-yiśraʾel wǎyyispᵉdû-lô*, "and all Israel came together to mourn for him". The same thing is expressed once more in 1 Sam 28,3 in a shorter form: *wǎyyispᵉdû-lô kǎl-yiśraʾel*, "and all Israel had mourned for him". I would not consider these two phrases as independent and thus not representing a formula proper, but rather a repeated phrase from the same source.[102]

In 1 Kings 14,13.18, where the sickness and death of Jeroboam's son Abijah are followed by the mourning of "all Israel": $w^e sap^e d\hat{u}$-$l\hat{o}$ $k\hat{a}l$-$yi\acute{s}ra^{\circ}el$ $w^e qab^e r\hat{u}$ $^{\circ}ot\hat{o}$, "All Israel will mourn for him and bury him" (v. 13), the prophet Ahijah tells Jeroboam's wife. When death has occurred, we are told: $w\breve{a}yyiqb^e r\hat{u}$ $^{\circ}ot\hat{o}$ $w\breve{a}yyisp^e d\hat{u}$-$l\hat{o}$ $k\hat{a}l$-$yi\acute{s}ra^{\circ}el$, "They buried him, and all Israel mourned for him" (v. 18). In the preceding verses death is referred to in similar phrases too: $\hat{u}met$ $h\breve{a}yy\alpha l\alpha d$, "the child will die" (v. 12) and $w^e h\breve{a}nn\breve{a}^c\breve{a}r$ met, "the boy died" (v. 17). This is, then, the death-burial pattern (cf. above 3.2.3.) in one of its variations. The mourning is built into, or combined with, it in slightly differing expressions.[103]

Falling outside the death-burial pattern but syntactically combined with a finite form of the verb $m\hat{u}t$ are two other positive statements about mourning. In Gen 23,2 we have at the beginning $w\breve{a}ttam\hat{a}t$ $\acute{s}ar\bar{a}$, "Sarah died", followed by the place of death Qirjath Arba, and then $w\breve{a}yyabo^{\circ}$ $^{\circ}\breve{a}braham$ $lispod$ $l^e\acute{s}ar\bar{a}$ $w^e libkotah$, "Abraham proceeded to mourn for Sarah and to bewail her". As we know, the question of the burial place is the main theme of this chapter (cf. above 3.2.4.).[104] In 2 Sam 11,26 Uriah's wife learns about her husband's death and proceeds to mourn for him: $w\breve{a}tti\acute{s}m\breve{a}^c$. . . $k\hat{i}$ met . . . $w\breve{a}ttispod$. Now it is evident that these combinations of $m\hat{u}t$ and spd do not constitute a formulaic use since the differences in form are too great. The same holds true of two other combinations, this time between $m\hat{u}t$ and $nih\breve{a}m$, "be consoled". In Gen 38,12 we read $w\breve{a}ttam\hat{a}t$ $b\breve{a}t$-$\breve{s}\hat{u}\breve{a}^c$. . . $w\breve{a}yyinnah\alpha m$ $y^e h\hat{u}d\bar{a}$ and in 2 Sam 13,39 (about David) $k\hat{i}$ $nih\breve{a}m$ $^c\breve{a}l$ $\breve{a}mn\hat{o}n$ $k\hat{i}$ met. Both refer to the completion of the mourning time, but do not constitute formulaic phrases.[105]

It would seem then, that the positive use of phrases about mourning for the dead do not form a part of the death-burial pattern, nor does it occur in other formulaic combinations with $m\hat{u}t$. This is perhaps somewhat astonishing, since mourning rites as a rule accompanied death and burial and one would accordingly expect this to be expressed in formulas or even patterns like those of death and burial.

50

3.4.2. Negative use of mourning phrases

A kind of indirect evidence of the importance of the mourning rites in connection with death and burial can be found in those instances where the observance of rites and customs for one reason or another is prohibited or forbidden. Our question is whether we can detect here some kind of formula or pattern. Four texts are here of primary concern. They are related to a dead person: *lamet* (Deut 14,1), *lemet* or *lămmet* (Jer 22,10), *ăl-met* (Jer 16,6) and *metîm* (Ez 24,17). They can be compared in respect of the corresponding verbal forms, which are all negated:

Deut 14,1		*loɔ titgodedû welɔ-tasîmû qărhā*
Jer 16,6	*welɔ yispedû*	*welɔ yitgodăd welɔ yiqqareăh*
Jer 22,10	*ɔăl-tibkû*	*weɔăl tanudû*
Ez 24,16	*welɔ tispod*	*welɔ tibkæ*

The variations in the individual forms are considerable: the forms are all imperfects: 2nd person pl in Deut 14,1 and Jer 22,10, but 3rd person pl in Jer 16,5 and 2nd person sing in Ez 24,16. There are combinations of two verbs except in Jer 16,6, where there are three, to which comes *loɔ yiqqaberû* at the beginning of the series. The only repeated combination being that of *gdd* and *qrh* (the latter as substantive and verb), there can at most be talk of fragments of a pattern.[106]

These variations also correspond with the reasons given for not observing the mourning rites. Deut 14,1 begins with the statement "You are the sons of the Lord your God", which is the reason why these particular rites, namely "gash" oneself and to shave oneself literally "between your eyes" should be avoided. They are considered to be heathen practices and therefore to conflict with the covenant between God and Israel.[107] In Jer 22,10 the prophet urges his people not to mourn for the dead (Josiah) but for him (Joahas) who has to go away into exile, "for he shall never return, never again see the land of his birth".[108] In contrast to these two short passages the two others, Jer 16,6-7 and Ez 24,16-17, are rather extensive. In Jer 16,4-5 we already encounter two pairs of negations: *loɔ yissapedû welɔ yiqqaberû* (v. 4) and *weɔăl telek lispôd weɔăl tanod lahæm* (v. 5). The reason is given: "for I have withdrawn my peace from this people, says the Lord, my love and affection".

In addition to the four negations already quoted (v. 6-7) there follow two more explicite exhortations: "no one shall give the mourner a portion of bread to console him for the dead, nor give him the cup of consolation, even for his father or his mother" (v. 7). No one will be able to observe the customal mourning rites during the coming catastrophe, says the prophet. What he does not convey is whether he approves of them as such or not.[109] In Ez 24,16, finally, the prophet himself is bereaved of his wife, but commanded not to mourn for her. In addition to the two verbs cited comes one further negation, not to "give way to tears", whereafter there follow positive exhortations intermingled with negative: "Keep in good heart; be quiet, and make no mourning for the dead; cover your head as usual and put sandals on your feet. You shall not cover your upper lip in mourning nor eat the bread of despair" (v. 17). After death has occurred the prophet retells the command not to observe the mourning rites. Like Jeremiah Ezechiel thus by his own non-observance of the mourning rites shall illustrate the magnitude of the coming catastrophe. However, whereas Jeremiah is prohibited from entering into human relationships such as marriage, Ezechiel is forced not to display any emotion when personally bereaved.[110]

The negative phrases about not observing the mourning rites when connected with forms of *mût* or/and *qbr* do not fall within the death-burial pattern, nor do they form a completely preserved pattern of their own. The existing repetitions could be explained either as fragments of such a pattern or alternatively as stemming from the fact that quite usual words for mourning are here accumulated and negated, albeit for different reasons. Since the first explanation would be hypothetical, we shall have to be content with the other.

3.5. Some special places of death

In 3.1. we found that an indication of the place of death or rather of burial belongs to what we called the death-burial pattern. These places were as a rule the ancestral homes of the deceased. The main exceptions were Rachel, Deborah, Miriam, Aaron and Moses, who died under extraordinary circumstances during the wanderings. All these places of death and burial can be said to form a variable element of the pattern, but not formulas as such. In this section, however, we shall focus our attention on some formulaic phrases about the place of death. One of them we have already encountered in connection with the death-burial pattern. It is the adverb šam or šammā, "there". We shall now consider all the instances where this expression is syntactically combined with a form of mût. Another group represent those cases where the place of death is expressed by bămmidbar, "in the desert".

3.5.1. mût ... šam/šammā

This adverb is of course a reference to a geographical place mentioned before. The verbal forms can be divided into "past" and "future" according to their meaning, the main forms being qal ipf cons and qal ipf complemented by a few examples of qal perf, qal perf cons and participle. I shall therefore discuss them within these two main groups.

3.5.1.1. wăyyamât/wăttamât šam

If we include in this group also the perfect forms, we are able to list the following eight (nine) instances:

Numb 20,1	wăttamât šam miryam wăttiqqaber šam	(Qadesh, v. 1)
Numb 20,26	wᵉăhᵃron yeʾasep ûmet šam	(Mount Hor, v. 25)
Numb 20,28	wăyyamât ʾăhᵃron šam bᵉroʾš hahar	(Mount Hor, v. 27)
Numb 33,38	wăyyăʿăl ʾăhᵃron ... wăyyamât šam	(Mount Hor, v. 38)
Deut 10,6	šam met ʾăhᵃron wăyyiqqaber šam	(Moserah, v. 6)
Deut 34,5	wăyyamât šam mošǣ ...	(Mount Nebo, v. 1)
Judg 1,7	waybîʾuhû yᵉrûšalăyim wăyyamât šam	(Jerusalem, v. 7)
2 Sam 6,7	wăyyamât šam ʿim ʾᵃrôn haʾᵃᵉlohîm	(treshing floor, v. 6)
1 Chron 13,10	wăyyamât šam lipnê ʾᵃᵉlohîm	(par. » v. 9)

Out of eight instances four are about Aaron, one about his sister Miriam and one about his brother Moses. The remaining two are about the Canaanite king Adoni-bezek, who was killed by the Israelites and Uzza, who accidentally touched the Ark and was killed on the spot.[111] Now it is quite possible that the (P) tradition about the death of Aaron is influenced by the (D) tradition about Moses: both die on the top of a mountain "at the commând of the Lord" (Deut 34,5, cf. Numb 33,38) and the grave place is in both cases unknown. According to Deut 10,6, however, Aaron died and was buried in Moserah.[112] Be that as it may, I think we are entitled to speak about a formulaic use of *šam* at least in the Pentateuchal instances. The other two differ in the way of death: it is a form of punishment and not a "natural" death in old age. The adverb *šam* is used as a reference to the place of death immediately before or in the near context. It is not stressed in Judg 1,7. In 2 Sam 6,7 = 1 Chron 13,10 it means "on the spot", which happened to be at the side of the Ark of God. In Numb 20,1 and Deut 10,6 it is stressed through repetition. In the four remaining cases there are the preparations for the unusual death of Aaron and Moses on the respective mountains, whereafter *šam* follows in an expectable but also pointed way. This would mean that although *šam* is quite a common adverb it is used not mechanically but somehow stressed in the six Pentateuchal instances, whereas in the two other cases it seems to be unstressed. If we disregard the function the "mechanical use" of *wǎyyamât šam* also adds to the formulaic combination of *mût* in past tense and the adverb *šam* discussed here.

3.5.1.2. yamût/lamût šam/šammā

In this paragraph I shall turn to those expressions where the adverb *šam/šammā* is combined with a verbal form (*mût*) in a present or future tense or with the infinitive. First I again simply list the instances:

Numb 14,35	*bǎmmidbar hǎzzǣ yittǎmmu wᵉšam yamutû*	(in this desert)
Numb 20,4	*ʾæl hǎmmidbar hǎzzǣ lamût šam*	(to this desert)
Is 22,18	*šammā tamût wᵉšammā* ...	(into a great wide land)
Jer 20,6	*ûbabæl tabôʾ wᵉšam tamût wᵉšam tiqqaber*	(Babel)
Jer 22,12	*kî bimqôm ᵃšær higlû ʾotô šam yamût*	(in the exile)
Jer 37,20	*bêt yᵉhônatan hǎssoper wᵉloʾ ʾamût šam*	(the house of J.)
Jer 38,26	*lᵉbiltî hᵃšibenî bêt yᵉhônatan lamût šam*	(rep. »)
Jer 42,16	*...šam yidbǎq ʾǎhᵃrêkæm miṣrǎyim wᵉšam tamutû*	(Egypt)
Ez 12,13	*wᵉhebeʾtî ʾotô babælā* ... *wᵉšam yamût*	(Babel)

Out of these nine instances two (Numb 14,35; 20,4) belong to a special group which I shall discuss in the next paragraph under the label "death in the wilderness". Another two (Jer 37,20; 38,26) relate to Jeremiah's imprisonment. In both cases we have farreaching similarities of expression, so that they may be considered variations of the same sentences. As to the variations we may point to the change of a finite verb form into a infinitive w^e*šam yamutû* - *lamût šam* (Numb 14,35; 20,4) and (w^e*lo*) *ʾamût šam* - (l^e*biltî*) *lamût šam* (Jer 37,20; 38,26). Were those expressions, however, the only we had, we would hardly be able to speak about a formula proper, except for *lamût šam*.

If we compare the five remaining instances, we can discern a formulaic use of the combination of an imperfect form of *mût* and *šam/šammā* and a common situation, that of exile. In Is 22,18 *šammā* is repeated in the same way as *šam* in Jer 20,6 (cf. Jer 42,16). In the first case there follows a longer description of the humiliation of Shebna, comptroller of the king's household. In the second case we have the death-burial pattern used about Pashur's coming fate in exile together with his friends to whom he has been a false prophet. In Jer 22,12 the prophet foretells the deportation of Shallum: "He shall never return; he shall die in the place of his exile and never see his land again". In Ez 12,13 the death of the "prince" (v. 12) in Babylon is foretold. It is stressed that his face will be covered so that he cannot see the land of his exile (v. 12, 13). A few of the dispersed will escape "sword, famine, and pestilence" (v. 16) to tell the story of "their abominations to the peoples among whom they go".[113] In Jer 42,16 the prophet warns those who try to escape to Egypt: "Sword" and "famine" will reach them there and "there will you die". In the following verse we have the complete triple formula "sword, famine and pestilence" as in Ez 12,16. We shall discuss this particular formula and its variations in greater detail below. Let it suffice here to point out that the places of exile are depicted by the prophets not as places of refuge from the enemy, but, at least in these particular cases, as places from which there is no return, where the same calamities will happen and death will occur. The formulaic use of the imperfect form of *mût* combined with *šam/šamma* corresponds to this common situation. Despite the variations in the personal forms this holds true not only for the cases discussed here but also for Numb 14,35 too.[114] As examples of death in the exile we may mention Am 7,17 and Ez 28,10, both however without the characteristic *šam* found in the cases discussed here.

3.5.2. Death in the wilderness

In paragraph 3.5.1.2. we have already dealt with two instances where the place of death was the desert, which was referred to by the adverb šam (Numb 14,35; 20,4). Here I shall consider those cases where bămmidbar or b^emidbar is connected more directly with a form of the verb mût. In accordance with the two preceding paragraphs I will group the material into two sections containing forms of past and future death.

3.5.2.1. met/wăyyamăt bămmidbar

Here I have found only four instances, all of which differ from each other. I shall list them, however, so that similarities and differences become clearer:

Numb 3,4   wăyyamăt nadab wa²ᵃbîhû ... b^emidbăr sînăy
Numb 14,2   lû-mătnû b^ecærœș mișrăyim ²ô bămmidbar hazzœ̆ lû-matnû
Numb 27,3   ²abînû met bămmidbar ... kî-b^ehæt²ô met
Jos 5,4   kol ²ănšê hămmilhamā metû bămmidbar ...

The first case is unusual in several respects: it has the qal ipf cons, the names of the dead are mentioned and so is the name of the wilderness. The second case is unreal and consists of two similar clauses, the order of the verb and the place of death being inverted. The two last examples resemble each other closely met/metû bămmidbar. Here we could speak of a formulaic use of the perfect forms and the place of death. However, there is not what we would call a common theme or motif, because all the cases are quite specific: Nadab and Abihu died because they committed a cult offence which is explicitly mentioned (Numb 3,4).[115] The fact that they left no sons is mentioned because of the genealogy of (the sons of) Aaron given here. Zelophehad died without a son, too, but in this case there arises a dispute about the right to inheritance. The claim is presented by his daughters (Numb 27,1ff.) and judgement is passed by Moses in their favour (Numb 27,5ff.)[116] However, in neither case is the circumstance that death had occurred in the wilderness essential. Jos 5,4 mentions the fact that all the fighting men who had left Egypt and were circumcised had died during the wanderings in the wilderness, whereas those men born in the wilderness were uncircumcised and thus had to be circumcised before entering the promised land.[117] Only Numb 14,2 displays the specific motif of "grumbling" in the wilderness. Here death is unreal, either anticipated as in the next paragraph, or preferable in retrospect as here.

It seems, then, that the fact that someone had died in the wilderness, a fact that in two cases (Numb 27,3 and Jos 5,4) is expressed i nearly the same way, does not make for a common motif. A formulaic expression could, however, be detected in these two cases.

3.5.2.2. lamût etc. bămmidbar

Characteristic of these cases is that they point to the future. Most of them are composed of a infinitive and the place of death. Only one imperfect was found and this was in itself a paronomastic formula (*môt yamutû*, Numb 26,65), which is a threat of death to be discussed below. If we leave it out, and also the cases with *šam* discussed above (3.5.1.2.), we have the following list:

Ex 14,11	*l^eqăhtanû lamût bămmidbar*
Ex 14,12	*kî tôb lanû . . . mimmutenû bămmidbar*
Numb 16,13	*hœ^{cæ}lîtanû . . . lăh^amîtenû bămmidbar*
Numb 21,5	*lamā hœ^{cæ}lîtunû . . . lamût bămmidbar*
Deut 9,28	*hôsî^ɔam lăh^amitam bămmidbar*

It is obvious that the similarities here are far greater than in 3.5.2.1. Twice we have the qal inf cstr *lamût* and twice the hif inf cstr *lăh^amît*. To the latter are added object suffixes, which, however, are different. It should be noted too, that in all four cases we have a verbal expression that denotes the taking away of the Israelites from Egypt: *l^eqăhtanû* (Ex 14,11), *hœ^{cæ}lîtanû* (Numb 16,13 and 21,5) and *hôsî^ɔam* (Deut 9,28). Only Ex 14,12 differs from this 'pattern' but this is due to the fact that it is a continuation of 14,11 and is constructed as a comparison between the conditions in Egypt and those in the wilderness. Whether we use the term formula or coined phrase here depends on whether we assume the existence of a common 'source' or not. A short look at the commentaries shows, that[118] Ex 14,11-12 is regarded as belonging to JE, Numb 16,13 to J, Numb 21,5 to E, whereas Deut 9,28 has to be D. This would mean, that the instances in no way belong to one 'source' and therefore we are entitled to speak of one formula or two depending upon whether we distinguish between the qal and hif infinitives.

As to the corresponding motifs we have in all cases to do with the "grumbling". In Ex 14,11-12 it is the earliest possible time: out of fear for the pursuing Egyptians the Israelites cried to the Lord and accused Moses of taking them out to die in the wilderness.[119] In Numb 16,13 the same accusation is thrown at Moses in connection with the rebellion against him initiated by Dathan and Abiram.[120] In Numb 21,5 it is the people who speak up against God and Moses. Finally, in Deut 9,28, the accusation is hypothetically directed to God: lest the surrounding peoples say, Moses implies in his prayer, that God destroyed his people in the desert, because He was not able to bring them to the promised land.[121] Now the difference between qal and hif forms does not stem from whether it is Moses or God who is accused, because both are used in each cases.

3.5.3. Summary

The adverb *šam* is combined in a formulaic way with forms of *mût* in two distinct ways. Referring to the past, there are the statements about Miriam's, Aaron's and Moses' death in Numb and Deut, where *šam* seems to be stressed in a special way. In the three cases outside the Pentateuch this was assumed not to be the case, although they add to the same formulaic use. Referring to the future *šam* meant one or another form of exile mainly in Jer, but also in Is and Ez. In the two remaining cases *šam* referred to a preceding *midbar*, both from Numb. Death in exile or in the desert are not very far from each other and in any case the formulaic use is evident here, too. The combinations of *mût* and *bămmidbar* were also considered separately for past and future forms of the verb. Here we found only four instances of past forms, which all differed from each other in form as well as in meaning. A formulaic use was considered in only two cases. Concerning future death in the wilderness, we found five cases, of which two had the form *lamût* and two *lăhᵃmît* plus suffixes. These were regarded as formulaic, whereas the fifth case, also being an infinitive, was dependent upon the first *lamût*. The common theme of all combinations of *mût* and *bămmidbar* was the 'grumbling' in the wilderness, although the subjects as well as the objects of this dissatisfaction differed.

3.6. Conclusions

There is a clearly distinguishable pattern with two constant elements namely the verbs *mût* and *qbr*. Both can take various forms, but this does not affect their formulaic character. Then we have a series of variables, the most common of which are the name of the deceased, the place of his grave and its geographical location. Sometimes the pattern includes other formulaic elements, such as the phrase of being gathered to one's kin, and those of dying at a ripe old age. These formulas are by no means restricted to the pattern, but are used freely alone or in combination with only one of the verbs. Sometimes the phrase of being gathered to one's kin replaces the death-and-burial pattern, which is the rule with the kindred phrase of lying down with one's fathers. The latter is nowhere used in combination with the verb *mût*. It is the Deuteronomistic formula for the normal death of a king of Israel and Judah. The phrase of being gathered to one's kin refers to the descension to Sheol, where the dead relatives are assembled. As its concrete background it may also refer to the use of secondary burials and ossuaries, where the remaining bones were gathered. The formula itself, however, is found in relatively late texts. This is the case with the cumulative use of formulaic elements within the death-burial pattern, too. But the pattern itself, with its two constant elements, occurs in texts of various ages. Thus we can conclude that the pattern is in itself old, but later it includes certain other formulaic elements which are used only about specific important persons such as Abraham, Isaac, Jacob, Aaron, Moses, Joshua, Gideon, David, Jehojadah and Job. In such cases some element of the pattern is usually left out. One element that could be expected within the pattern, namely that of ritual mourning, is generally missing: only two cases were found, one of them about Samuel. Certain tendencies to formulaic use of expressions about mourning were found, especially about the absence of mourning in prophecies. However, here too we found no real formulas. In some cases we found a formulaic use of a distinct expression for the place of death (and burial). One case was the use of the adverb *šam,* 'there', which especially when used by Jeremiah, but also by Isaiah and Ezechiel, referred to exile. Another expression was *bămmidbar,* which collocated with the motif of "grumbling in the desert".

What can we conclude about the functions of the formulas discussed here? The death-burial pattern itself obviously has a narrative function of marking the end of the story. It is thus used not only about the patriarchs themselves, but occasionally about a mother of the people (Rachel), not only about the brother heroes Moses and Aaron, but also about their sister Miriam. Moreover, it is by no means restricted to the most important figures, but also used in the lists of the 'minor judges'. Otherwise the formulaic elements connected with the pattern about the patriarchs or used more or less freely are restricted to the really important figures, about whose death something more than simply stating the fact of death and burial is found to be appropriate. In this way they are distinguished from the minor agents, but also from the kings who died an ordinary death. The same can be said of the formulaic expressions about the place of death. Usually it is the patrimony, the family grave, the royal tombs. In some extraordinary cases, however, the place has to be stressed in a special way: when death occurs *en route,* in exile or in the desert — whether it be real or unreal. So there are formulas for the 'usual' or 'common' way of death and burial and there are special formulas to mark the importance of an 'unusual' person, and an 'exceptional' place of death and burial.

4. DEATH MARKING TIME

In this chapter I shall first consider some prepositional expressions which have the function of marking the time relation 'until', 'at' and 'after' someone's death. Then I shall proceed to the succession formulas and to certain genealogies which have a chronological function. It goes without saying that the prepositional expressions come rather close to those discussed in Chapter 2. It is also true that succession and genealogy sometimes occur within or are connected with the death-burial pattern discussed in Chapter 3. However, the emphasis in the phrases to be discussed here lies more on this time marking or chronological function than on the actual death of the persons mentioned. In the genealogies this is often expressed through the age of the persons, which has an explicit chronological function.

4.1. Until the death of . . .

I shall here examine some phrases about events taking place or not taking place within the span of time up to someone's death. The preposition *ʿăd* indicates the limit of this span of time, but unlike phrases discussed above it is not the approaching of death that is essential here, but rather the "rest of life". The examples divide into two distinct groups, one consisting of *ʿăd* followed by the construct form *môt* and a noun or personal name signifying a person and one consisting of the stereotype formula *ʿăd-yôm môtô*, "to the day of his death".

4.1.1. ʿăd-môt . . .

Of the five examples in this section four represent the same phrase, namely *ʿăd-môt hăkkohen hăggadôl*, "till the death of the high priest" (Numb 35,25.

28, cf. v. 32; Jos 20,6). The fifth instance has the personal name $š^el\omō$, "to the death of Solomon" (1 Kings 11,40). In the first case the span of time is that of asylum for a homicide: "The community shall protect the homicide from the vengeance of the kinsman and take him back to the city of refuge where he had taken sanctuary. He must stay there till the death of the duly anointed high priest" (Numb 35,25). Provided that the killing was unintended and that he remains within the boundaries of the city of refuge, he is protected and can return to his own property "after the death of the high priest" (v. 28). There is no way of releasing him earlier – e.g. by accepting payment for him (v. 32).[122] In Jos 20,2ff. this law is referred to, the cities of refuge are named and their functions defined. It is not surprising that this phrase should be formulaic: legal formulations show by their very nature a tendency toward formulaic language in general. The only variations here are the qualifications for the high priest: he must be duly anointed (Numb 35,25) and he must be the ruling high priest (Jos 20,6). That the death of the high priest is a way of marking time should be clear enough from Numb 35,28: "The homicide must remain in the city of refuge till the death of the high priest ($^{c}ăd-môt$ $hăkkohen$ $hăggadôl$); after the death of the high priest ($w^{e}ʾăh^{a}rê$ $môt$ $hăkkohen$ $hăggadôl$) he may go back to his property" (cf. below 4.3.). So we can speak of a formula including $hăkkohen$ $hăggadôl$. Whether it is originally connected with the institution of the cities of refuge is open to discussion,[123] since it is not found in Deut 19, but only in Numb 35 and Jos 20, and it is not quite clear which of the three texts, if any, contains the original formulation. However, they are hardly independent of each other. If we restrict the phrase to $^{c}ăd-môt$ ..., then we have to include 1 Kings 11,40 about the asylum of Jeroboam, who fled to King Shishak of Egypt after his unsuccessful rebellion against Solomon. Here we have not a legal precept but a historical remark about what had taken place. But the function of the phrase is the same: not until the death of Solomon could Jeroboam return. The role of Solomon here and that of the high priest in the law discussed are of course entirely different, but interestingly enough asylum is the common denominator. Thus $^{c}ăd-môt$ . . . can be called a formula marking the limit of two different asylum situations.[124]

4.1.2. ʿǎd-yôm môtô

A more distinct formula is ʿǎd-yôm môtô, which in this form is found in Judg 13,7; 1 Sam 15,35; 2 Kings 15,5 = 2 Chron 26,21; Jer 52,11.34. The same formula but with a feminine suffix (ʿǎd-yôm môtah) is found in 2 Sam 6.23. In Judg 13,7 the formula marks the closing of the whole span of Samson's time as a Nazirite which began with his birth (min hǎbbǽtœn). This second prepositional expression completes the first in the way two opposites sometimes do; that is, they express a totality, in this case of Samson's life. In 1 Sam 15,35, however, the time from the final breach between Samuel and Saul to the first's death covers the last years of Samuel, since he was already old (1 Sam 8,1), when the question about introducing the kingdom was raised. It was a remarkable thing, however, and many decisive things happened before his death (1 Sam 25,1; 28,3, cf. above 3.2.1.). The king and the seer who had anointed him did not see each other during these years.

In 2 Kings 15,5 (= 2 Chron 26,21) the time marked is the years of Azariah's (Uzziah's) leprosy, when he had to hand over the actual rule to his son Jotham.[125] In the closing chapter of Jer we first read about the blinding of King Zedekiah and about his custody in Babylon for the rest of his life (Jer 52,11).[126] Easier was the fate of Jehojakin, who was released from prison by Evil-Merodach "and lived as a pensioner of the king the rest of his life" (Jer 52,33). This period is expressed in the following verse by means of the pair of phrases: ʿǎd-yôm môtô and kǎl-yᵉmê ḥǎyyâw, both meaning "the rest of his life".[127] In 2 Sam 6,23, finally, we are told that Saul's daughter Michal had no child to her "dying day", which should be regarded as a penalty for her contemptuous criticism of King David's dance before the ark of the Lord (v. 20).

A review of the use of this formula shows that it is used about rather unpleasant ways of ending one's life, such as Samuel's controversy with Saul, Azariah's illness, Zedekiah's imprisonment, and Michal's childlessness. However there are also what might be called positive developments such as Samson's time as a Nazirite and Jehojakin's rehabilitation. It would seem then that this formula as such is a rather neutral way of marking the remaining years of a person's life. It assumes the meaning of "the rest of one's life", once completed with a beginning point "from birth" (Judg 13,7) and once equated with the expression "all the days of his (remaining) life" (Jer 52, 33-34).

It should be noted that we have the expression *yôm-hămmawœt* in Eccl. 7,1 and 8,8. It does of course refer to the end of life, but in the first case there is a favourable comparison with the beginning of life and in the second it is stated that man has no knowledge of his end. In neither case does the expression have the time marking function.

4.2. At the death of ...

From the rather clear cases determined by the preposition *ʿăd* discussed above, we turn to expressions in which the preposition *bᵉ* is followed by the construct form or a suffix form of *mawœt*. The time indication is here more difficult to determine because of the character of the preposition. Sometimes this is a way to introduce the object, which is undoubtedly the case in Ez 18,32 and 33,11. But also the question whether *bᵉ* expresses simultaneity or something that happened immediately after death must be resolved from case to case.

4.2.1. *bᵉmôt* ...

I shall here discuss five instances spread over quite different parts of the Hebrew Bible: Gen 21,16; Numb 26,10; Judg 2,19; Prov 11,7 and Esth 2,7. Of special interest are again the time relation and the context situation.

In Gen 21,16 Hagar's words *ʾăl ʾœrʾœ bᵉmôt hăyyœlœd* has been translated "how can I watch the child die" (NEB) or "Let me not look on as the child dies" (NJV). Both renderings presuppose of course simultaneity between watching and dying and also that *bᵉ* expresses a time relation and does not simply introduce the object of her watching.[128] Turning to Numb 26,10 *bᵉmôt haʿedā* has been rendered as "when that band died" (NJV) and "and so their company died" (NEB) referring to Korah and his followers. This happened in connection with an uprising by Korah against Moses and Aaron, which was followed by divine punishment in the form of a natural catastrophe, where the rebels were swallowed up by the earth and burnt up by fire (cf. Numb 16,1ff.). Death clearly takes place here in immediate connection with the natural catastrophe; here it happened in reality and was not antecipated as in the case of Hagar and Ishmael. In Judg 2,19, however, death must have occurred first: $w^e hay\bar{a}$ $b^e m\hat{o}t$ $h\check{a}\check{s}\check{s}\hat{o}pe\d{t}$ can be rendered "But as soon as the judge was dead" (NEB). What then took place belongs to the Deuteronomistical pattern, namely the relapse into deeper corruption than before, followed by divine punishment and rescue through a new judge and so on. Here $b^e m\hat{o}t$ expresses a time immediately before this sequence of events; it is their starting point.[129] Simultaneity is again presupposed in Prov 11,7 where $b^e m\hat{o}t$ $^{\circ}adam$ $ra\check{s}a^c$, or simply $^{\circ}adam$ as some MSS read, marks the end of hope — regardless of how we interpret the following words.[130] Finally we have Esth 2,7 where Mordecai's adoption of Esther had happened $\hat{u}b^e m\hat{o}t$ $^{\circ}ab\hat{\imath}ha$ $w^{e\circ}immah$, that is "after the death of her father and mother" (NEB), since adoption must have been preceded by the death of her parents.[131]

Of five instances we would regard three as expressing simultaneity between $b^e m\hat{o}t$ ... and the immediate context, whereas two cases (Judg 2,19 and Esth 2,7) have $b^e m\hat{o}t$ ... as a prerequisite for the following events. However, there too this event or these events follow "as soon as" death has occurred or immediately after, so that simultaneity is very near, indeed. As to the contextual situations there does not seem to be any other similarities than the unpleasant event death is to be regarded as. Rather all five situations represent quite different conditions out of which or in connection with which other things emerge. From a purely formal point of view, however, we could regard $b^e m\hat{o}t$ ... as a formula, since the construction of the phrase is always the same. The variable is the person(s) dead but the constant element would count as a formula. On the other hand, the lack of any specific function in the context rather speaks in favour of regarding this expression as an 'idiom', which would explain why it is quite freely used.

4.2.2. $b^e m\hat{o}t\hat{o}$

This expression occurs seven (or six) times and has in three (or five) cases a clear chronological or time marking function. These cases are:

Numb 33,39 "he (Aaron) was a hundred and twenty-three years old when he died";

Deut 34,7 "Moses was a hundred and twenty years old when he died";

2 Chron 24,15 "Jehoiadah (was) . . . a hundred and thirty years old when
        he died";

2 Chron 32,33 "all Judah and the people of Jerusalem paid him (Hezekiah)
        honour when he died";

Judg 16,30   "so the dead whom he (Samson) killed at his death were
        more than those he had killed in his life".

Although all five cases occur in concluding phrases about death and burial
(cf. above ch. 3), three of them give the actual age of the deceased – every
time a high figure (123, 120 and 130 years). In the case of Hezekiah it is the
honour he received from his people at his death. This could be compared with
Judg 16,30 which is a kind of summing up of Samson's life coming to an unusual end in the Philistine temple. He was duly buried in his family grave and
there is a mention of his twenty years as judge over Israel. From this we may
conclude, that although neither of these statements about Hezekiah and
Samson gives the age of the deceased, but rather other circumstances show-
ing their importance, nevertheless they occur in concluding phrases about
death and burial.

The two remaining cases do not have to do with the death of a historical
person but instead with reflections about what endures and does not endure
when a man dies:

Ps 49,18   "for when he dies he can take none of it along; his goods
        cannot follow him down";

Prov 14,32   "An evil man is brought down by his wickedness; the up-
        right man is secure in his own honesty/ at his own death"
        (MT);

If we prefer to read $b^e tumm\hat{o}$, "in his honesty/innocence" in Prov 14,32
(with LXX and Peshitta), which undoubtedly makes a better parallel with
$b^e ra^c at\hat{o}$, "by his wickedness" than MT:s $b^e m\hat{o}t\hat{o}$, "at his death",[133] we have
only one case left, namely Ps 49,18. Here the futility of richness is demon-
strated: earthly belongings do not follow a man in his grave. This is well in
keeping with the sapiential character of the psalm as such.[134]

From the above examples we can conclude that the expression $b^e m\hat{o}t\hat{o}$ is
not restricted to one specific context. In three cases it is connected with the

number of years someone had attained "at his death"; in two other cases it refers to the death of a historical person, too, but is connected with other circumstances which distinguish him "at his death". In the one remaining case it occurs in a reflection about the fate of a rich man "at his death". Now this means that the time marking function is most obvious in the three first cases, it also has this function in the following two, referring to what actually happened at Hezekiah's and Samson's death. In the sapiential reflection of Ps 49,18, however, we meet a phenomenon that always repeats itself, namely that a rich man must "at his death" be parted from his goods. If we followed MT's reading in Prov 14,32, the same would hold true here: it is about something that always and universally repeats itself. Thus if we wish to speak about $b^e m \hat{o} t \hat{o}$ as a formula, we have to restrict it to the three first, or with caution to five cases, whereas Ps 49,18 shows that we have another use of the expression, too. This would be easily explained if we assumed that $b^e m \hat{o} t \hat{o}$ were an idiomatic expression which can rather freely be used in various contexts. But here the position of the expression within the concluding phrases about a person, which follow a certain pattern, favour a formulaic use at least in Numb 33,39; Deut 34,7 and 2 Chron 24,15, and with reservation in 2 Chron 32,33 and Judg 16,30, too.

4.3. After the death of ...

The prepositional phrase $\partial a h^a r \hat{e} \ m \hat{o} t$ ... is a relatively common and clear expression of dating something after someone's death. Although the construction of the phrase is nearly the same in all cases, I shall try to make some distinctions based upon syntactic grounds.

In the phrase $k a^a \check{s} \alpha r \ met$ ... the death referred to lies in the past in two cases of three, which thus have a temporal meaning. I shall therefore discuss them in this paragraph.

4.3.1. wayhî $\partial a h^a r \hat{e} \ m \hat{o} t$ ...

This phrase occurs at the beginning of a sentence in Gen 25,11; Jos 1,1; Judg 1,1 and 2 Sam 1,1. It is followed three times by another ipf cons form and once (2 Sam 1,1) by a perf form. This seems to be a rather particular way of expressing the transition from one epoch to another: from Abraham to Isaac (Gen 25,11), from Moses to Joshua (Jos 1,1), from Joshua to the Judges (Judg 1,1) and from Saul to David (2 Sam 1,1). These epochs are tied to individual leaders and so their deaths become time markers. It goes without saying that death as such is not the point here and therefore not dwelt upon. The death of the leader is usually described earlier and, when referred to in this connection, it is a kind of chronological remark.

Were it not for Gen 25,11 we would have to regard the phrase as a Deuteronomistic "transition phrase". However, we can now call it a *transition formula* instead and it is indeed one of the most characteristic time marking formulas to be found in the Hebrew Bible. We will now proceed to some variations of it, where the time marking function is less obvious.

4.3.2. $w^{e,}\breve{a}\dot{h}^a r\hat{e}\ m\hat{o}t$ ...

This phrase is also found at the beginning of a sentence or clause in Numb 35,28; 2 Chron 24,17 and, slightly modified, in 1 Chron 2,24 ($w^{e,}\breve{a}\dot{h}\bar{a}r$ $m\hat{o}t$- . . .). It is obviously used as chronological remark, but not in the same epoch-marking way as the previous phrase. It is used about the time after the death of the high priest, when the homicide was allowed to leave his asylum (Numb 35,28 cf. above 4.1.1.). In 1 Chron 2,24 it is used in an etiological list about Hezron's death and Caleb's fathering of Ashhur. In 2 Chron 24,17 it introduces the events after the death of the high priest Jehoiadah, whose death and burial are mentioned in the preceding verses (cf. 4.2.2.). The contexts are rather different: a legal statement, an etiological list and a narrative passage. It is not an equivalent to the previous phrase then, but a formula which is rather freely used.

4.3.3. $\textdegree\breve{a}\dot{h}^a r\hat{e}\ m\hat{o}t$ ...

This phrase comes rather close to the preceding, but there is a difference in its syntactic position: it does not begin a new sentence or clause, but comes somewhere in the middle or at the end. Examples found are Gen 26,18;

Lev 16,1; 2 Kings 14,17 = 2 Chron 25,25; 2 Kings 1,1; 2 Chron 22,4; Ruth 2,11. Again the contexts differ in content, but they are all narrative passages. After Abraham's death the wells dug by him were stopped up by the Philistines (Gen 26,18). After the death of Aaron's two sons the Lord gave Moses instructions as how to enter the sanctuary (Lev 16,1). After Ahab's death Moab rebelled against Israel (2 Kings 1,1). Amaziah of Judah lived fifteen years after the death of King Jehoash of Israel (2 Kings 14,17 = 2 Chron 25,25). Ahaziah of Judah followed the evil ways of the house of Ahab after the latter's death (2 Chron 22,4). Boaz was told, what Ruth had done after the death of her husband (Ruth 2,11). One of these instances could be regarded as introducing a new epoch (2 Kings 1,1), two others have to do with royal chronologies (2 Kings 14,17 = 2 Chron 25,25; 2 Chron 22,4). The three remaining could be said to mark new situations and how they were faced (Gen 26,18; Ruth 2,11) or should be faced (Lev 16,1). The last of the three is a narrative introduction to legal regulations, while the other can be said to be purely narrative or give the chronological framework to a narrative passage. Thus we have here all the functions represented by the two earlier phrases discussed.

4.3.4. ˀ*ăḥᵃrê môtî*

This is a repeated phrase found in Deut 31,27.29. Moses fears that the Israelites, being stubborn and defying the Lord when he is still alive (*bᵉˁôdænnî ḥăy*), will continue to do so much more after his death (ˀ*ăḥᵃrê môtî*). This fear he continues to state: "For I know that after my death you will . . ." (v. 29). It is quite clear, that he regards his death not as a turning point, but as a moment when things become even worse than before, during his lifetime, when he himself was able to act as a mediator. It is a new situation that his people will face and his death is a time marker. It would seem, then, that this variation is a casual modification of the usual form of the phrase due only to the circumstance that Moses himself is speaking, or rather, that Deut is stylized as a long address by Moses to the people.

4.3.5. *kăᵃšær met*

The first of three instances employs the phrase *kăᵃšær-met* to express a comparison between the death of Moses and that of Aaron (Deut 32,50). This use of *kăᵃšær* is not temporal and is accordingly translated "just as Aaron your brother died" (cf. above 4.3.1.). In the other two cases the use of *kăᵃšær met* is temporal. Judg 8,33 begins with *wăyhî kăᵃšær met gidᶜôn*, "after Gideon's death", where the meaning is the same as in Judg 2,19 (cf. above 4.2.1.), i.e. "as soon as" the judge was dead the Israelites returned to idolatry according to the so called Deuteronomistic pattern. In 2 Sam 12,21 David's behaviour in connection with his son's death is astonishingly described to himself by his servants: "while the boy lived you fasted and wept for him, but now that he is dead (*wᵉkăᵃšær met*) you rise up and eat" (NEB). Also without correcting MT's reading *băᵃbûr* to *bᵉᶜôd*[135] the temporal distinction between "still alive" and "now dead" ought to be clear enough. It follows, then, that the phrase *kăᵃšær met* . . . in two of three cases has the temporal meaning of a time immediately after death has occurred, whereas in one instance it has the comparative meaning "as", "like". Since the Hebrew phrase is the same in all three cases, all of them count as a formula, although its meaning differs in accordance with the context. This would be the obvious conclusion, if we adopt the strictly formal criterion of a formula being "a repeated word group". One may ask whether an additional criterion again would be required. If one cannot postulate that formulas must have a specific function within similar contexts, one should nevertheless require that a formula must have the same meaning, whether it occurs in similar or in different contexts. If so, Deut 32,50 cannot be counted as an example of a formulaic use of the phrase in question.

4.3.6. *Summary*

The time marking function of *ᵃḥᵃrê môt* . . . was found in all the variations discussed above. However, the contexts themselves were different, so that we cannot speak about a specific function in a certain context or even similar contexts. This would hold true only for 4.3.1., which is a transition formula marking off whole epochs. Among the other variants we found some comparable cases too, but here the contexts differed more. This does not mean, however, that the character of formula would apply only to those cases with the specific epoch-marking function. As long as we have to do with a death of historical personalities, we cannot merely refer to a common use, i.e. death being a time marker, after which something takes place. We are tempted here again to speak about idiomatic expressions which have quite a clear meaning but which are not restricted to specific contexts, but can be used rather freely. Unfortunately the biblical material here does not allow for a distinction between 'formula' and 'idiom' as was stated in the introduction. We can only point out that there are formulas with a specific function within a certain type of context, and then there are others with a wider application. Among these one has to consider if they are not 'idioms' instead.

One major difference between *'ăḥᵃrê môt* . . . and *kǎ-ᵃšœr met* . . . is that the second one does not have one distinct meaning: it was twice used in a temporal sense with a similar meaning as *'ăḥᵃrê môt* . . ., but in addition to this there is one case with a comparative meaning, "just as" (Deut 32,50). Thus only in its temporal use can this phrase be called a formula, and that with hesitation too, since both remaining cases (Judg 8,33 and 2 Sam 12,21) are found in rather different contexts. However, there is a similarity in this temporal sense in all the cases discussed above, which justifies our attempt to treat them together as formulas marking time.

4.4. Succession

We have already met the succession formula *wǎyyimlok tǎḥtǎw* (3.3.3.). Its most common use can be found in the Deuteronomistic pattern used about more than twenty Judean and Israelite kings. This pattern contains the formula *wǎyyiškǎb ʿim ᵃbotâw* (cf. above 3.3.1.), a formula about burial in the royal tombs, and the succession formula, which as a rule applies to dynastic succession. This pattern expresses peaceful succession, but it is restricted to Israelite and Judean kings; about foreign rulers and in cases of violent death we have combinations between forms of *mût* and the succession formula. Since I restrict my investigation to formulas containing the stem *mût*, I shall consequently turn to these combinations now. There are two main types to be discussed, namely combinations with the qal ipf consecutive *wǎyyamât* and with hif ipf consecutive with object suffix *wǎymîtehû*.

4.4.1. wăyyamât ... wăyyimlok tăḥtâw

In Gen 36,32-39 we have a list of eight Edomite kings which is quoted *verbatim* in 1 Chron 1,44-50. It belongs apparently to the chronological framework of 'P' and is regarded as rather old.[136] The kings do not form a dynasty, but seem to have been elected. Although this duplicate list does not qualify as a formula, it can be regarded as one basic form of the pattern. The first king is introduced by his given personal name, his father's name and his native town (Gen 36,32). The name is reiterated after *wăyyamât* whereafter the corresponding data of the successor follow. Personal details of the last king's wife are exceptionally added in Gen 36,39 (= 1 Chron 1,50). The list is one of five Edomite lists in Gen 36, after the end of the *tôl^edot yiṣḥaq* (Gen 25,19 - 35,29) and the beginning of the specific Jacob story (Gen 37). It has thus found its appropriate place here telling us what became of Jacob's brother, Esau, something which is expressed immediately in the heading of the chapter: *w^e>ellæ tol^edôt ʿeśaw hû> ^eædôm*, "this is the line of Esau – that is, Edom" (36,1). It is genealogy in the first place and chronology in the second.

In 2 Sam 10,1 (par 1 Chron 19,1) we have a note about the death of the Ammonite king Nahash[137] and the succession through his son Hanun. Here the chronological function is clear enough: the succession pattern is directly linked to the chronological formula *wăyhî >ăḥ^arê-ken*, "some time afterwards". David regarded this time as favourable for renewed contacts with the Ammonites, something that resulted in war, however.

In 1 Chron 29,28 we have the case already discussed where the pattern used about Solomon's succession to David has adopted the phrases about good old age and richness (cf. 3.3.2. and 3.3.3.). It follows after the chronological data of David's kingships in Hebron and Jerusalem (v. 26-27), so that its chronological function is clear, too.

The whole Chapter of 2 Kings 1 is devoted to King Ahaziah's accident (v. 2), his inquiry about his recovery and the prophet Eliah's intervention. Eliah foretells the king's death (*kî-môt tamût* v. 16, cf. below 6.2.2.). Thereafter the pattern continues: *wăyyamât* followed by the remark about the fulfilment of the prophetic word, the succession formula, the year of the Judean king and the note that he had no son as an explanation for why he was succeeded by his brother. Again the chronological function is clear.

The succession formula occurs twice in 2 Kings 8,15 and 13,24. It is used about the Aramean successions in Damascus: how Hazael succeeded Ben-Hadad, and how he himself was succeeded by his son Ben-Hadad. Hazael had inquired from the prophet Elisha whether his master would recover from his illness and got the ambiguous answer that he would, but that the Lord had told Elisha, that in fact he would die (2 Kings 8,10). We do not know precisely what Hazael was supposed to have done as the subject of *wayyiqqāḥ hămmăkber wăyyiṭbol bămmăyim wăyyiproš ʿăl-panăw*, "when he took the netting (blanket?) and dipped it in water and spread it before (over?) his face".[138] The result is nevertheless clear: *wăyyamăt wăyyimlok ḥᵃzāʾel tăḥtăw.* In Ackadian sources Hazael is known as an usurper, but was he the king's murderer, too? We do not know.[139] In 13,24 the time had come when Hazael himself was to be succeeded, and here there is no ambiguity: *wăyyamăt ḥᵃzaʾel . . . wăyyimlok bæn-ḥᵃdăd bᵉnô tăḥtăw.* Both the successions mark the beginning and the end of Hazael's rule, under which Israel had to endure many hardships. This is something that Elisha could foresee and weep over in advance (8,11f.) and which is retrospectively confirmed (13,22ff.). The formula has thus been used by the Deuteronomist to mark the chronology of a really important epoch of foreign rule.

It would be tempting to regard 1 Kings 16,22b as an abbreviation of the same pattern: *wăyyamăt tibnî wăyyimlok ʿămrî,* which would then mean that Tibni died a peaceful death and was succeeded by Omri. On the other hand, in LXX we have the words "and his brother Joram", which do not look like a secondary addition.[140] If both brothers died at the same time, however, we have to consider a violent death,[141] a result of the power struggle hinted at in the first half of the verse. If so, the phrase could be regarded as euphemistic or obscure, but also — given the ambiguity of 2 Kings 8,15 — as an expression used for lack of more detailed information. On the other hand, the fact that *tăḥtăw* is missing here can be seen as an indication that there was no real succession at all and that Omri came to power after an interregnum (cf. the four years gap between the chronologies in v. 10 and 23), during which he fought Tibni.

The succession Joash - Amaziah as related in 2 Kings 12,21f. (par 2 Chron 24,25.27) was brought about through assassination: *hikkuhû wăyyamot,* cf. 2 Chron 24,25: *wăyyăhărguhû . . . wăyyamot* (cf. below 6.10.1.). The Deuteronomist then has the ordinary burial formula "and he was buried with his forefathers in the city of David", whereas the Chronicler goes out of his way to point out that "he was buried in the city of David, but not in the burial place of the kings" (v. 25). The Deuteronomist then immediately has the succession formula, while the Chronicler inserts (v. 26-27) some notes on the identity of the killers before also giving the same formula. It is interesting in this connection to note the sequence of two verbs for the slaying.

In the following section we shall look at the particular conspiracy pattern. The difference between this case and usual conspiracies is that while King Joash was assassinated by his servants and followed by his son as the legitimate successor, the conspiracy usually ends with the succession of the conspirator himself. The chronology involved follows at the beginning of the following chapter (2 Kings 13,1 par 2 Chron 25,1) in both versions.

The assassination of the Assyrian king, Sennacherib, by two of his sons is expressed by *hikkuhû b̆ăhærœb* but without any form of *mût* (2 Kings 19,37 = Is 37,38). His succession by a third son, Esarhaddon, is nevertheless expressed by the succession formula. What happens here is rather similar to the case of Joash.

4.4.2. *wăymîtehu . . . wăyyimlok tăhtâw*

Whereas the sequence *wăyyamât . . . wăyyimlok tăhtâw* was sometimes ambiguous as to whether the succession occurred in a peaceful way or not, this sequence is a clear expression of succession through killing or assassination of the predecessor by the successor. Moreover, whereas both verbs in the previous formula had different subjects, the subject here is the same. Since it is a question of narrative forms, the crucial sequence is usually not restricted to these two verbs, but can comprise four or five. I shall here list these verbs:

1 Kings 15,27f.	*wăyyiqšor . . . wăyyăkkehû . . . wăymitehû . . . wăyyimlok tăhtâw*
1 Kings 16,10	*wăyyabo> . . . wăyyăkkehû wăymîtehû . . . wăyyimlok tăhtâw*
2 Kings 15,10	*wăyyiqšor . . . wăyyăkkehû . . . wăymîtehû wăyyimlok tăhtâw*
2 Kings 15,14	*wăyyabo> . . . wăyyăk >æt- . . . wăymîtehû wăyyimlok tăhtâw*

2 Kings 15,25   wǎyyiqšor . . . wǎyyǎkkehû . . . wǎymîtehû wǎyyimlok
tǎḥtâw

2 Kings 15,30   wǎyyiqsâr-qœšœr . . . wǎyyǎkkehû wǎymîtehû wǎyyimlok
tǎḥtâw

Although there are no two absolutely similar sequences here, it is easy to discern a common pattern comprising four verbs; in 2 Kings 15,14 we have a fifth (wǎyyǎ‘ǎl) preceding wǎyyaboʾ. The first verb is four times wǎyyiqšor ‘alâw followed by the name of the name of the usurpator, who is the common subject of the whole series. In addition to this there is the fact that we have wǎyyiqšor also in 1 Kings 16,9, which means that here too we have a series of five verbs. In all cases we have the form wǎyyǎkkehû, except in 2 Kings 15,14 where the equivalent wǎyyǎk ʾœt- occurs. Thus it is only the first verbs which vary, whereas the three concluding verbs are the same. Let us have a brief look at the other data given in each case:

1) the *name of the conspirator,* including his father's name:

1 Kings 15,27	Baasha son of Ahijah
2 Kings 15,10	Shallum son of Jabesh
2 Kings 15,14	Menahem son of Elah
2 Kings 15,25	Pekah son of Remaliah
2 Kings 15,30	Hoshea son of Elah

About Baasha we are informed about his tribe (Issachar) and in two other cases about the conspirator's 'previous occupation', namely:

1 Kings 16,9	Zimri, "who was in service commanding half of the chariotry"
2 Kings 15,25	Pekah . . . "his (Pekahiah's) lieutenant";

2) the *place of the conspiracy* with occasional details:

1 Kings 15,27	Gibbeton
1 Kings 16,9	Tirzah
2 Kings 15,10	Ibleam (uncertain reading)[142]

2 Kings 15,14   Samaria
2 Kings 15,25   Samaria

3) the *time of conspiracy* according to the year of the reigning Judean king:

1 Kings 15,28	the third year of Asa king of Judah (Baasha)
1 Kings 16,10	the twenty-seventh year of Asa king of Judah (Zimri)
2 Kings 15,13	the thirty-ninth year of Uzziah king of Judah (Shallum)
2 Kings 15,13	after one full month (Menahem)
2 Kings 15,27	the fifty-second year of Azariah king of Judah (Pekah)
2 Kings 15,30	the twentieth year of Jotham son of Uzziah (Hoshea)

In only three of six cases is the time for the conspiracy given within the pattern, in the case of Menahem it is mentioned before, and in the cases of Shallum and Pekah, after the sequence. That is also the case regarding the name of the *victim of the conspiracy,* whose name is mentioned in the pattern in 2 Kings 15,14 (Shallum) and 2 Kings 15,30 (Pekah). In the other cases the name is to be found in the context before or after the pattern.

It is obvious from these examples that we have a "conspiracy pattern" built upon four or five verbs in imperfect narrative forms. The first verb thereby expresses the conspiracy (*wăyyiqšor*) and is only once missing. The three last verbs are invariably the same and occur in the same order (*wăyyăkkehû wăymîtehû wăyyimlok tăḥtâw*). The other constant elements are the name of the conspirator, the place and time of the conspiracy. Although the time occurs only three times in the pattern, in the remaining cases it can be inferred from the context. Thus it is clear enough that this pattern has a chronological function, at the beginning and the end of the Deuteronomistic history of the Northern Kingdom.

4.4.3. Summary

Comparing the two types of succession patterns we have observed, that they have in common the succession formula *wăyyimlok tăḥtâw* at the end of the sequence. While the first was characterized by another narrative wăyyamất, the second showed a series of narratives beginning with wăyyiqšor, and followed by the expression for assassination wăyyăkkehû wăymîtehû. This conspiracy pattern is restricted to the Deuteronomistic work and used about six Northern Israelite conspiracies. The first pattern is used about Israelite and Judean as well as about foreign rulers. Here we found some border cases where the narrative wăyyamất was preceded by expressions for killing (2 Kings 12,21f./2 Chron 24,25.27), where a form of mût was missing (2 Kings 19,37 = Is 37,28) or where the expression was ambiguous as to the way of death (1 Kings 16,22). In all three cases the throne was violently seized, but in 1 Kings 16,22 there was no succession from Tibni to Omri, since both fought over the throne. Although this chapter includes three conspiracies, only the first (v. 9-10) is described by means of the pattern. The reason why v. 18 does not have the succession pattern is obviously that Zimri took his own life by burning himself in the royal palace. Moreover, the third phrase took the form of a power struggle between two rival successors, which ended with the victory of Omri. Both cases were singular and could therefore not be expressed with the coined conspiracy pattern of the Deuteronomistic writer.

The chronological function of the succession expressed by these patterns is usually quite obvious by inclusion of the year of succession in the pattern or in the context. Only regarding foreign rulers was this not the case, since the chronology here is not the primary concern of the biblical writer.

4.5. Genealogy and age

We sahll now turn to some data about genealogy and age found chiefly in the 'P' stratum of Genesis, but also in some other phrases. We have to distinguish between those genealogies which make up all we know about the persons involved (Gen 5) and the genealogical phrases about death and progeny of persons about whom more details stemming from various sources have been reported. We shall start with the first kind of genealogies. It should be noted, too, that most of the phrases discussed here contain the pair of opposites to be discussed in a separate chapter (ch. 8). However, since I consider this use of opposites to belong to a chronological and genealogical framework, I shall accordingly deal with these phrases here.

4.5.1. From Adam to Noah

In Gen 5 we have a basic formulaic pattern, which shows a deviation only about the first and the last of its persons, namely Adam and Noah. This pattern runs in the following way:[143]

wǎyhî-A X šanîm wǎyyôlæd ʾæt-B	A was X years old when he begot B
wǎyhî-A ʾǎhᵃrê hôlîdô ʾæt-B	After the birth of B, A lived
Y šanîm wǎyyôlæd banîm ûbanôt	Y years and begot sons and daughters
wǎyyihyû kǎl-yᵉ mê-A Z šanîm	All the days of A came to Z years,
wǎyyamot	then he died

This pattern is repeated in Gen 5,6-8, 9-11, 12-14, 15-17, 18-20, 25-27 and 28,30-31. It is used about the respective ages of Seth (912), Enosh (905), Kenan (910), Mahalalel (895), Jared (962), Methuselah (969) and Lamech (777). Adam being the first in line has an additional remark "a son in his likeness, after his image" (v. 3) and Hanoch, the pattern being basically the same, is given two such remarks: "Enoch walked with God" (v. 22a) and "Enoch walked with God, and then was no more, because God took him" (v. 24). Their respective ages are also given: Adam 930 years (v. 5) and Enoch 365 years (v. 23).

As for Noah, in v. 29 we have an etymology of his name: "This one will bring us relief from our work and the toil of our hands, out of the very soil which YHWH had placed under ban". He lived 500 years before he begot Shem, Ham and Japhet (v. 32). When 'P' returns to his age after the flood another hundred years have elapsed, since after living 350 more years he reaches a total age of 950 years (Gen 9,28-29). But still the same pattern is maintained: wǎyhî instead of wǎyhî in 5,32, but then wǎyhî ʾǎhǎr in 9,28 and wǎyyihyû ... wǎyyamât in 9,29.

The genealogical interest of 'P' in reaching as far back as possible[144] seems to be manifest in this list. Together with the Cainite list, Gen 4,17-24 which gives no ages, this genealogy points back to a common source in Mesopotamia. There are, however, certain differences which ought to be stressed: a) there is no resemblance in the names between the biblical and the Mesopotamian antediluvian lists, b) the relatively high ages of the 'P' list are rather modest in comparison with the latter, and c) the biblical lists are interested in patriarchs not kings. The numerical significance of Hanoch's age being the solar number of 365 and of Lamech's 777 years being composed of 7 and 77 have parallels outside the Bible too.[145] Furthermore, the mere fact of genealogy used to mark epochs and to secure links with the remote past is of course the same. That this should be expressed in a stereotyped way by using such patterns is not surprising at all. Perhaps the deviations are more interesting than the likeness. They tell us something important about three persons in the list: Adam, Hanoch and Noah. While the story about Adam is already told and that of Noah follows, the remarks about Hanoch within the pattern are all we know about him and therefore all the more important.

4.5.2. From Terah to Job

The notes about age are in several cases given immediately before the phrases about death. This is the case particularly in the chronological framework of 'P' in Genesis. Here we do not find a stereotype pattern like that in Gen 5, but rather far reaching similarities. We shall try to find out whether and in which cases we are justified in speaking about a pattern here:

Gen 11,32   wǎyyihyû yᵉmê-tærǎḥ ... wǎyyamàt tærǎḥ ...
Gen 23,1-2   wǎyyihyû ḥǎyyê śarā ... šᵉnê ḥǎyyê śarā wǎttamàt ...
Gen 25,7-8   wᵉᵃ ellæ yᵉmê šᵉnê-ḥǎyyê ᵃbraham ᵃšær-ḥay ...
             wǎyyigwǎˤ wǎyyamàt ...
Gen 25,17   wᵉᵃ ellæ šᵉnê ḥǎyyê yišmaᵃel ... wǎyyigwǎˤ wǎyyamàt
             ...
Gen 35,28-29 wǎyyihyû yᵉmê yiṣḥaq ... wǎyyigwǎˤ yiṣḥaq wǎyyamàt
             ...
Gen 47,28-29 wǎyḥî yǎᵃqob ... wǎyyiqrᵉbû yᵉmê-yiśraᵃel lamût ...
Gen 50,22.24.26 wǎyḥî yôsep ... ᵃanokî met ... wǎyyamàt yôsep ...
Job 42,16-17 wǎyḥî ᵃiyyôb ... wǎyyamàt ᵃiyyôb ...

From these examples we can discover only two introduction phrases which are repeated, namely wǎyyihyû yᵉmê ..., "the days of x came to ..." (Gen

11,32; 35,28) and *wăyḥî* x . . ., "x lived . . .". While the first occurs only in 'P', the second is an idiom occurring in connection with *mût* in Gen 47,28-29 ('P'/'J'), in Gen 50,22 ('E')[146] and in the epilogue to Job. Within the 'P' framework we have other similarities such as *š^enê ḥăyyê* . . . (Gen 23,1; 25,7; 25,17), and the combination of the phrases about age with the death-burial pattern (Gen 25,7-9; 35,28-29 cf. Gen 25,17). Then there is outside 'P' the combination with other phrases about dying (Gen 47,29, cf. 2.2.1.; Gen 50,24, cf. 2.1.1. and Job 42,17, cf. 3.3.2.). In all cases the phrase about age is followed by the corresponding phrase about the actual death of the person, except for Gen 47,28-29,[147] where Jacob speaks about his impending death. In the case of Joseph the key phrases are spread over a wider context, Gen 50,22-26, so that one can ask whether we really have here a formulaic pattern. But if we take the different phrase about age as one element and the phrase about actual death as the other, then of course we have a kind of age and death pattern in most of the cases, except for Gen 47,28-29 and perhaps also Gen 50,22-26. In so doing, we have allowed for rather large variations regarding both elements. This pattern would be restricted to and typical again of 'P', save for the instance of Job. Turning to the combination 'P'/'J' in Gen 47 and to 'E' in Gen 50 we would transcend the limits of this pattern, although there too age and death are combined.[148]

As to the function of this pattern, we must be content to say that it is used in the general chronological framework of 'P' and that the author of the Job epilogue has chosen to conclude the tale with phrases similar to those used about the patriarchs in Genesis. The similarities in form with the 'P' list in Gen 5 are also quite apparent but here the genealogy was the chief motif and the pattern included itself the whole life span of the patriarch, whereas the function here is to contribute a conclusion to the *tôl^edôt* story of the respective patriarch.[149]

4.5.3. Dying without sons

Here we may include a short note about the lack of male offspring. We have already mentioned the case of 2 Kings 1,17, where we were told that Ahaziah was followed by his brother Jehoram because he had no son (*kî lo[>]-hayā lô ben*, cf. 4.4.1.). This seems to be a quite precise and unrepeated piece of information about the lack of a legitimate heir to the throne. When we turn to the Chronicler we find two different phrases about the lack of sons. First we have the twice repeated phrase *wǎyyamât* plus name and *loʾ banîm*. It is used about Seled and Jether in 1 Chron 2,30.32. The importance of this information is due to the fact that dying without a son meant the extinction of the family. For comparison we may turn to v. 34, where we read about Sheshan: *wᵉloʾ hayā lᵉšešan banîm kî-ʿim banôt*, "Sheshan left no sons but daughters". There is a contradiction between this information and v. 31, where a son is mentioned. This obviously means that we have another list in v. 34ff. What is more interesting in this connection is of course the more detailed information: Sheshan had offspring through his daughter and his slave. Finally in 1 Chron 23,22 we have the same phrase about Eleazar: *wǎyyamât* plus name and *wᵉloʾ-hayû lô banîm kî ʿim-banôt*, "When Eleazar died, he left no sons but daughters". In this Levitical genealogy the line is continued through marriage between the daughters of Eleazar and the sons of his brother Kish. This would mean that there is a clear intention behind the statement that one left no sons but daughters, because it was precisely through the daughters the line was nevertheless continued. To sum up: we have two phrases about the lack of sons both restricted to the genealogical lists of the Chronicler. The first simply states that there was no son, which means that the line was cut off. The other adds the information about daughters, through which the line was then continued. One can of course then ask: whose line? In 1 Chron 2,34 it is implied that it was indeed Sheshan's line, since his daughter was married to his Egyptian slave. But in the case of Eleazar, it would obviously be the line of his brother Kish, since his sons married the daughters of Eleazar. It should also be added that these genealogies do not include chronological data in the manner of the kings and their successors.

A quite unique case is that famous Deuteronomistic remark about Michal's childlessness as a punishment for her contempt of David and his dancing before the Ark of the Lord: *loʾ-hayā lah yœlœd ʿǎd yôm môtah*, "she had no child to her dying day" (2 Sam 6,23). But here it is her personal tragedy, not that of the royal dynasty that is at stake.

4.6. Conclusions

We found several formulas not only expressing time but having a chronological function. The construct form *môt* preceded by the prepositions *ʿăd* (4.1.), *bᵉ* and *ʾăhăr* or *ʾăhᵃrê* could for the most cases also be viewed as idioms used to express before, at and after the death of someone. Their meaning was simple and they could be used in various contexts. There were, however, several cases where this observation does not suffice. When there was a clear similarity in the function of a certain phrase, we had to regard it as formulaic. Such cases were, for example, 4.1.1. and 4.3.1. But also in other expressions, where a common use or function was absent, we were inclined to speak about formulas instead of idioms, since the material was too scarce to provide a criterion for distinguishing formulas from mere idioms. Such cases were 4.1.2., 4.2.1., 4.2.2., 4.3.2., 4.3.3., 4.3.4., 4.3.5.

Under the heading "succession" (4.4.) we discussed two different patterns, both consisting of the succession formula *wăyyimlok tăhtăw* as the final link in a chain of narratives. The first pattern had only one other constant element, namely the narrative of *mût,* while the other showed a sequence of three or four other narratives, usually introduced with the conspiracy formula *wăyyiqšor ʿalăw* ... This second formulaic pattern was used about conspiracies by the Deuteronomist, whereas the first had a wider application and was used mainly about peaceful succession, although some of them were ambiguous as to their real meaning. Their chronological function within the closing words about the respective king's reign or as an introduction to the successor was mostly clear. Here there is no doubt that the term formula or rather formulaic pattern is justified in view of the form as well as of the function of the repeated elements.

5. CAUSES OF DEATH

There are several repeated phrases which express the cause of death. Common to them is that the cause itself is introduced by the preposition b^e. Within this group of phrases we shall distinguish between the *reason,* that is mostly sin or disobedience toward God, and the *way* of death, that is starvation, plague, death in war or by the sword, etc. I shall, however, begin this chapter by discussing certain stereotype *questions* about the causes of death. They are formally different from the statements about the causes: common to them is the interrogative *lammā.*

5.1. Why should you die?

In only one case is there an explicit reference to premature death: *lammā tamût b^elo> ͨittæka,* "Why should you die before your time?" (Eccl 7,17). It follows after two exhortations: "do not be over-wicked and do not be a fool". It is clear from this that premature death is thought of as a consequence of something to be done or not to be done. The actual reason for death is also explicitly mentioned once: *lammā yûmăt mæ ͨaśā,* "Why should he be killed, what has he done?" (1 Sam 20,32). This is what Jonathan asks his father Saul because the latter's intention to kill David.

The two questions quoted refer to reasons for the death of an individual. There are also similar questions about collective groups: *w^elammā namût nægdæka,* "why should we die before you?" (Gen 47,15) and *lammā namût l^eͨênͨeka,* "why should we die before your eyes?" (v. 19), both put to Joseph by the Egyptians. Both are conditioned by their request for bread: *habā-llanû læhæm,* "give us bread!" (v. 15) and could therefore also be rendered "lest we die" (NJV) or "or we shall die" (NEB), i.e., as a consequence of hunger. In Deut 5,22 *lammā namût* is explained with the words "for this fearsome fire will consume us". The anticipated cause of death here is the fire on Mount Sinai. In Jer 27,13 a similar question is put to the king: *lammā tamûtû ʾăttā wᵉˁămmᵉka*, "why should you and your people die?" and in Ez 18,31 and 33,11 the question runs: *lammā tamûtû bêt yiśraʾel*, "why should you die, you men of Israel?" In the first instance the reason for death is submittance to the king of Babylon. In Ez 18 and 33, however, it is not clear whether it is an individual or a collective who is threatened, but the context speaks for the latter alternative.[150] Sins, then, are misdeeds of the past, which are considered to be the cause of deportation and exile. This again would have fatal consequences for the national survival of the people, if they did not repent.

We saw that they need not be rendered as questions like "why should . . .", but could easily be regarded as meaning "lest we die" or "or we shall die" or "let us not die". They are thus assumed to be negated, because this alternative should obviously be chosen to avoid the danger or threat. This would mean that they are rhetorical. They are a means of forcefully pointing toward an impending danger and imply a request to prevent or remove this threat. This can be done according to special circumstances: by being wise and not wicked (Eccl 7,16f.); by giving the people bread (Gen 47,15.19); by having Moses as a mediator on Mount Sinai (Deut 5,22); by giving up resistance to the Babylonians (Jer 27,12) and by repenting (Ez 18,31 and 33,11).

Formally the questions can all be viewed as variations of the same formula. Since their function and meaning are obviously the same, or at least similar, they constitute a formula proper: a rhetorical question with the function of pointing to a danger which would inevitably lead to death unless it were removed.

5.2. Death because of sin

Next I shall discuss the instances where the cause of death is expressed through the substantives *ˁawôn*, *ˁæwæl*, *hetʾ*, or *hăttaʾt*. All of them are words indicating wrongdoing, iniquity, sin. I shall divide them into two groups by combining the first two and the last two.

84

5.2.1. *mût* – *bă͑ᵃwôn(ô)*/*b^e͑ăwlô*

The combination of *mût* (qal) with a form of *ᶜawôn* is found in the following phrases:

Ez 3,18; 33,8   *hû' raša' bă͑ᵃwônô yamût;*
Ez 3,19; 33,9   *hû' bă͑ᵃwônô yamût;*
Ez 18,17   *hû' lo' yamût bă͑ᵃwôn 'abîw;*
Ez 18,18   *w^e hinnē met bă͑ᵃwônô;*
Ez 7,16¹⁵¹   *kullam yamûtû 'iš bă͑ᵃwônô;*
Jer 31,30   *kî 'im-'iš bă͑ᵃwônô yamût;*

The main differences are the negation in Ez 18,17 and the perfect form in Ez 18,18. Knierim regards the phrase as formulated by Ezechiel after the model of legal, declaratory forms (Deut 24,16) and partly "prophetical formulations". Since it cannot be found in older sources it cannot be regarded a formula proper.¹⁵² According to our criteria, however, the instance in Jer would count as a formulaic use, although the *Sitz im Leben* is not the sacral law, but the prophetical preaching. However, there it has its proper function, even if it is rather loose in comparison with the legal declarations from which it is adapted.

There is still another combination of *ᶜawôn* and the consecutive *wametû* to be considered below (Ex 28,43, cf. 5.2.3. and 6.1.). If we turn to the hif.-forms we have two almost identical phrases:

1 Sam 20,8   *w^e 'im-yœš-bî ᶜawôn h^a mîtenî 'āttā,* "if I am guilty kill me yourself";

2 Sam 14,32   *w^e 'im-yœš-bî ᶜawôn wœh^œ mitanî,* "if I have done any wrong, put me to death".

The introduction *w^e 'im yœš* . . . is also repeated twice in 1 Sam 14,41 (in the fuller reading according to LXX). Knierim assumes that it is an example of a formulaic use in the passing of judgement in a kind of discussion.¹⁵³ It can of course also be regarded as a coined phrase, namely by the Deuteronomistic redactor.

Ezechiel alone has the combination of ʿæwæl and mût:

Ez 18,26   bᵉʿ ăwlô ᵃšær-ʿasạ̄ yamût, "it is because of the wrong he has
                         done that he dies";
Ez 33,13   ûbᵉʿ ăwlô ᵃšær ʿasạ̄ bô yamût;
Ez 18,26; wᵉʿasạ̄ ʿawæl ûmetʿ ᵃlêhæm, "... and takes to evil ways and
33,18   dies because of them".

While the second instance is a slightly extended form of the first, the
third – twice repeated – is constructed with two paratactical forms without
the relative clause. Compared with the earlier formula, there are certain
similarities: bᵉʿ ăwlô ... yamût / bặ⁻ᵃwônô yamût. The main difference is the
relative clause inserted in this second phrase. If the first were to be considered
a creation by Ezechiel, this would be a variation found only here. It can thus
be regarded as formulaic, too, and in the same way as the first an adaptation
from priestly legal formulations. According to Zimmerli Ez 18 and 3,17-21
and 33,1-9 show a fixed 'Schulsprache'. More important, according to him,
are the declaratory legal phrases in 18,10ff.14ff., which, from a formal point
of view, are close to the classical apodictic law.[154]

5.2.2. bᵉḥæṭʾô / bᵉḥăṭṭaʾtô ... mût

Turning to the substantives ḥeṭʾ and ḥặṭṭaʾt as causes of death, we shall start
with the largest group of similar phrases:

Numb 27,3   kî-bᵉḥæṭʾô met, "he died for his own sin";
Deut 24,16   ʾîš bᵉḥæṭʾô yûmatû, "a man shall be put to death only   for
                         his own sin";
2 Kings 14,6 kî ʾim-ʾîš bᵉḥæṭʾô yamût;
2 Chron 25,4 kî ʾîš bᵉḥæṭʾô yamûtû;
Ez 3,20   bᵉḥăṭṭaʾtô yamût, "he will die for his sin";
Ez 18,24   ûbᵉḥăṭṭaʾtô ᵃšær-hataʾ bam yamût, "for the sins he has
                         done he will die".

Within this group there are certain differences: Numb 27,3 gives a concrete case (Zelophehad) where someone died (perf) because of his sin, while the other instances state a *principle.* Here again we have one variation with *bᵉḥæṭˀô,* where Deut 24,16 is the original form and 2 Kings 14,6 and 2 Chron 25,4 quotations. Then we have two cases with *bᵉḥăṭṭaˀtô* employed by Ezechiel. I think we can regard them all as variations of the same formula. Now we shall consider another group of three cases:

Am 9,10   *băḥærœb yamûtû kol ḥăṭṭaˀê ᶜămmî,* "they shall die by the sword, all the sinners of my people";

Ez 18,4.10   *hănnœpœš hăḥoṭˀet hîˀ tamût,* "the soul that sins shall die".

Whereas Am 9,10 does not exhibit any formulaic combination of the two stems, Ezechiel gives still another variation of the *principle,* that each shall die through his own sin. This difference between a concrete case and the principle is something that seems to have escaped Knierim, who takes them all together.¹⁵⁵

5.2.3. *ḥeṭˀ/ mišpăṭ mawœt*

In Deut and Jer there are five similarly constructed expressions for "guilt of capital offence":

Deut 19,6   *wᵉlô ˀên mišpăṭ-mawœt,* "yet he was not guilty of capital offense";

Deut 21,22   *wᵉkî yihyœ bᵉˀîš ḥeṭˀ mišpăṭ-mawœt,* "If a man is guilty of a capital offense";

Deut 22,26   *ˀên lănnăᶜᵃrā ḥeṭˀ mawœt,* "the girl is not guilty of a capital offense";

Jer 26,11   *mišpăṭ-mawœt laˀîš hăzzœ,* "condemns this man to death";

Jer 26,16   *ˀên-laˀîš hăzzœ mišpăṭ-mawœt,* "this man ought not to be condemned to death".

There seems to be an underlying pattern consisting of the following elements: $hyh/\partial\hat{e}n - mi\check{s}p\breve{a}t/het\partial/het\partial\ mi\check{s}p\breve{a}t - maw\alpha t - b^e/l^e$. Deut has all three variations, while Jer has only one of the technical terms[156] for capital offense. One may ask whether these cases really are expressions for the *reason* of death and not for death as a *consequence* instead. In Deut 19,6 the verdict implies that "the blood-avenger pursuing the manslayer in hot anger, may overtake him and kill him", and the consequence of this is, that "he was not guilty of a capital crime, since he had never been the other's enemy". In Deut 21,22 the premise is that "a man is guilty of a capital offense" and as a consequence put to death ($w^eh\hat{u}mat$). In Deut 22,26 one can interpret the verdict "not guilty of a capital offense", either as the reason why "you shall do nothing to the girl", or as the consequence of prevalent circumstances, namely "though the engaged girl cried for help, there was no one to save her", i.e. from rape. In Jer 26,11 the reason for the prophet being condemned to death is that he prophesied against the city, and conversely in v. 16, why he should not be condemned, "for he has spoken to us in the name of the Lord our God".

Thus it seems that the formulaic phrase about being guilty/convicted of a capital offense and condemned to death lies more in the conclusion than in the premise. If, however, we view the phrase as an expression of an *intermediate* act between the reason and the ultimate consequence we come closer to the truth. This can be illustrated by two examples. In Numb 18,22 we have the expression $la\acute{s}e\partial t\ het\partial\ lam\hat{u}t$, meaning to "incur guilt and die". The reason is that the Israelites trespass on the Tent of Meeting, and the consequence of this is death. In the same way we can interpret the comparable expression of Ex 28,43: $w^elo\partial\ yi\check{s}\partial\hat{u}\ \varsigma aw\hat{o}n\ wamet\hat{u}$, "that they may not incur guilt and die". Not incurring guilt may be viewed as the consequence of being properly dressed according to v. 42f. On the other hand *wamet\hat{u}* is the typical expression of death as a consequence, in this case of an improper way of serving at the Tent of Meeting. In fact we have in these examples two more formulaic expressions of the act of incurring guilt with its dire consequence. These examples also make it clear why expressions of incurring guilt sometimes seem to be linked more closely to the deed, sometimes to the punishment. It depends on the shift of focus. Logically guilt is the consequence of a violation, but the reason for a death sentence. This intermediate link seem to be presupposed and accordingly frequently left out on the sentence or expression level. When it is expressed, we have this intermediate link in a formulaic phrase as here. Thus we can see it as a bridge between the formulas as well as the themes of this chapter and the next.

5.2.4. Function and Sitz im Leben

As for the *function* of the phrases discussed in this paragraph I wish to refer to Knierim,[157] who considers civil law as the original *Sitz im Leben*, as can be seen in Deut 21,22; 22,26. However, Numb 18,22 and 27,3 – both belonging to 'P' – show a "slipping away" from the civil to the sacral realm. In the remaining cases – including Am 9,10 – it is a question of legal formulations, not within a legal procedure but transferred to preaching (Deut 24,16; 2 Kings 14,6; 2 Chron 25,4; Ez 18,4.20; 3,20).

In this realm the word combination *mût - ḥṭʾ* is considered formulaic, but regarding the variations in the previous cases he holds that they should be considered as only "bedingt formelhaft".[158] In my opinion this holds true for Numb 18,22; 27,3 as well as for Deut 21,22; 22,26. In addition to this there is the non-formulaic combination in Am 9,10. We should not forget 2 Sam 12,13, where another non-formulaic phrase states that, although *ḥăṭṭaʾt* is a sufficient cause for death, this can be avoided because "The Lord has removed your sin, you shall not die".

5.3. Ways of Death

Here I shall deal with phrases which express ways of death. Formally they are constructed around the combination of *mût/mawœt* with prepositional expressions: (*băm*)*milḥamā, băhœrœb, băddœbœr* and *baraʿab*. We shall discuss these combinations in the above order. While the first two refer to death in war more directly, the following two 'pestilence' and 'famine', usually come in the footsteps of war. Thus they all represent a special kind of evil death, and not ways of death in general.

5.3.1. mût/mawœt (băm)milḥamā

First I shall turn to the syntactical combinations of mût/mawœt with milḥamā, "battle". In narrative form we have Absalom's death referred to by his adherents: wᵉʾ ăbšalôm ... met bămmilḥamā, "but Absalom ... has fallen in the battle" (2 Sam 19,11). The legal provisions for exemption from military service allow for three different cases, but each time repatriation and its motivation are stated in the same way: pœn yamût bămmilḥamā, "lest he die in battle" (Deut 20,5-7). These are then repetitions and do not qualify as a formula. There are also two poetical combinations of mût/mawœt with milḥamā. Here the parallel line introduces another, albeit equivalent, way of death:

Is 22,2   ḥᵃlalăyik loʾḥăllê-ḥœrœb/   "Your slain are not the slain of the
                wᵉloʾ metê milḥamā   sword / nor the dead of battle";
Job 5,20   bᵉraʿab padᵉka mimmawœt/   "In time of famine he will save
                ûbᵉmilḥamā mîdê ḥœrœb   you from death / in battle from
                                          the sword".

In Is 22,2 we can distinguish the word pairs ḥalal/met and ḥœrœb/milḥamā. In Job 5,20 the word pairs are raʿab/milḥamā and mawœt/ḥœrœb. This means that the syntactical construction of the lines does not convey any repeated word pair in these two passages, in which case it would qualify as a formula.[159] What is perhaps most interesting here is the fact that milḥamā by reason of parallelism can be equated not only with ḥœrœb (Is 5,22) but also with raʿrab (Job 5,20). This means that all of them are considered to be expressions of death in war: famine is a consequence of or it accompanies battle, and the chief instrument of battle is the sword.

5.3.2. mût băḥœrœb

Proceeding to the combinations of mût with băḥœrœb, we shall start with three cases were mût stands in qal ipf:

Am 7,11   băḥœrœb yamût yărâbʿam,   "Jeroboam shall die by the
                                          sword";

Am 9,10 *băḥærœb yamûtû kol ḥăṭṭaʾê ʿammî,* "all the sinners of my
                                         people shall die by the
                                         sword";

Jer 34,4/5 *loʾ tamût băḥærœb/ bᵉšalôm tamût,* "You shall not die by
                                         the sword/ you will die
                                         a peaceful death".

The two phrases from Amos have the same word order, beginning with *băḥærœb* followed by qal ipf 3rd person sing. of *mût,* and can therefore be called coined phrases, and not formulas proper since they are restricted to Amos only. Jer 34,4/5 is otherwise constructed, but has instead the interesting, antithetical parallelism of *băḥærœb* and *bᵉšalôm.* Although *ḥærœb* has been rendered each time by 'sword', this parallelism shows that it means 'war' as opposed to 'peace'.[160] It could obviously be rendered in this way also in Am 9,10 and, with some reservations, in Am 7,11 too.

The functions of Am 7,11 and 9,10 on the one hand and Jer 34,4/5 on the other are also different: whereas Amos threatens death as something unescapable to King Jeroboam (or his 'house', v. 9) and "the sinners of my people",[161] Jeremiah gives King Zedekiah a chance of survival if he listens to the words of the Lord.[162]

There are also combinations between hif.-forms of *mût* and *băḥærœb.* The assassination of Queen Ataljah is called for through an imperative *hamet băḥærœb,* "put to the sword" (2 Kings 11,15), while the corresponding expression in 2 Chron 23,14 has the hof ipf *yûmắt băḥærœb,* "let . . . be put to the sword". When this command is then enacted, 2 Kings 11,20 reads *hemîtû băḥærœb,* "they put to the sword", which is repeated in 2 Chron 23,21. It is obvious that 2 Chron here is dependent upon 2 Kings,[163] which means that we do not have any real formulas here. What we have is the order to kill by the sword, which is then carried out. Two other combinations represent parts of promises made by king Solomon not to kill his brother, Adonijah, *ʾim yamît . . . bœḥarœb,* "that he will not put . . . to the sword" (1 Kings 1,51) and not to kill Shimei, who had cursed David: *ʾim ʾᵃmîtᵉka bœḥarœb,* "I would not put him to the sword" (1 Kings 2,8). One of these oaths is made in 3rd person sing, the other in 1st person sing. Common to all four instances is the word 'order' between the verbal form and the prepositional expression. However, only the latter combination is formulaic, since 1 Kings 1,51 and 2,8 employ the "oath formula",[164] which is not restricted to the Deuteronomistic writer alone.

There are several phrases where the syntactical connection between *mût* hif and *hærœb* is looser than in the examples mentioned above. Since, moreover, they differ quite substantially from each other, we are hardly able to find any formulas here. There are, however, several similarities worth mentioning: *wǎyyǎkkû . . . bǎhærœb wǎyyamœt ʔotô* (Jer 41,2) about the assassination of Gedaljah and *wǎyyǎk . . . wǎymîtehû wᵉhærœb ʔên bᵉyǎddawid* (1 Sam 17,50) about David slaying Goliath. Both combine *nkh* (hif) and *mût* (hif) in a paratactical way, but while the sword in the first case is the instrument, it is expressly stated that David killed Goliath without a sword. It is, then, the combination of the verbs that is equally expressed, whereas the mention of the sword in the second case is an additional remark which denies the instrumental function of a sword here – a remarkable fact. We may also compare Abimelech's short order to his armour-bearer in Judg 9,54 *šᵉlop hǎrbᵉka ûmôtᵉtenî*, "draw your sword and kill me" and David's killing off Goliath (1 Sam 17,51): *wǎyyiqqǎh ʔœt-hǎrbô wǎyyišlᵉpah mittāʕrah wǎyymotᵉtehû*, "and grasping his sword, he drew it out of the scabbard and killed him". Killing is expressed by *mût*(polel) and preceded by the action of drawing the sword, which in Judg 9,54 is expressed only by the verb *šlp* plus *hærœb* but in 1 Sam 17,51 by a paratactical combination of *lqh* and *šlp* plus the object *hærœb* and the prepositional expression *mittāʕrah*. Common to both the act of drawing the sword *šlp hærœb* and the act of killing *mût* (polel).

In this connection I wish to mention 1 Kings 19,17, where *mût* (hif) has *hǎnnimlaṭ mehærœb*, "anyone who escapes the sword", as its object. In the two preceding verses the prophet Elijah is summoned to anoint three men: Hasael to be king over Aram, Jehu to be king over Israel and Elisha to be his follower as prophet. Then follows a threat as the purpose of his action:

wᵉhayā hǎnnimlaṭ mehærœb hᵃzaʔel	"Anyone who escapes the sword of
yamît yehûʔ	Hazael, Jehu will slay,
wᵉhǎnnimlaṭ mehærœb yehûʔ	and anyone who escapes the sword
yamît ˀœlîša ͨ	of Jehu, Elisha will slay".

92

Although there are no quite similar expressions elsewhere, we can point to the thrice repeated threat in 1 Kings 14,11; 16,4 and 21,24 and some other similarly constructed threats to be discussed below. What they have in common is that, by linking several enemies or ways of death, they express the inescapability of death.[165]

About the several kinds of combining *mût* with *hærœb* we can conclude, that there are formulas where *băhærœb* is combined with either *mût* or *hemît* and there are several looser combinations of *hemît* and *hærœb*. It seems that the combinations with hif.-forms do not always refer to death in war, but also to assassination (Ataljah, Gedaljah) or slaying of an individual. However, it should be remembered that the killing of Goliath and Abimelech also took place during battle or war.

5.3.3. *mût/hemît bara^cab/băs̩s̩ama^ɔ/băddœbœr*

Here I shall discuss the combinations of *mût* in qal- and hif -forms combined with one of three ways of death, namely *ra^cab*, "hunger", *s̩ama^ɔ*, "thirst" and *dœbœr*, "plague", "pestilence". In the following paragraphs I shall turn to combinations of these and *hærœb*.

As the only way of death *ra^cab* occurs three times. In Ex 16,3 the Israelites complain to Moses and Aaron of having been brought from the fleshpots of Egypt into the wilderness *l^ehamît ɔæt-kâl-hăqqahal hăzzœ̄ bara^cab*, "to let this assembly starve to death". This is a variation of the theme "death in the wilderness" (cf. 3.5.2.1.). In Is 14,30, after the death of King Ahaz, the Philistines are threatened through a divine oracle with the words *w^ehemătti bara^cab šâršek ûš^{e,ɔ}erîtek yăh^arog*, "the offsprings of your roots I will kill by starvation and put the remnant of you to death". Besides the combination of *hemît* with *bara^cab* we also have here the word pair *hemît/hrg* as a result of parallelism. It is questionable whether we should consider *hemît bara^cab* as formulaic only on the basis of these two examples, since the third is totally different: *wăyyamât tăhtâw mipp^enê ra^cab*, "he will die of hunger where he lies" (Jer 38,9). When we turn to *s̩ama^ɔ* as the way of death, however, we find in Ex 17,3 one instance that is formally very close to Ex 16,3 and also represents a variation of "death in the wilderness": *l^ehamît ɔotî w^{e,ɔ} æt-banăy w^{e,ɔ}æt-miqnăy băs̩s̩ama^ɔ*, "to let me and my family and my herds die of thirst". Another instance found in Judg 15,18 has *mût* instead of *hemît*: *wᵉ⁻ăttā ᵓamût băṣṣama* , "and I must now die of thirst" in the mouth of Samson. A combination of 'hunger' and 'thirst' as ways of death is to be found in 2 Chron 32,11: *lamût bᵉraᶜab ûbᵉṣamaᵃ*, which belongs to Sennaherib's message to the beleaguered Jerusalem.

Turning, finally, to combinations of *mût* and *dæbær* we find two totally different examples. Jeremiah prophesies an evil fate for Zedekiah and his people as the outcome of the Babylonian siege of Jerusalem: *bᵉdæbær gadŏl yamûtû,* "they shall die of a great pestilence" (Jer 21,6). This follows after another phrase indicating that God himself is the slayer: "I will strike down (*wᵉhikketî*) those who live in this city, men and cattle alike". In the historic psalm 78 the slaying of the Egyptian firstborn (v. 51) is preceded by two parallel phrases where *mawæt* and *dæbær* form a word pair: "not shielding their lives from death/ but abandoning their bodies to the plague" (v. 50b). Since this word pair is nowhere repeated, however, it cannot be considered a formula.

On formal grounds we should consider the combination *hemît baraᶜab* and the phrases *lᵉhamît . . . baraᶜab/băṣṣamaᵓ* together with the combination *lamût bᵉraᶜab ûbᵉṣamaᵓ* as being formulaic. These phrases are used to describe death either during or as a consequence of war, or "death in the wilderness". Is 14,30 is a threat, the three other cases indicate the evil intentions of the leaders to let the people die of hunger and thirst. Here one could also speak about a common function: the expression is used in agitations against these leaders, namely Moses and Aaron (Ex 16,3; 17,3) and Hezekiah (2 Chron 32,11).[166]

5.3.4. *mût bahæræb – baraᶜab*

Next I shall discuss combinations of *mût* on the one hand and *hæræb* and *raᶜab* on the other:

Jer 11,22	*hăbbăhûrîm yamutû băhæræb/*	"their young shall die
	bᵉnêhæm ûbᵉnôtêhæm yamutû baraᶜab	by the sword their
		sons and daughters
		shall die by famine";

Jer 44,12 *yippolû bắhœrœb baraᶜab yittắmmû* "some shall fall by

    miqqaton wᵉᶜắd-gadôl bắhœrœb ûbaraᶜab the sword, others will

    yamutû   meet their end by

                  famine. High and low

                  alike will die by

                  sword or by famine".

These instances belong to the "double pattern",[166] which can also be found in Jer 14,15.16.18; 16,4; 42,16; 44,27 and Lam 4,19, but without the syntactical connection to *mût*. Since this very combination is formulaic, sometimes as phrases with *bắhœrœb* and *baraᶜab* immediately connected as in Jer 44,12, and sometimes as word pairs in parallel lines as in Jer 11,22, we can speak of a pattern containing *mût*. In Jer they form threats of war, which is their function.

The combination of these two ways of death could be viewed as a shortening of the triple formula *hœrœb - raᶜab - dœbœr* to be discussed below. On the other hand the parallelism between *bᵃhûrîm* and *banîm-banôt* in 11,22 and between *yippolû* and *yittắmmû* in 44,12 require only two ways of death. When we turn to Ez 33,27, it seems obvious that the triple formula is intended, but the middle link[167] *raᶜab* has been changed so that we have *bắhœrœb yippolû / lᵃhắyyä nᵉtắttîw lᵉɔåklô / bắddœbœr yamutû*. Here again we can point to 1 Kings 14,11 (repeated in 16,4 and 21,24), where, however, both ways of death are to be considered variations of the same, namely to be food for wild animals, dogs and birds. We also note that this way of death is thought of as the fate of those who have already fallen and now lie in the town or in the field, whereas Ez 33,27 speaks of being food for wild animals as a parallel to falling by the sword and dying by pestilence. Moreover, this replaces *mût baraᶜab* in the complete triple formula, to which we shall now turn.

5.3.5. *mût bắhœrœb – baraᶜab – bắddœbœr*

In its simplest form and combined with *mût* the triple formula can be found in Jer:

21,9; 38,2: *yamût băhœrœb (û)bara^cab ûbăddœbœr;*

42,17: *yamûtû băhœrœb bara^cab ûbăddœbœr;*

42,22: *băhœrœb bara^cab ûbăddœbœr tamûtû;*

27,13: *lammā tamûtû [>]ăttā w^{ec}amm^eka băhœrœb bara^cab*
ûbăddœbœr.

Subjects are "whoever remains in the city" (21,9; 38,2); "all the men who are bent on going to Egypt and settling there" (42,17.22) and Zedekiah, king of Judah and his people (27,13). The most impressive similarity of these phrases lies in the constant order of the three ways of death, whereas deviations concern the people spoken about or addressed and in the order of the verb *mût* and the triple formula: 42,22 has the verb after the formula, whereas the other cases have the verb before. When we proceed to other occurrences of this same pattern, we shall find deviations in the order of the ways of death as well as in the fact that they are not linked directly to each other. The usual order in Jer is *hœrœb – ra^cab – dœbœr* as in the cases above, and this pertains also to most cases without *mût*, namely 14,12; 24,10; 27,8; 29,17.18; 32,24.36 and 44,17. However, in 18,21 we have *ra^cab – hœrœb – dœbœr*: in 34,17 *hœrœb – dœbœr – ra^cab* and in 15,2 and 21,7 *dœbœr – hœrœb – ra^cab*, which means that the formula is not completely fixed.[168]

When we turn to Ezechiel we find more extensive alterations of the triple formula, here too combined with *mût*:

5,12 *š^elištêk băddœbœr yamûtû*   "One third of your people shall
      ûbara^cab yiklû b^etôkek   die by pestilence and perish by
      w^ehašš^elišît băhœrœb yipp^elû   famine in your midst, one third
                                   shall fall by the sword";

6,12 *harahôq băddœbœr yamût*   "Far away they will die
      w^ehăqqarôb băhœrœb yippôl   by pestilence; at home they will fall by the
      w^ehănniš[>]ar w^ehănnaṣûr bara^cab yamût   sword; any who survive or are spared will die by famine";

7,15 *hăhœrœb băhûṣ w^ehăddœbœr w^ehara^cab mibbayit*   "Outside is the
      [>]ăšœr baššadē băhœrœb yamût   sword, inside are pestillence
      wa[>]ăšœr ba^cîr ra^cab wadœbœr yok^alœnnû   and famine: in the country men will die by the sword, in the city famine and pestilence will carry them off".

In Ez 5,12 and 6,12 the triple form is extended to the verbs used: *yamûtû* – *yiklû* – *yipp^elû* (5,12) and *yamût* – *yippôl* – *yamût* (6,12). In 5,12 the people are divided into three parts although the middle part is not expressly mentioned. In 6,12 the division follows another pattern: *harahôq* – *hǎqqarôb* – *hǎnnaṣûr*, if, following LXX, we take *w^ehǎnniš^əar* to be an interpolation.[169] In 7,15 we have a division built upon the contrast between inside and outside and the ways of death are accordingly divided into one plus two: *ḥærǣb* – *dǣbǣr* and *ra^cab*, with inverted order between the last two when explained at the end of the verse. In the same vein 6,12 is an elaboration of 6,11, where the triple formula is combined with *npl: bǎḥǣrǣb bara^cab ûbǎddǣbǣr yippolû*, i.e., the same firm composition and word order found in Jer. Otherwise Ezechiel has variations in the order of the triple elements:

5,12   *bǎddǣbǣr – ûbara^cab – bǎḥǣrǣb*
6,12   *bǎddǣbǣr – bǎḥǣrǣb – bara^cab*
7,15   *hǎḥǣrǣb – w^ehǎddǣbǣr – w^ehara^cab / bǎḥǣrǣb – ra^cab – wadǣbǣr*

In Ez 12,16 we meet the formula once more: *meḥǣrǣb – mera^cab – ûmiddǣbǣr*, but as in 6,11 they are not connected with the verb *mût*. This means that Ez employs the triple formula 5 times, 3 of which are combined with *mût*. Jer for his part uses it no less than 15 times, 5 of which are directly combined with *mût*. It is quite possible that Ez has borrowed the formula from Jer and, in so doing, made alterations of his own.[170] This would explain the relative firm composition in Jer in comparison to the rather free use in Ez. The double formula (7.3.4.) is to be found only in Jer and Lam. The triple formula is restricted to Jer and Ez. The fact that both of them are formulaic in form as well as in function (threats of war) also makes their combination with the verb *mût* formulaic. The alterations found especially in Ez enable us to speak of a *pattern*, where all the elements of the triple formula are – sometimes rather forcibly[171] – introduced to describe the complete extinction by war and what follows in the footsteps of war: famine and pestilence.

5.4. Conclusions

The reason for discussing the above phrases in one chapter was their similarity in form. They introduce the causes of death by way of a prepositional expression, mainly b^e plus a substantive. We have seen that this cause can be viewed either as the *reason* for death or as the *way* of death. In the first case we dealt with four substantives used in a formulaic way, mainly in Ez but also elsewhere. Although most of the phrases seem to have originated from civil or sacral law, they had been transferred from this *Sitz im Leben* to another, namely Deuteronomistic and prophetic preaching about the law. Their common theme was that a man dies because of his own sin, provided of course that he has committed a sin that required punishment. In the second case we dealt with another five substantives expressing ways of death. Although some combinations with *mût* indicated death through hunger and thirst, most were found to be expressions for death through war. This was especially the case with the double and triple formulas used in Jer and the alternative versions of the triple formula in Ez. In combination with *mût* this triple formula expressed the *totality* of death by war: what does not fall by the sword will fall victim to starvation and plague. Another formulaic use of *mût* in combination with the sword was found in oaths, but here the threat or promise not to kill was directed to individuals by the king. These and other cases of individual threats show, I think, that in the final analysis premature death was considered not only as 'evil', but as a punishment by God. Thus the question of 1 Sam 20,32 always seems to worry Old Testament writers: "Why should he be killed, what has he done?". Here the reason and way of death come together: when reasons are given they point to the guilt of men, and when extinctions of collective groups are theatened, these too are thought of as punishments for sins.

6. DEATH AS CONSEQUENCE

In the previous chapter I dealt with formulaic expressions about the *cause* of death, here I will deal with death as a *consequence.* Since cause and consequence are logically inseparable from each other, one may ask what the different ways. It is not only the question of shifting the focus from cause to in characteristic or formulaic ways, sometimes again the consequences. There connected to the stem *mût,* it is this stem itself which here has the stereotype form expressing the consequence of things which can be expressed in very different ways. It is not only the question of shifting the focus from cause to consequence, but the fact that sometimes it is the causes which are expressed in characteristic or formulaic ways, sometimes again the consequences. There are of course several different ways of expressing consequences: one is through the perfect consecutive of the verb *mût,* another the imperfect consecutive, a third the simple imperfect or the paronomastic imperfect, etc. Accordingly, the functions and meanings differ, too: it can be the consequence of something that has actually happened, it can be the consequence threatened if something should happen, it can be a law prescribing certain punishment for certain offences, etc. I shall also include the negated forms expressing, that the dire, consequence was in fact avoided, or how it should be avoided. Finally I shall discuss a few phrases constructed upon the noun *mawæt* which can be considered threats too.

In this chapter I shall classify the material on formal grounds alone, since there does not seem to be any possibility of classifying it according to content such as actual killings, threats, death penalties, etc. Only in retrospective shall we be able to see whether some form is preferred in order to express some special content.

6.1. The qal perfect consecutive

Since the perfect consecutive forms usually express a consequence which has not yet taken place, they can be used in threats – be they spontaneous or legal. I shall here discuss the qal forms only and later turn to the hif'il and hof'al forms.

Let us first consider two cases where the guilty person has to be found or the guilt of a particular person has to be established:

Gen 44,9   *ᵃšær yimmaṣeᵓ ᵓittô meᵃbadǽka wamet,* "whichever of your servants it is found with shall die";

1 Kings 1,52   *wᵉᵓim-raʿā timmaṣeᵓ-bô wamet,* "but if he is found troublesome, he shall die".

In both cases the conditions are defined in advance. In the case of Joseph's brothers they voluntarily suggest how to find out whether there is a thief among them and what the punishment should be.[172] In the case of Adonijah, it is King Solomon who defines the conditions under which his rival shall live or die. One might suspect here a formulaic phrase consisting of the combination of *mṣᵓ*(nif) and *mût*. The main difference in its use, however, is that in the first case *someone* guilty is to be found within a group of several people, while in the other case it is the question whether *something* evil should be found in one person. This difference does not, however, prevent us from regarding the use of at least *wamet* as formulaic, since it follows after the conditions have been defined, i.e. as a consequence. If we take 1 Sam 26,10, we have still the same consequence (*wamet*), but here as an alternative form of punishment and without the condition that something be found in Saul which requires his death.[173]

When we come to legal formulations, we should distinguish between mortal consequences belonging to the crime and consequences which constitute the punishment. The first kind of consequences can best be studied in the Book of the Covenant and some other cases:

Ex 21,12	"Whoever strikes a man so that he dies (*wamet*) shall be put to death";
Ex 21,20	"When a man strikes his slave, male or female, with a rod, and he dies (*ûmet*) then and there, he must be avenged";
Ex 21,28	"When an ox gores a man or woman to death (*wamet*) . . .";
Ex 21,35	"When a man's ox injures his neighbour's ox and it dies (*wamet*) . . .";
Ex 22,1	"If the thief is seized while breaking in and he is beaten to death (*w^ehukkā wamet*), there is no bloodguilt in this case";
Deut 19,11-12	"When one man is the enemy of another, and he lies in wait for him, attacks him and strikes him a blow so that he dies (*w^ehikkahû næpæš wamet*) . . . they shall hand him over to the avenger of blood, and he shall die (*wamet*)";
2 Sam 11,15	"Put Uriah opposite the enemy where the fighting is fiercest and then fall back, and leave him to meet his death (*w^enikkā wamet*)".

It ought to be stressed that *wamet/ûmet* as a consequence is often connected with the verb *nkh* (nif'al, hif'il or hof'al). When both are used together they obviously express the consequence of the criminal act ('Tatfolge'), which is formulated in various ways, according to the circumstances. I shall return to the punishment later. It should be noted that the first sentence (Ex 21,12) is formulated in the participial style typical of apodictic laws,[174] while the others use the conditional particles *w^ekî* (21,20.28.35, Deut 19,11) and *ʾim* (22,1) which are characteristic of casuistic laws.[175] 2 Sam 11,15 is of course no punishment at all, but David's instruction to have Uriah killed.

Before we proceed to capital punishment as a consequence we should pay some attention to non-legal formulations about death as a consequence. In Gen 19,19; 33,13; 44,22.31 we have four cases where death is a consequence of a certain act that should be avoided. The impossibility of the proposed act is first expressed *w^eʾanokî loʾ ʾûkăl*, "I cannot" and *loʾ-yûkăl hănnăʿăr*, "the boy cannot" (19,19 and 44,22). But the construction of cause and consequence is then different each time: *pæn* . . . *wamattî,* "lest . . . and I die" (Gen 19,19); *ûdᵉpaqûm* . . . *wametû,* "if they are driven hard . . . (all the flocks) will die" (Gen 33,13); *wᵉᶜazⱥb ᵓæt-ᵓabîw wamet,* "if he were to leave him his father would die" (Gen 44,22) and *wᵉhayā kirᵓôtô kî-ᵓên hănnăᶜăr wamet,* "when he sees that the boy is not with us, he will die" (v. 31).

Although the consecutive form here invariably occurs at or near the end of the sentence, we cannot regard this as a sufficient criterion for calling it formulaic. This order between cause and consequence is of course quite natural. If we turn back to the legal formulations of the Book of the Covenant, there are some significant differences: first, the criminal act is stated in a similar way – except for Ex 21,12 – then the result of this act is expressed through *wamet* and finally sentence is pronounced. Thus, one can say that when the crime is expressed by *wamet,* this has a given place within a formulaic pattern, which means that it has a formulaic use.

Sometimes a mortal consequence can stem from contact with sacred objects:

Numb 4,15 *wᵉloᵓ yiggᵉᶜû ᵓæl-hăqqodæš wametû,* "so that they do not come in contact with the sacred objects and die";

Numb 4,20 *wᵉloᵓ yaboᵓû lirᵓot kᵉbăllăᶜ ᵓæt-* "but not go inside and witness the dismantling of the *hăqqodæš wametû,* sanctuary lest they die".

We may point to Ex 28,43 (5.2.3.) about incurring guilt, which has a similar form: *wᵉloᵓ* + qal ipf . . . *wametû.* Whereas death in Numb 4,15.20 is the immediate consequence[176] of touching or even looking at holy things, Ex 28,43 gives the indirect result, namely incurring guilt, of not being properly dressed. As we suggested guilt may be presupposed even when not directly stated, and Numb 4,15.20 seem to be an indication that this interpretation is correct at least regarding contact with holy objects. All three are provisions for the priests, namely how they should avoid the fatal consequences which may follow from these contacts.

wamet as an expression for death as consequence of punishment is also combined in Deut with the stoning formulas:

Deut 13,11:   ûs^eqăltô ba^{,a}banîm wamet
Deut 17,5:   ûs^eqăltam ba^{,a}banîm wametû
Deut 22,21:   ûs^eqalûha … ba^{,a}banîm wametā
Deut 22,24:   ûs^eqăltæm [,]otam ba^{,a}banîm wametû
Deut 21,21:   ûr^egamuhû kâl-[,]ănšê ^cîrô ba^{,a}banîm wamet

Although the formula with *sql* is considered to be older than the corresponding one with *rgm*, they are nevertheless equivalent expressions for stoning to death.[177] Outside Deut the *sql* variant is used without the verb *mût* in Ex 8,22; 17,4; 21,28-32 and 19,13, which shows that the formula itself expresses death as a consequence of this particular punishment. In addition to this is the fact that it is used with imperfect and imperfect consecutive forms in 1 Kings 21,10ff., in the story about Naboth, to which I shall return below. Turning to the *rgm* version it is found in legal formulations following the formula *mût yûmat(û)* (Lev 20,2.27; 24,16; Numb 15,35), and is also used together with the imperfect consecutive in two cases (Numb 35, 36; 1 Kings 12,18 = 2 Chron 10,18). In this connection we shall restrict our observations to the cases listed above. In Deut we have very small variations due only to the person(s) addressed and those liable to the penalty. The crimes thus punished are idolatry (Deut 13,11; 17,5), adultery (Deut 22,21. 24) to which comes the liquidation of a "defiant son" (Deut 21,21). There is still one formulaic use of the perfect consecutive of *mût* in connection with death sentences, all instances again in Deut:

Deut 17,12   ûmet ha[,]îš hăhû[,]
Deut 18,20   ûmet hănnabî[,] hăhû[,]
Deut 24,7   ûmet hăggănnab hăhû[,]
Deut 22,25   ûmet ha[,]îš ^{,a}šœr-šakăb ^cimmah

Instead of the demonstrative *hăhû[,]* we have a relative clause in the last example. Otherwise the formal similarity is striking. All four examples belong to the casuistic laws, but the offences differ widely from each other: rejection of the priest's or judge's decision (17,12); prophesying what God has not commanded or in the name of other gods (18,20); rape of a girl in the country, where she could not be heard (22,25) and kidnapping a fellow Israelite, who is then harshly treated and sold (24,7). Nevertheless, the use is formulaic,[178] since it is the conclusion of a casuistic law: the conclusions refer to persons introduced in a conditional way. Between the introduction and the conclusion we have the circumstances under which the offence was committed, all according to a rather strict pattern. The verdict *ûmet* ... does not, however, indicate what punishment exactly is prescribed. Here it differs from concluding *wamet/ûmet* in the cases of stoning: while this could be seen as the ultimate outcome of the penalty, *ûmet* ... is used in an absolute way for the penalty as such.

6.2. The qal imperfect

We have already discussed many examples of the qal imperfect of *mût* used in threats and predictions. The stress in these examples lay on either the extraordinary places of death (ch. 3) or the causes of death (ch. 5). When I here turn to those imperfect forms which express death as a consequence, the main group will consist of paronomastic expressions. First, however, I shall discuss some cases with the imperfect alone. Regarding the difference between the perf.cons. and the impf.cons. it has been suggested that the first expresses the death sentence as something given and unavoidable, whereas the second stresses that it is the desired consequence.[179]

6.2.1. ... *w^eyamot*

We have two cases, where the threatened consequence is preceded by the hif. of *yṣ*:

| Judg 6,30 | *hôṣe˕ ˒æt-binka w^eyamot,* | "bring out your son, he must die"; |
| 1 Kings 21,10 | *w^ehôṣî˒uhû w^esiqluhû w^eyamot,* | "and then take him out and stone him to death". |

In both cases the 'guilty' person has already been found out by searching (Judg 6,30) or by false accusation (1 Kings 21,10). The alleged offence in both cases is a 'religious' one (against Ba'al and YHWH). In the case of Gideon the threat is averted, while in the case of Naboth it is carried out. In the first case $w^e yamot$ is the sole expression of the penalty, in the second we have a synthetic expression, "stone to death", as was the case in Deut (cf. above 6.1.). Despite these differences, we can speak of a formulaic combination of $ys^{,}$ in hif. imperative and $w^e yamot$.

6.2.2. môt tamût

This paronomastic formula occurs 12 times in threats of death or in proclamations of death sentences:

Gen 2,17:   "you will certainly die" (NEB); "you shall be doomed to die" (NJV);

Gen 20,7:   "I tell you that you are doomed to die" (NEB); "know that you shall surely die" (NJV);

1 Sam 14,44:   "Then Saul swore a great oath *that Jonathan should die*" (NEB);

1 Sam 22,16:   "Ahimelech, you must die" (NEB);

1 Kings 2,37.42: "you shall die; make no mistake about that" (NEB);

2 Kings 1,4.6: "you shall die" (NEB);

2 Kings 1,16:   "you will die" (NEB);

Jer 26,8:   "and threatened him with death" (NEB);

Ez 3,18; 33,8.14: "I pronounce a sentence of death ..." (NEB).

Although none of these instances occurs in legal texts, most of them can nevertheless be viewed as pronouncement or threat of death sentences. God threatens death in Gen 2,17 *if* the man should eat from the tree of the knowledge of good and evil and in Gen 20,7 *if* king Ahimelech should *not* send Sarah back. The king acts with corresponding authority in 1 Sam 14,44 (Saul pronouncing a death sentence on Jonathan); 1 Sam 22,16 (Saul condemning Ahimelech to death);[180] 1 Kings 2,37.42 (Solomon threatening Shimei with death *if* he leaves Jerusalem). In some cases we have a divine judgement pronounced by a prophet; 2 Kings 1,4.6.16 (Eliah repeating God's decision about King Ahaziah). In Ez 3,18; 33,8.14 God hypothetically pronounces judgement upon 'a wicked man' and in Jer 26,8 it is the mob led by priests and prophets which condemns Jeremiah to death.[181] Here we have a spontaneous act, the reaction to the prophet's message, while threats and sentences in the other cases are conditioned by a violation of God's or the king's will and authority. That this is the case in 2 Kings 1,4ff. too, we can conclude from the introductory word in v. 4 $w^e laken$, "now, therefore", namely because King Ahaziah has consulted the oracle of Baal Zebub, the god of Philistine Ekron. As a criterion for distinguishing between threats and pronouncements of judgement we may regard the occurrence of *conditions*. Accordingly we have threats in Gen 2,17; 20,7; 1 Kings 2,37.42 and judgements in 1 Sam 14,44; 22,16; 2 Kings 1,4.6.16; Jer 26,8; Ez 3,18; 33,8.14. We should note, however, that Jer 26,8 is only a preliminary judgement and accordingly in a way to be considered a threat of judgement. In all cases it is a question of transgressions of concrete commandments and they are committed by individuals.[182] The formulaic function is thus beyond dispute.

6.2.3. *môt yamût(û)*

In this form the formula occurs only four times and only once in the plural:

Numb 26,65: "for the Lord had said *they should all die* in the wilderness";

1 Sam 14,39: "even if it lies in my son Jonathan, *he shall die*";

2 Sam 12,14: "*the boy* that will be born to you *shall die*";

2 Kings 8,10: "but the Lord has revealed to me that *in fact he will die*".

Again none of the instances occur in legal texts. In Numb 26,65 we have an account of what had happened to the Israelites in the wilderness: God had doomed them all to die except for Caleb and Joshua. In 1 Sam 14,39 Saul swears an oath not to spare even his son Jonathan, if he is guilty of the failure to obtain an answer from God – something that was actually found to be the case. Saul then condemns his son to death with another oath (v. 44, cf. above), although Jonathan was eventually rescued through the intervention of the people (v. 45f.).

In 2 Sam 12,14 the prophet Nathan announces the fate of David's first son by Bathsheba: the punishment shall be exacted not from the king directly but from his son, who will die. In 2 Kings 8,10 King Ben-Hadad of Aram asks the prophet Elisha about his illness and receives the ambiguous answer that he shall recover, although the Lord had revealed "that in fact he will die", a message that was communicated to Hazael (cf. 4.4.1.).

In three cases we have judgements passed by God and in one (1 Sam 14, 39) a threat pronounced under oath[183] by King Saul. Numb 26,65 differs from the other cases in that it concerns a judgement pronounced and carried out in the past. Furthermore, only two cases concern concrete transgressions by individuals, namely 1 Sam 14,39 and 2 Sam 12,14. In the second case the transgressor himself is spared and his offspring, the fruit of his transgression, is doomed to die. Taken all together, these phrases can perhaps be regarded simply as variations of the formula *môt tamût* discussed above due to the fact that the condemned person is not present.[184] This could be claimed for three of the four cases, namely 1 Sam 14,39; 2 Sam 12,14 and 2 Kings 8,10.

6.2.4. *môt namût*

This phrase occurs only twice. In Judg 13,22 Manoah speaks to his wife after the angel of God has appeared before them: "we are doomed to die, we have seen God". His wife draws, however, the opposite conclusion from the fact that God had accepted their sacrifices (v. 23). 2 Sam 14,14a seems to be a statement about the common fate of man: "we shall all die like water is spilt on the ground and lost". Its function in the context is not clear: is it thought of as a contrast between "man's ineluctable end in death" and "a living death which is not ineluctable, viz. the condition of Absalom in exile" (14b)?[185] Common to both these statements is the inescapability of death, be it the result of a fateful encounter with God, as in Judg 13,22, or simply the common fate of mankind, as in 2 Sam 14,14a. However, the difference is obvious too, namely between the common fate of man — although already envisaged in a way in Gen 2,17 — and the actual consequence of seeing God (cf. Ex 3,6; 33,20.23; Lev 16,12f.; Is 6,4 and Judg 6,22).

6.2.5. Conclusions

The formulaic use of qal imperfect forms of *mût* is particularly manifest in the case of *môt tamût*, which is the formula used when a threat of death or a death sentence is addressed to the guilty person.[186] If we regard the presence of conditions as a criterion for distinguishing threats from pronouncements of death sentences, both are represented in the material. However, sentences are also conditioned, but then the conditions are laid down in advance (in laws, etc.), while in conditioned threats they are closely related to the threat itself. If we turn to the other variants of the paronomastic formula, they are not used in the same strict manner. Sometimes they are used about more than one person (*môt yamûtû* in Numb 26,65 and *môt namût*). Sometimes they are used about people in the past (Numb 26,65) or without reference to any guilt (2 Sam 14,14; 2 Kings 8,10). In the last case one cannot really speak of death as a consequence either. In the case of *môt yamût* it can be regarded as a variation of *môt tamût* or formulated in accordance with it. The same cannot be said about the plural forms since there is no legal setting or function. The paronomastic form can be regarded as way of underscoring the seriousness of the threat or the sentence. Otherwise this seems to be the basic form of a threat or pronouncement of death, a question to which we shall return below.

6.3. Negated qal imperfect forms

Avoiding death is mostly expressed through a negated form of *mût*. I shall here discuss the qal imperfect forms and later turn to the hif'il and hof'al forms. I shall classify the material according to the different personal forms and to some extent also according to the negations used. But since the negation $(w^e)lo^{\circ}$ is by far the most common, I shall include the few cases with other negations $(w^e)pæn$ and $(w^e)^{\circ}\breve{a}l$ to the corresponding forms with the first negation.

6.3.1. $(w^e)lo^{\circ}/pæn\ ^{\circ}amût$

If we exclude 1 Sam 20,14 on text critical grounds,[187] there are only three instances left negated by $(w^e)lo^{\circ}$ and one by *pæn*:

Deut 18,16	The people begs Moses to mediate on Mount Horeb in order to save its life: "Let us not hear again the voice of the Lord our God, nor see this great fire again, or we shall die ($w^e lo^{\circ}$ ${}^{\circ}am\hat{u}t$)";
Jer 37,20	Jeremiah petitions King Zedekiah not to take him to the house of Jonathan the scribe lest he die there ($w^e lo^{\circ}$ ${}^{\circ}am\hat{u}t$ šam);
Ps 118,17	The psalmist utters a formula of confidence: "I shall not die but live (lo° ${}^{\circ}am\hat{u}t$ $k\hat{i}$ ${}^{\circ}\alpha h y\bar{\alpha}$) to proclaim the works of the Lord";
Gen 26,9	Isaac explains his lying to King Ahimelech regarding Rebecca: "I thought I should die because of her" (${}^{\circ}am\breve{a}rt\hat{i}$ $p\alpha n$-${}^{\circ}am\hat{u}t$ ${}^{\varsigma}al\hat{e}ha$).

No two cases are entirely similar: in Jer 37,20 I have regarded šam as part of a repeated phrase (cg. above 3.5.1.2.) and in Ps 118,17 we have the pair of opposites mût - ḥyh to be discussed below (8.1.). On the other hand, three cases express avoidance of an immediate threat and only in Ps 118,17 could the phrase be seen to express a general trust in the future. It is also the only case where the negation does not have the waw copulativum. Finally, this is the only phrase used in a poetical context, while the others occur in direct discourse and in narrative expressions. We would regard the expression $w^e lo^{\circ}$ ${}^{\circ}am\hat{u}t$ in Deut 18,16 and Jer 37,20 as formulaic: here it can be translated "lest I die". However, here too we have a difference between collective speaking in Deut 18,16 and individual speech in Jer 37,20 in which also the adverb šam appears. Gen 26,9 expresses avoidance of death as a consequence, too, but here the expression is too different in form and function to be regarded as formulaic. Ps 118,17, if formulaic, belongs to quite another type of formula.

6.3.2. (w^e)lo${}^{\circ}$ tamût

This phrase occurs seven[188] times:

Judg 6,23	Gideon realizing that he had seen the angel of the Lord fears for his life but is reassured: "... do not be afraid you shall not die" (ʾal tîrāʾ lōʾ tamût);
1 Sam 20,2	David, asking Jonathan why his father persecuted him, gets the answer: "God forbid! You shall not die" (ḥalîlā lōʾ tamût);
2 Sam 12,13	David, realizing that he has sinned against the Lord, is told by Nathan that God has transferred his sin and he shall not die himself (gam yhwh hæʿᵉbîr ḥaṭṭatᵉka lōʾ tamût). Instead his son by Bathsheba is doomed to die.
2 Sam 19,24	David on his way back across the Jordan is asked if Shimei should not be killed because he had cursed the king. David swears an oath that Shimei shall not die (lōʾtamût);
Jer 11,21	The people of Anatoth had threatened Jeremiah with death if he continued to prophesy in the name of the Lord (lōʾ tinnabeʾ bᵉšem yhwh wᵉlōʾ tamût bᵉyadenû);
Jer 34,4/5	Jeremiah's word to King Zedekiah (cf. above 5.3.2.): "you shall not die by the sword; you will die a peaceful death (lōʾ tamût bāḥœræb/ bᵉšalôm tamût)";
Jer 38,24	Zedekiah warns Jeremiah not to tell anobody of their meeting: "Let no one know about this, and you shall not die (wᵉlōʾ tamût)".

The majority of these statements are parts of oaths or reassurances that a person shall not die, although there would have been a sufficient reason or fear that this might happen: lōʾ tamût (Judg 6,23; 1 Sam 20,2; 2 Sam 12,13; 19,24; Jer 34,4/5). In two cases, however, the statement is made conditional. The threatened person — both times Jeremiah — has to behave in a certain way in order to avoid death (Jer 11,21; 38,24). This condition is also formally distinguished by the waw copulativum: wᵉlōʾ tamût. These cases are thus comparable to Deut 18,16 and Jer 37,20 above (6.3.1.). However, the statements with a simple lōʾ tamût can also be viewed as consequences, at least indirectly: David's life is spared because his guilt has been 'transferred' (2 Sam 12,13); Shimei's life is spared because of the oath sworn by David (2 Sam 19,24);[189] King Zedekiah will be captured but not killed as a consequence of divine decision (Jer 34,2ff.); Gideon has seen "the angel of the

110

Lord face to face" and has reason to fear for his life, but he is reassured that he will not die (Judg 6,23); Jonathan reassures David that his father cannot have planned to kill David without telling his son.

6.3.3. (wᵉ)lo>/pæn / wᵉ>ăl yamût

Out of a total of 15 cases we have 8 negated by wᵉlo>, 4 by lo>, 2 by pæn and 1 by wᵉ>ăl. They are:

Ex 9,4   As a result of God's distinction between Israel's herds and those of the Egyptians, nothing that belongs to Israel will die (wᵉlo> yamût ... dabar, cf. above 2.6.);

Ex 21,18   The outcome of a quarrel being that a man strikes another with a stone or a spade, but the other is not killed (wᵉlo> yamût); there follow other casuistic provisions;

Ex 28,35   Aaron shall wear the ephod when he serves in the Tent of the Presence (NEB): "and so he will not die" (wᵉlo> yamût);

Lev 16,2   Aaron shall not enter the sanctuary at any time but at the appointed time "on pain of death" (wᵉlo> yamût);

Lev 16,13   The cloud of incense will hide the cover which is over (the Ark of) the pact, so that he shall not die (wᵉlo> yamût);

Numb 35,12   The cities of refuge shall hide the killer so that he shall not die (wᵉlo> yamût) before he stands his trial;

Jos 20,9   These cities were intended for any man who killed another inadvertently, to ensure that no one should die at the hand of the avenger of blood ... (wᵉlo> yamût bᵉyăd) until he stood trial ...;

Is 51,14   The oppressor's fury should not frighten the people because those who are trembling shall soon be free and not die (wᵉlo>-yamût lăššăḥăt) (the meaning of the preceding words is uncertain);

Ez 18,21.28; Repentance by a sinner will save his life: "he shall live; he
33,15   shall not die" (ḥayō yiḥyæ lo> yamût, 3 times);

Prov 23,13   "Do not withhold discipline from a boy; take the stick to him, and save him from death" (lo> yamût cf. v. 14: wᵉnăpšô miššᵉ>ôl tăṣṣîl);

Gen 38,11   Judah promises Tamar his son Shelah if she remains in her
             father's house as a widow, for he was afraid that he too
             would die (pœn-yamût găm-hû⁾ kᵉ⁾œḥâw) like his brothers;
Deut 20,5.6.7. Any man who has built a new house and has not dedicated
             it (v. 5), or has planted a vineyard and has not begun to use
             it (v. 6), or has pledged himself to take a woman in mar-
             riage and has not taken her (v. 7), shall return home from
             the army "lest he die in battle" (pœn-yamût bămmilḥamā,
             cf. above 5.3.1.) and another man fulfil what he has left un-
             done;
Deut 33,6   Moses' blessing to Reuben: "May Reuben live and not die
             (yᵉḥî rᵉ⁾ûben wᵉ⁾ăl-yamot) though few be his numbers".

The eight first instances all have the copulative form wᵉlo⁾ yamût. Although the cases differ from each other, most of them are legal or cultic. Five
can be said to express the fatal outcome, if certain precautions are not taken
to prevent this (Ex 28,35; Lev 16,2.13; Numb 35,12; Jos 20.9), while three
state that death will in fact be avoided (Ex 9,4; 21,18; Is 51,14). Of the four
cases with a simple lo⁾ three belong to the formula ḥayô yiḥyœ̄ lo⁾ yamût to
be discussed below. Like Prov 23,13 — the remaining case — it presupposes,
that death is the outcome of guilt and can be avoided through repentance or,
as here, by education. Three of the four cases with pœn again are found in the
wider formula pœn yamût bămmilḥamā (cf. 5.3.1.). Here too death is prevent-
ed ot thought to be so through the removal of the endangered person (Deut
20) or, in the case of Tamar, the person, who represents the danger. Finally, in Deut 33,6 we have the negated jussive form parallel with the preceding
opposite yᵉḥî. This blessing is a simple wish unconditioned by any human
measures.

Thus it turns out that the great majority of the cases express a conditional
avoidance of death. They are not formally distinguishable from those cases
where death is actually avoided (Ex 9,4), where it is predicted that death will
not occur (Is 51,14), or where the wish that the tribe of Reuben may not die
out is expressed in the form of a blessing (Deut 33,6).

However, some of these cases are indirectly thought of as consequences,
too: sparing the lives of the Israelite cattle is the consequence of God's
distinction between them and the Egyptian cattle (Ex 9,4); avoiding death in

Ex 21,18 is the consequence of a non-fatal blow, which results only in enjurement; not succumbing to the oppressor in Is 51,14 is the consequence of divine protection, and of course the blessings in Deut 33 presuppose divine intervention in the lives of the Israelite tribes (cf. v. 2ff., 7.11, etc.). This would mean, then, that all the cases discussed above are in some way to be considered consequential on avoidance of death. In the very last case of Deut 33,6, however, the stress is upon the positive element and the negated opposite has the function of underscoring this (cf. 8.1.).

We may consider $w^e lo^{\jmath}$ yamût as a formula and the Deuteronomic *pœn-yamût bămmilhamā* as a coined phrase. The simple $lo^{\jmath}$ yamût or pœn yamût or $^{\jmath}ăl$ yamot are to be considered elements of more comprehensive formulaic expressions to be discussed below.

6.3.4. $w^e lo^{\jmath}/ pœn/ w^{e\jmath}ăl$ namût

The formula $w^e nihyǣ w^e lo^{\jmath}$ namût occurs three times:

Gen 42,2	in the mouth of Jacob in his order to his sons to go down to Egypt to buy corn "so that we may keep ourselves alive and not starve" (NEB); "that we may live and not die" (NJV);
Gen 43,8	in the mouth of Judah, who declares that this time they ought to take their youngest brother with them: "we shall save our lives ... and none of us will starve" (NEB);
Gen 47,19	in the mouth of the Egyptians: "give us seed-corn to keep us alive, or we shall die ..." (NEB); cf. *lammā namût* above 5.1.

We shall return to the complete formula below (8.1.). It is, as such, an expression for avoiding death, all three times conditioned by the possibility of obtaining bread or corn from Egypt, which is administered by Joseph.

In Ex 20,19 the Israelites on Mount Sinai ask Moses to mediate between them and God: $w^{e\jmath}ăl-y^e dăbber$ *immanû $^{\jmath æ}lohim$ pœn-namût*, "but if God speaks to us we shall die" (NEB); "but let not God speak to us, lest we die" (NJV). Cf. above 6.3.1. $w^e lo^{\jmath}$ $^{\jmath}amût$ (Deut 18,6). Finally 1 Sam 12,19 gives the petition of the people to Samuel to pray for them so that God should not kill them because of their sin when they asked for a king: *hitpállel b^e·ǎd- ^a badêka ʾæl-yhwh ʾ^æ lohêka w^ė>ǎl namût,* "Pray for us your servants to the Lord your God, to save us from death" (NEB). In these cases it is the fear of God, whose presence (Ex 20,19) or thunder and rain are experienced as a threat, that makes them turn to their mediator for help. There seem to be no difference in meaning between *pæn namût* and *w^ė> ǎl namût.* The meaning of *w^e lo> namût* is essentially the same, although its function is to underscore the positive statement by negating its absolute opposite.[190]

6.3.5. *w^e lo>/ (w^e)pæn tamûtû/ t^e mutûn*

Here we have seven cases with the negation *w^e lo>* and two with *(w^e)pæn.* They are used interchangeably and we shall present them in the same order in which they occur:

Gen 3,3.4. The woman relating God's prohibition to eat from the tree in the middle of the garden: *pæn t^e mutûn,* "lest you die" (NEB). The serpent's reply: *lo>-môt t^e mutûn,* "you are not going to die" (NJV); "Of course you will not die" (NEB). This is the single case where the paronomastic formula *môt tamût* is negated;[191]

Gen 42,20 Joseph testing his brothers' truthfulness: *w^e ye>amenû dibrêkæm w^e lo> tamûtû,* "that your words be verified and that you may not die" (NJV); "thus your words will be proven true, and you will not die" (NEB);

Lev 8,35 Aaron and his sons are commanded to "stay at the entrance of the Tent of Meeting day and night for seven days, keeping the Lord's charge – that you may not die" (*ûš^e mǎrtæm mišmæræt yhwh w^e lo> tamûtû*) (NJV);

Lev 10,6.7.9. "Do not dishevel your hair and do not rend your clothes, lest you die (*w^e lo> tamûtû*) . . . You must not go outside the entrance of the Tent of Meeting, lest you die (*pæn tamutû*) . . . Drink no wine or ale, you and your sons with you, when you enter the Tent of Meeting, that you may

not die (*w^elo͗ tamutû*) (NJV); NEB has all three times
"lest you die";

Numb 18,32 "but you must not profane the sacred donations of the
Israelites, lest you die" (*w^elo͗ tamûtû*);

2 Kings 18,32 Rab-Shake, the chief officer of the Assyrians, addressing
the people of Jerusalem: "until I come and take you to a
land like your own . . . life for you all, instead of death"
(NEB): *wiḥyû w^elo͗ tamutû,* "that you may live and not
die".

Avoiding death is here conditioned by the observing of certain cultic
(Lev 8,35; 10,6.7.9; Numb 18,32) or otherwise divinely authorized prohibitions (Gen 3,3.4.) or human commands (Gen 42,20; 2 Kings 18,32). It is
obvious that the formula has the same meaning throughout. Only Gen 3,4 has
the form of a direct statement, whereas the other cases present the condition
for avoiding death.

6.3.6. *(w^e)lo͗ yamûtû*

This formula is encountered six times, all being cultic or legal texts: in
addition to this there is 2 Chron 25,4 with the trice repeated *lo͗ yamûtû;*

Ex 30,20.21 "When they enter the Tent of Meeting they shall wash
with water, that they may not die (*w^elo͗ yamutû*) . . . they
shall wash their hands and feet, that they may not die
(*w^elo͗ yamutû*)" (NJV);

Lev 15,31 "You shall put the Israelites on guard against their un-
cleanness, lest they die . . . (*w^elo͗ yamutû*)";

Numb 4,19 "Do this with them, that they may live and not die
(*w^eḥayû w^elo͗ yamutû*) when they approach the most
sacred objects . . ." (NJV). The formula of opposites, cf. below: 8.1.;

Numb 17,25 "Put Aaron's staff back before the Pact, as a lesson to
rebels, so that their mutterings against Me may cease, lest
they die (*w^elo͗ yamutû*)" (NJV);

Numb 18,3   "but they must not have any contact with the furnishings of the sanctuary or with the altar, lest both they and you die (*w^elo> yamutû găm-hem găm-ʾăttæm*)" (NJV);

2 Chron 25,4   "Fathers shall not die for their children, nor children for their fathers; a man shall die only for his own sin" (NEB): (*lo> yamûtû ʾabôt ʿăl-banîm ûbanîm lo> yamûtû ʿăl-ʾabôt kî ʾîš b^eḥæpô yamûtû*); (cf. 5.2.2. and the variant *lo> yûm^etû* in Deut 24,16; 2 Kings 14,6).

The difference between the conditional formula *w^elo> yamûtû* and the statement *lo> yamûtû* is again quite clear. The first expresses the avoidance as the consequence of following the ritual prescriptions explicitly stated. Or from another point of view, it threatens death, if these prescriptions are not observed. The statement *lo> yamûtû* (2 Chron 25,4) is also referred to as a Mosaic law but it does not involve any specific conditions other than the negative one that no one should die for the sins of his father or his son. The positive conclusion was discussed above (5.2.2.).

6.3.7. Conclusions

Avoiding death expressed through a negated qal imperfect form can almost without exception be viewed as a consequence of something. The formal difference between *lo>* and *w^elo>* usually corresponds to a clear difference in meaning. In the first case we have statements about actual avoidance of death, in the second about the possibility of avoiding death, if certain conditions are present. Negations with *pæn* would then belong to the second category, while the two cases with *w^eʾăl* differ from each other. Deut 33,6, being an unconditioned wish, belongs to the first group whereas 1 Sam 12,19, being conditioned, belongs to the second.

There are, however, also cases where we have *w^elo>* without any conditions mentioned: Ex 9,4; 21,18 and Is 51,14. This does not mean, that they are not thought of as consequences (cf. 6.3.2.). To these examples we have to add the synthetic expression consisting of the verb *ḥyh* in a positive form and of a negated form of *mût*: Deut 33,6; Gen 42,2; 43,8; 47,19; 2 Kings 18,32; Ps 118,17. Their function and meaning will be discussed in greater detail below.

In the case of Deut 33,6, however, we can say that $w^{e\lambda}\tilde{a}l\ yamot$ is a logical counterpart to $y^e\hat{h}\hat{\iota}$ and one does not expect any conditions.

The statements with an unconditional $lo^{\jmath}$ differ from each other in function and meaning: Ps 118,17 has a synthetic expression for the psalmist's trust (6.3.1.). The oaths and reassurances discussed in 6.3.2. can be interpreted as consequences of a certain pattern of behaviour although the conditions are laid down in only two cases (Jer 11,21; 38,24). This is also the case with Prov 23,13 (cf. 6.3.2.). Gen 3,4 is the serpent's denial of the divinely threatened consequences and 2 Chron 25,4 (Deut 24,16; 2 Kings 14,6) a denial of commonly held concepts about one specific reason for death (cf. 5.2.2. and 6.3.5.).

6.4. The hif 'il perfect consecutive

Threats of death or death sentences are sometimes expressed in these forms, which I here list in a single group:

Ex 1,16:   "and if it is a boy, kill him ($w\check{a}h^amitt\tilde{æ}n\ {}^{\jmath}ot\hat{o}$)";
Ex 21,29:   "and the ox kills ($w^ehem\hat{\iota}t$) a man or a woman . . .";
Numb 14,15:   "if you then kill ($w^ehem\check{a}tt\tilde{a}$) this people to a man";
2 Sam 13,28: "strike Amnon, then kill him ($w\check{a}h^amitt\tilde{æ}m\ {}^{\jmath}ot\hat{o}$)";
2 Sam 14,32: "if I have done any wrong, put me to death ($w\tilde{æ}h^{æ}mitan\hat{\iota}$)";
Is 14,30:   "but the offspring of your roots I will kill ($w^ehem\check{a}tt\hat{\iota}$) by starvation ($bara^cab$)";
Is 65,15:   "So may the Lord God slay you ($w\tilde{æ}h^{æ}m\hat{\iota}t^eka$)";
Hos 2,5:   "I will leave her to die of thirst ($w\check{a}h^amitt\hat{\iota}ha\ b\check{a}\dot{s}\dot{s}ama^{\jmath}$)";
Hos 9,16:   "I will slay ($w^ehem\check{a}tt\hat{\iota}$) the dearest offspring of their womb".

Looking at the closest formal similarities we found certain groups which may constitute formulas:

1) $w^ehem\check{a}tt\hat{\iota}$ etc. (Is 14,30; Hos 2,5; 9,16) with God as subject of a threat and a people as object. In Is 14,30 the people addressed are the Philistines, while Hos threatens Israel/Ephraim. Is 65,15 threatens the unfaith-

ful part of Judah (cf. v. 11) and does so in an oath laid in the mouth of "my chosen". Thus only the first three cases would qualify as a formula proper. We can, however, describe them all as *direct threats*, i.e. they are not conditioned in any way.

2) *wah^{a}mittæn* etc. (Ex 1,16; 2 Sam 13,28; 14,32) with human killing as a consequence. The conditions are of different kinds: that the Hebrew child is a boy (Ex 1,16); that Absalom gives the order to kill Amnon (2 Sam 13,28) and that Absalom is found guilty before his father, the king (2 Sam 14,32). While the first two can be called *conditional orders* to kill, the third is the *inevitable consequence,* if Absalom should be found guilty (cf. 5.2.1.) and is therefore formulaic in the same way as 1 Sam 20,8 and 1 Sam 14,41.[192]

3) *w^{e}hemît* (Ex 21,29) and *w^{e}hemàttâ* (Numb 14,15) both express consequences and causes at the same time. The difference between the "goring ox" in the legal formulation of Ex 21,29 and God's killing of his people in Numb 14,15 are too great to regard the expressions as formulaic. They are, however, both hypothetical.

Thus I regard 1) and 2) as examples of a formulaic use of the hif 'il perfect consecutive of *mût*.

6.5. The hif 'il imperfect

Here we do not have any paronomastic formula like *môt tamût* and *môt yûmat* but instead simple imperfect forms expressing threats and consequences of different kinds:

Gen 42,37	"You may kill (*tamît*) both my sons, if I do not bring him back to you";
Numb 35,19.21	"The blood-avenger shall put the murderer to death (*yamît*) upon encounter";
Judg 20,13	"Hand over the scoundrels in Gibeah, and we will put them to death (*ûn^{e}mîtem*)";
1 Sam 11,12	"Hand the men over to us to be put to death (*ûn^{e}mîtem*)";

/

1 Kings 19,17   "Anyone who escapes the sword of Hazael Jehu will slay
(yamı̂t), and anyone who escapes the sword of Jehu
Elisha will slay (yamı̂t)";

2 Kings 7,4   "if they spare us (y^{e}hǎyyunû), we shall live (niḥyæ̂);
if they put us to death (y^{e}mı̂tunû), we can but die
(wamatnû)";

Is 11,4   "and with a word he shall slay (yamı̂t) the wicked;

Job 5,2   "The fool is destroyed (tamı̂t) by his own angry passions".

Of these examples Is 11,4 and 1 Kings 19,17 are direct threats pronounced
as divine punishments through a prophet. However, while in Is 11,4 this is
acted out through the Messianic king, 1 Kings 19,17 gives a series of three
anointed actors to execute the punishment. Numb 35,19.21 repeat yamı̂t in
the context of casuistic laws,[193] while Gen 42,37 is a self-imposed threat[194]
followed by a condition (ʾim-loʾ). 2 Kings 7,4 is largely built upon the pair
of opposites (ḥyh - mût), to which I shall return below. In Judg 20,13 and
1 Sam 11,12 we have the request to hand over certain people (t^{e}nû ʾæt-
(ha)^{ʔ}našı̂m) followed by the threat ûn^{e}mitem. It should be considered either
a formula or a coined phrase. Together with Numb 35,19.21. this phrase is
the only formulaic expression here.

There are, however, four oaths expressing the intention not to kill:

1 Sam 30,15   hiššabֿ^{e}ʿā lı̂ beʾlohı̂m ʾim-t^{e}mı̂tenı̂
1 Kings 1,51   yiššabǎֿ-lı̂ . . . ʾim-yamı̂t ʾæt-ʿǎbdô bæharæb
1 Kings 2,8   waʾæššabǎֿ lô bǎyhwh leʾmor ʾim-^{ʔ}mı̂t^{e}ka bæharæb
Jer 38,16   wǎyyiššabǎֿ . . . leʾmor ḥǎy-yhwh . . . ʾim-^{ʔ}mı̂tæka

As we can see clearly from these examples the oaths follow a pattern built
upon the verb šbֿ(nif ʾal) plus l^e (or ʾæl) followed by the suffix indicating the
person receiving the oath and then the oath formula itself beginning with ʾim
and the verbal form. Sometimes the oath is introduced by the formula ḥǎy-
yhwh (cf. below 6.7.). Thus it is not only the oath itself that constitutes the
formula, but it is the whole pattern which is formulaic and the oath forms
an element in this pattern.[195]

Finally we have some cases with a negated hif'il imperfect:

Judg 15,13:   "No; we will only bind you and hand you over to them,
               we will not kill you (w^ehamet lo³ n^emîtæka)";
1 Sam 5,11:   "Send the Ark of the God of Israel away; let it go back
               to its own place, or it will be the death of us all
               (w^elo³-yamît 'otî w^e₃æt-'ammî)";
1 Kings 2,26: "You deserve to die (kî ³îš mawæt ³attā) . . . but in spite
               of this day's work I shall not put you to death (lo³
               ^{3a}mîtæka)";
Jer 38,25:   "Let no one know about this, and you shall not be put
               to death (w^elo³ n^emîtæka)";
2 Chron 23,14: "Do not kill her (lo³ t^emîtûha) in the house of the
               Lord".

Here we can distinguish between two unconditioned reassurances (lo³)
found in Judg 15,13 and 1 Kings 2,26, and another two which are con-
ditioned (w^elo³) by certain measures (1 Sam 5,11; Jer 38,25). The last case
is not a reassurance but an order not to kill in a certain place, but rather
outside it. In spite of the similarities between the two former cases on the
one hand and the latter two on the other, their respective contexts are too
different to allow us to call them formulas, or even formulaic, when we take
in account not only formal but also functional similarities.

Summing up our findings in this paragraph, we can say that the hif'il
imperfect forms are not used in formulas to the same extent as some qal
forms and – as we shall see – also certain hof'al forms. The most striking
exception is the formulaic pattern used about or in oaths. Apart from this
there were only two formulas used in casuistic laws and another two cases
about delivery for killing. We shall return below to the use of hif'il forms in
expressions about actual killing.

6.6. The hof'al imperfect

While the hif'il forms are not very common in threats and legal formulations
about capital punishment, this is the case with the hof'al imperfect forms.

120

I shall begin with the simple *yûmat*, then turn to the corresponding negative forms before proceeding to the paronomastic *môt yûmat*.

6.6.1. *yûmat* etc.

Ex 21,29:	"and the ox kills a man or a woman, then the ox shall be stoned, and the owner shall be put to death (*yûmat*) as well";
Ex 35,2:	"Whoever works on that day shall be put to death (*yûmat*)";
Lev 24,16:	"Whoever utters the Name of the Lord shall be put to death (*môt yûmat*): all the community shall stone him to death: alien or native, if he utters the Name, he shall be put to death (*yûmat*)";
Lev 24,21:	"but whoever strikes a man and kills him shall be put to death (*yûmat*)";
Numb 1,51; 3,10.38; 18,7:	"any unqualified person who comes near it shall be put to death (*yûmat*)";
Deut 13,6:	"That prophet or that dreamer shall be put to death (*yûmat*) for ...";
Deut 17,6:	"Sentence of death shall be carried out (*yûmắt hămmet*) on the testimony of two or three witnesses";
Deut 24,16:	"a man shall be put to death (*yûmatû*) only for his own sin";
Jos 1,18:	"Whoever rebels against your authority, and fails to carry out all your orders, shall be put to death (*yûmat*)";
Judg 6,31:	"Whoever pleads his cause shall be put to death (*yûmắt*) at dawn";
1 Sam 20,32:	"Why should he die (*yûmắt*), what has he done?";
2 Sam 19,23:	"Why should any man be put to death (*yûmắt*) this day in Israel?";
1 Kings 2,24:	"as the Lord lives ... this very day Adonijah shall be put to death (*yûmắt*)";
2 Kings 11,8:	"and anyone who comes near the ranks is to be put to death (*yûmat*)";

2 Kings 14,6:	"a man shall be put to death (*yûmat*) only for his own sin";
Jer 38,4:	"the man must be put to death (*yûmăt*)";
Prov 19,16:	"To keep the commandments keeps a man safe, but scorning the way of the Lord brings death (*yûmat* Q: *yamût*)";
2 Chron 15,13:	"all who would not seek the Lord the God of Israel were to be put to death (*yûmat*)";
2 Chron 23,7:	"anyone who tries to enter the house is to be put to death (*yûmat*)";
2 Chron 23,14:	"Bring her outside the precincts and let anyone in attendance on her be put to the sword (*yûmắt bæḥarœb*)".

There are several points which draw our attention in the above list:

1) The four times repeated formula in Numb 1,51; 3,10.38; 18,7: "any outsider who encroaches shall be put to death" provides for capital punishment in the case of violations of certain cultic instruments (the Tabernacle) and their functions, which are the reserved domain of the Aaronite priesthood only.[196]

2) The position of *yûmat* at the end of the phrase or the sentence in accordance with some kind of formulaic pattern is very characteristic, although there are exceptions mainly in narrative contexts (Judg 6,31; 1 Sam 20,32; 2 Sam 19,23; 1 Kings 2,24; Jer 38,4; 2 Chron 23,14).

3) *yûmat* can be viewed as part of such apodictic patterns beginning with *kol* plus participle (Ex 35,2); *kol* ᵃ*šœr* (2 Chron 15,13); *kol* ᵓîš ᵃ*šœr* (Jos 1, 18); ᵃ*šœr* (Judg 6,31); participle (Lev 24,16; 2 Kings 11,8; Prov 19,16; 2 Chron 23,7.14); noun (Numb 1,51; 3,10.38; 18,7); or in certain cases with casuistic formulations, such as *wᵉᵓim* (Ex 21,29) and *kî-ᵓim* (2 Kings 14,6).

This would mean that phrases with *yûmat* are to a large extent formulaic or influenced by legal, i.e. formulaic style.[197] It should be added that we have only one case with the hof'al perfect consecutive *wᵉhûmat*, namely Deut 21,22, which also belongs to a casuistic pattern: "When a man is convicted of

122

a capital offence and is put to death ($w^e h \hat{u} m a t$), you shall hang him on a gibbet . . .". The only case of a simple perfect ($hum^e t\hat{u}$) again does not express a threat but refers to a case of actual killing (2 Sam 21,9).

6.6.2. lo² yûm^e tû

The negated forms are few indeed, only three cases, two of which are duplicates:

Lev 19,20   *lo² yûm^e tû kî-lo² huppašā* "They shall not be put to death, because she has not freed";

Deut 24,16;   *lo² yûm^e tû ²abôt ²ăl-*
2 Kings 14,6   *banîm ûbanîm lo² yûm^e tû ²ăl- ²abôt*

Cf. 2 Chron 25,4 which reads *yamûtû* instead of *yûm^e tû* (6.3.5.), and is therein followed by most of the old versions.

Lev 19,20, in a casuistic law, makes an exception from the death penalty for a man who has intercourse with a "slave-girl who has been assigned to another man and neither ransomed nor given her freedom". As for Deut 24,16 (and the influenced cases 2 Kings 14,6 and 2 Chron 25,4) it represents a kind of *new law* comparable to Jer 31.29f. (and Ez 18,22f.). While the latter points to the future, Deut 24,16 is promulgated in a specific historical situation, which, however, we are not able to determine. Since its form is apodictic we can assume, following Knierim,[198] that it has its *Sitz im Leben* in the sacral instruction about the law within the cult. This would mean, then, that although it is repeated in a different context, it is nevertheless a formula, although a rather late one.

6.6.3. môt yûmat/yûm^e tû

This paronomastic phrase is found mainly in the legal codes of the Pentateuch, and there in certain easily distinguishable contexts: in the Book of the Covenant (Ex 21,12.15-17; 22,18), in the Law of Holiness (Lev 20) and finally some isolated examples in the Pentateuch (Gen 26,11; Ex 31,14.15;

Lev 24,16.17; 27,29; Numb 15,35; 35,16.17.18.21.31.) and outside the Pentateuch in Judg 21,5 and Ez 18,13. Although *môt yûmat* is itself a formula, it is usually also part of a larger pattern, which we shall try to describe from case to case, thereby classifying the material according to the above contexts.

a) The participial laws in the Book of the Covenant.

Ex 21,12   *măkkē ʾîš wamet môt yûmat*
     21,15   *ûmăkkē ʾabîw wᵉʾimmô môt yûmat*
     21,16   *wᵉgoneb ʾîš ûmᵉkarô wᵉnimṣaʾ bᵉyadô môt yûmat*
     21,17   *ûmᵉqăllel ʾabîw wᵉʾimmô môt yûmat*
     22,18   *kâl-šokeb ʿim-bᵉhemā môt yûmat*

If we assume that the shortest form is the original, this is preserved in 21,12.15.17, while v. 16 has the addition *ûmᵉkarô wᵉnimṣaʾ bᵉyadô*, "whether he has sold him or still is holding him" and 22,18 the initial *kâl-*, "anyone" before the participle. Taking these into account we have a strict pattern beginning with the qal active, pi'el or hif'il participle expressing the person who commits the crime, followed by the object and, in two cases, by the consequence (*wamet* in 21,12 and *ûmᵉkarô . . .* in 21,16) and ending with the sentence formula. This pattern is apodictic, but Ex 22,18 occurs within a context of casuistically formulated laws and may have been displaced from its original context in the series. If we speak of a five-word pattern,[199] we should note that the constant elements are the participle at the beginning and the *môt yûmat* formula at the end, while the two middle elements vary.

b) Lev 20

Here, too, we have a series of *môt yûmat* laws but not in participial style but with certain other easily distinguishable features:

v. 2   *ʾîš ʾîš . . . ʾᵃšær yitten mizzărʿô lămmolæk môt yûmat . . .*
v. 9   *ki-ʾîš ʾîš ᵃšær yᵉqăllel ʾæt-ʾabîw wᵉʾæt-ʾimmô môt yûmat . . .*
v. 10   *wᵉʾîš ᵃšær yinʾăp . . . ʾæt-ʾešæt reʿehû môt yûmat . . .*
v. 11   *wᵉʾîš ᵃšær yiškăb ʾæt-ʾešæt ʾabîw ʿærwăt ʾabîw gillā môt yûmat*

124

v. 12 w^{e}ˀiš ˀ^{a}šær yiškăb ˀæt-kăllatô môt yûm^{e}tû š^{e}nêhæm . . .

v. 13 w^{e}ˀiš ˀ^{a}šær yiškàb ˀæt-zakar mišk^{e}bê ˀiššā . . . môt yûmatû . . .

v. 15 w^{e}ˀiš ˀ^{a}šær yitten š^{e}kâbtô bibhemā môt yûmat . . .

v. 16 w^{e}ˀiššā ˀ^{a}šær tiqrăb ˀæl-kăl-b^{e}hemā . . . môt yûmatû . . .

v. 27 w^{e}ˀiš ˀô-ˀiššā kî-yihyǣ bahæm ˀôb ✱ô yidd^{e}ˁonî môt yûmatû . . .

The common structure of these laws is again obvious: at the beginning we have ˀiš ˀiš/ w^{e}ˀiš ˀ^{a}šær, "anyone who", followed by a qal imperfect form of the verb and the môt yûmat formula. In addition to these elements there is the blood-guilt formula: dam-bô (v. 9) or d^{e}mêhæm bam (v. 10.11.12.13. 16.27) at the very end of the pattern.[200] It is assumed that this pattern reflects a later stage of development[201] than the participial pattern discussed above. There are, however, different opinions as to what the original form may have been. If the blood-guilt formula belongs to the original pattern, v. 2 may be a later adaptation of this pattern. It has also been assumed that v. 27 originally followed after v. 2,[202] both laws expressing the prohibition against certain foreign cultic practices. V. 9 corresponds in meaning to Ex 21,17 and v. 10-16 are directed against sexual offences. Some of them have an additional moral point: ˁærwăt ˀabîw gillā, "it is the nakedness of his father that he has uncovered" (v. 11): tæbæl ˁaśû, "they have committed incest" (v. 12) and tô ˁebā ˁaśû, "the two of them have done an abhorrent thing" (v. 13).[203]

c) Numb 35

16   w^{e}ˀim biklî barzæl hikkahû wăyyamot roṣeăh hûˀ môt yûmat haroṣeăh

17   w^{e}ˀim b^{e}ˀæbæn . . . hikkahû wăyyamot roṣeăh hûˀ môt yûmat haroṣeăh

18   ˀô biklî ˁeṣ- . . . hikkahû wăyyamot roṣeăh hûˀ môt yûmăt haroṣeăh

21   ˀô b^{e}ˀêbā hikkahû b^{e}yadô wăyyamot môt yûmăt hammakkǣ roṣeăh hûˀ

31   w^{e}loˀ tiqhû kopær l^{e}næpæš roṣeăh ˀ^{a}šær-hûˀ rašaˁ lamût kî-môt yûmat

Although these laws, with the exception of v. 31, are similarly formulated they do not have the same strictly worded form as the previous examples from Ex 21 and Lev 20. They are commonly held to be later adaptations of the old patterns.[204] They are "kasuistisch aufgelöst" and do not use the *môt yûmat* formula to denote a capital punishment on behalf of the community, but rather in the hands of the avenger of blood (cf. v. 19.21).[205] The crime is in all cases – again with the exception of v. 31 – the same, namely intentional murder and the variation is to be found in the weapon used. V. 31 forbids the acceptance of payment for the life of the killer – he shall be put to death as the previous laws (v. 16-21) already stated.

d) Other legal statements

Ex 31,14   *ûš^emårtœm ˀœt-haššåbbat kî qodœš hî˟ lakœm m^eḥallêha môt yûmat*

Ex 31,15   *. . . qodœš låyhwh kål-ha^cošœ̄ m^elaˀkā b^eyôm haššåbat môt yûmat*

Lev 24,16   *w^enoqeb šem-yhwh môt-yûmat . . . b^enåqbô-šem yûmat*

Lev 24,17   *w^{e˟}îš kî-yåkkœ̄ kål-nœpœš ˀadam môt yûmat*

Lev 27,29   *kål-herœm ˀ^ašœr yåḥˀrȧm min-haˀadam loˀ yippadœ̄ môt yûmat*

Numb 15,35 *môt yûmȧt haˀ îš ragôm ˀotô baˀ^abanîm kål-ha^cedā . . .*

There are no close similarities between these laws, except for the repeated statements about the sabbath. Also the other are directed against cultic offences – except Lev 24,17. Lev 24,16 is formulated in the same participial style as Ex 21,12 etc., whereas Lev 24,17 has the same content as Ex 21,12 but represents a "kasuistische Auflösung" of this old law. It would seem then that Lev 24,16 is quite old but has later been augmented, and Lev 24,17 is a later variation of an old law[206] (Ex 21,12). Ex 31,14 and 15 prescribes the death penalty for violating the sabbath and Numb 15,32-35 has been regarded as a "priestly midrash" reinforcing the commandment to sanctify the sabbath. Lev 27,29, finally, does not concern capital punishment for a certain offence or crime, but is a kind of "Bann gegen Götzendiener".[207]

e) Other formulations with *môt yûmat*:

Gen 26,11   *hånnogeå^c baˀîš hȧzzœ̄ ûb^{e˟}ištô môt yûmat*

Judg 21,5   *kî hăśś^{e}bû'ā hăgg^{e}dôlā hay^{e}tā ... le'mor môt yûmat*

Ez 18,13   *lo' yihyæ 'et kăl-hăttô'ebôt ha'ellæ 'aśā môt yûmat damô bô yihyæ*

These three remaining examples occurring outside legal texts do not exhibit formal similarities with each other. Interestingly, however, Gen 26,11 has the participial form found in Ex 21 and is only one word longer (*ûb^e'iśtô*) than the five-word pattern would allow. It is either an adaptation of this pattern or perhaps older than this.[208] Judg 21,5 and Ez 18,13 are again concerned with sacral things, in the first case in connection with the holy war and in the second with cultic offences. Both have the form of curses threatening the offender with death. It should be evident, that they all use legal patterns including the legal formula *môt yûmat* in prescribing the death penalty for specific crimes.

6.6.4. Conclusions

The hof'al imperfect is used comparatively frequently for threats or prescriptions of the death penalty. Most remarkable is, of course, the use of the paronomastic formula *môt yûmat,* which occurs 28 times, mainly in legal contexts. In the old legal codes we met it in two series of laws (Ex 21 and Lev 20) and here it was used about non-sacral offences and formulated in accordance with relatively strict patterns. This form was loosened and the formula itself used for cases where the punishment was undertaken by the avenger of blood instead of the community (Numb 35) and in various legal formulations about sacral offences (Ex 31,14f.; Lev 24,16 etc.). The three cases found in non-legal texts were apparently formulated under the influence of this legal formula. It would seem that the same also holds true for some of the cases with only *yûmat.* This is the case especially with legal formulations Ex 21,29; 35,2; Lev 24,11.16 (and the negated form Lev 19,20); Numb 1,51; 3,10.38; 18,7; Deut 13,6; 21,22 (perfect consecutive); 17,6; 24, 16. It is obvious that *yûmat* in Deut has the same meaning as *môt yûmat* elsewhere, i.e. for capital punishment. The use of qal (*yamût*) in this sense is also peculiar to Deut. But the influence of the legal formula *môt yûmat* is perhaps also discernible in narrative contexts such as Jos 1,18; 2 Kings 11,8;

14,6; 2 Chron 15,13; 23,7.14. An indication of this is given by the participles at the beginning of the phrase and *yûmat* at the end. We therefore have to take into account a distant development from the strict form and restrictive use of the formula in the old legal codes through a long period of adaptation and more extensive use in later legal formulations and then, parallel to this, its influence on narrative texts, etc.

6.7. Threats and laws with *mawæt*

The overwhelming majority of the cases discussed above are verbal forms (qal, hif'il and hof'al) expressing threats and laws prescribing the death penalty for certain crimes or offences. At the end of the chapter we shall turn to a few combinations with the noun *mawæt* expressing the same . It should be added here that there are a great many other combinations with *mawæt* which are expressions mainly for the nether world and will thus be discussed below. I shall here distinguish between threats and laws because it is possible even on formal grounds alone.

We have five cases, all found in narrative texts:

1 Sam 20,31   *wᵉˑắttā šᵉlắh wᵉqắh ʾotô ʾelắy kî bæn-mawæt hû*ˀ
1 Sam 26,16   *hắy-yhwh kî bᵉnê-mawæt ʾắttæm*
2 Sam 12,5   *hắy-yhwh kî bæn-mawæt haˀîš haˁośǽ zoˀt*
2 Sam 19,29   *kî loˀ hayā kâl-bêt ʾabî kî ʾim-ʾắnšê-mawæt lắˀᵃdonî . . .*
1 Kings 2,26   *ˁᵃnatot lek ˁàl-śadǽka kî ʾîš mawæt ʾattā*

It seems that it is really a question of two distinct formulas here, one consisting of *kî* plus *bæn/bᵉnê mawæt* plus a pronoun, personal or demonstrative, and the other conforming to this pattern with *ʾîš* instead of *bæn* (1 Kings 2,26) or in a looser formulation (2 Sam 19,29). Two cases with *bæn/bᵉnê mawæt* occur in solemn oaths (1 Sam 26,16 and 2 Sam 12,5) distinguished by the oath formula *hắy-yhwh*.[209] The others, too, come close to oaths. It seems quite feasible to translate them with "deserve to die" as NEB does. They can also be said to express threats although they do not always mean that the threatened person will really die.

128

6.8. 'Fall' and 'die'

In 2.4.2. we encountered the phrase w^e*hinnē nopel met* as a special expression for recognition of death. In 5.3. both verbs occurred as equivalents (Jer 44,12; Ez 5,12; 6,11.12; 33,27) expressing death caused by war or following in the footsteps of war. While *npl* and *mût* here formed a word pair on parallel lines and took the qal imperfect forms, we shall now look at some phrases where both verbs are combined in a narrative sequence, mostly in the qal imperfect consecutive.

In 2 Sam 2,23 we read about Abner killing Asahel: *wǎyyippâl-šam wǎyyamǎt tǎḥtâw*, "and he fell dead in his tracks". The place where he fell is referred to in the same verse as *ᵓœl-hǎmmaqôm ᵃ꜔šœr-napǎl šam ᶜᵃšā꜔el wǎyyamot*, "the place where Asahel lay dead". In 2 Sam 1,4 David is informed about the disastrous battle on Mount Gilboa: *w^egǎm-hǎrbē napǎl min-haᶜam wǎyyamutû w^egǎm ša꜔ûl wîhônatan b^enô metû*, "and many of the people have fallen, and Saul too and Jonathan are dead". Common to these expressions is that *npl* and *mût* are used as equivalents and with the same subjects – apart from the concluding *metû* in 2 Sam 1,4. The function of this use of the equivalents seems to be to stress the 'falling' and thus make the description more impressive.

We have another two instances where *npl* and *mût* cannot be considered equivalents describing the same action, but rather two separate actions of which *mût* can be viewed as the consequence of *npl*. Thus we read in 1 Sam 31,5, how Saul's armour-bearer takes his own life during the above mentioned battle: *wǎyyippol gǎm-hû꜔ ᶜǎl-ḥǎrbô wǎyyamǎt ᶜimmô*, "he too fell on his sword and died with him", i.e. with Saul, who had drawn his sword and "fallen on it" (*wǎyyippol ᶜalêha*, v. 4). Although the subjects of *npl* and *mût* are again the same, the first, together with the sword as instrument, describes the suicidal act, the consequence of which is death (*wǎyyamǎt*). The parallel in 1 Chron 10,5 reads *ᶜǎl-hǎḥœrœb* instead of *ᶜǎl-ḥǎrbô*. In Job 1,19 another 'falling' causes death, but here it is the house which, struck by the whirlwind, falls on the sons of Job: *wǎyyippol ᶜǎl hǎnn^eᶜarîm wǎyyamûtû*. This means that the subjects of these two acts are different.

Summing up the combinations of *mût* and *npl* within the same phrase we have variations and differences concerning the verbal forms, the subjects and the actions:

1) the sequences *wǎyyippol* – *wǎyyamàt* and *napǎl* – *wǎyyamot* are synthetic expressions for the same act committed by the same subject (Asahel); This is also the case of *napǎl* – *wǎyyamutû* in 2 Sam 1,4a. The additional *metû* in 2 Sam 1,4b, however, has a different subject (Saul and Jonathan as distinguished from the people).

2) 1 Sam 31,5 uses *wǎyyippol* and *wǎyyamàt* for two consecutive acts by the same person, but nevertheless distinguishable from each other.

3) Job 1,19 also uses *wǎyyippol* and *wǎyyamûtû* in a sequence of cause and consequence but, the subjects being different, this combination is not comparable to those above.

These distinctions would mean that the synthetic expressions in 2 Sam 2,23 (twice) and 2 Sam 1,4a qualify as either formulaic or idiomatic. Since the function seems to be only to give a vivid expression by using the two verbs as equivalents, one should speak rather of an idiom. The two other combinations (1 Sam 31,5 and Job 1,19) are not repeated and here the verbs simply describe two different acts, although in 1 Sam 31,5 by the same subjects.

6.9. Trying and denying

Expressions about attempts to kill are usually formulated through the word combination *biqqeš l^ehamît*. The variations in form are not large at all:

Ex 4,24   *wǎyyipg^ešehû yhwh wàybaqqeš h^amîtô*
1 Sam 19,2   *m^ebǎqqeš šaʾûl ʾabî lǎh^amîtœka*
2 Sam 20,19   *ʾǎttā m^ebǎqqeš l^ehamît ʿîr w^eʾem b^eyiśraʾel*
1 Kings 11,40 *wǎybǎqqeš š^elomō l^ehamît ʾœt yàràbʿam*
Jer 26,21   *wǎybǎqqeš hǎmmœlœk h^amîtô*
Ps 37,32   *ṣopœ rašǎʿ lǎṣṣǎddîq ûm^ebǎqqeš lǎh^amîtô*

The common elements of all these phrases are the pi'el ipf or ipt forms of *bqš* and the hif'il infinitive of *mût*. In Gen 37,18 for example we have a

9

similar phrase: *wăyyitnăqq^elû ʾotô lăh^amîtô.* But here the verb expressing the attempt or intention is different. A purely formal definition of formula would qualify the above instances as a formula about attempts to kill. In three cases the person who makes the attempt is a king (1 Sam 19,2; 1 Kings 11,40; Jer 26,21), in one case the army commander Joab (2 Sam 20,19), in one the Lord (Ex 4,24) and in one "the wicked" (Ps 37,32). It can be said that in all cases, except perhaps the case of Jeroboam, the victim is innocent in the eyes of the writer. However, situational contexts differ considerably and thus we are not able to speak about a distinct function of the supposed formula. I would therefore prefer to speak of an *idiom expressing attempts to kill.* It should also be noted that not all of the examples can be regarded as consequences: as such I would consider 1 Kings 11,40 and Jer 26,21 (both with the pi'el imperfect consecutive), while the other cases simply state that someone attempted to kill without indicating a cause – result connection.

There are a few combinations expressing the wish to kill; or not to kill someone, mostly with YHWH as the subject:

Judg 13,23   *lû ḥapeṣ yhwh lăh^amîtenû* (Manoah to his wife)
1 Sam 2,25   *kî-ḥapeṣ yhwh lăh^amîtam* (about the sons of Eli)
Ez 18,23   *hæḥapoṣ ʾ^æḥpoṣ môt raša^c*
18,32   *kî loʾ ʾæḥpoṣ b^emôt hămmet*
33,11   *hăy-ʾanî ... ʾim-ʾæḥpoṣ b^emôt haraša^c*

We have here two clearly distinguishable phrases, one with the form *ḥapeṣ yhwh lăh^amît* plus suffix used twice in Dtr, and one that is negated in some way or another in Ez: *æḥpoṣ (b^e)môt raša^c/hămmet.* It is questionable whether we should speak of one formula, or rather two repeated phrases here, peculiar to Dtr and Ez. I prefer to regard them as two distinct phrases, since Ez 18,23 is a rather emphatic choice of the opposite alternative, namely repentance and life, which is also expressly stated in Ez 18,32 and 33,11. This means that all three cases belong to formulaic combinations of the opposites discussed below (8.2.).

Comparing Judg 13,23 and 1 Sam 2,25 with the idiom discussed above about attempting to kill, there is the common element of the hif'il infinitive *l^ehamît.* They are expressions of God's intentions, which come rather close to the attempt in, say, Ex 4,24, although the contexts are widely different. Ez with his idiom, on the other hand, rules out entirely the suggestion, that God should have such intentions, and stresses that the opposite, in fact, is the case.

6.10. Slaying

Combinations of *nkh* (hif.) and *mût* (qal/hif.) occur in legal as well as in narrative texts. I already discussed some legal formulations about slaying in connection with the expression *wamet(û)* (6.1.), i.e., cases where the slaying was expressed through *măkkē* (Ex 21,12), *yăkkē* (Ex 21,20), *wᵉhukkā* (Ex 22,1) and *wᵉhikkahû* (Deut 19,11) all followed by *wamet*. In addition to these examples there was 2 Sam 11,15 with the combination *wᵉnikkā wamet*. Both verbal forms expressed together the act of slaying and pointed to a hypothetical act or a plan to kill (1 Sam 11,15). Now I shall turn to cases where both verbs are used in a similar synthetic way, but point to actual killing in the past. Before doing this I shall briefly draw attention to the expression *hikkahû wăyyamot* in Numb 35,16.17.18 and 21 with the instrumental *bᵉyadô*, "with his hand", inserted. This formulation can be translated "strikes him ... and he dies" or "struck him ... and he died", but it is nevertheless a legal and hypothetical formulation. Although confined to Numb 35 alone, it is also a formulaic expression occurring in a casuistic pattern which includes phrases about the weapon, about the crime as murder and finally stating the sentence.[210]

6.10.1. hikkā ... mût

In narrative texts there are some examples with combination of *nkh* (hif.) and *mût* (qal):

2 Sam 1,15   *wăyyăkkehû wăyyamot*
2 Sam 10,18   *wᵉᵓet šôbak šăr-ṣᵉbaᵓô hikkā wăyyamât šam*
2 Sam 11,21   *mî-hikkā ᵓæt-ᵓᵃbîmœlœk ... wăyyamât bᵉtebeṣ*
2 Sam 20,10   *wăyyăkkehû bah ... wăyyamot*
2 Kings 12,21f. *wăyyăkkû ᵓæt-yôᵓaš ... hikkûhû wăyyamot*
2 Kings 25,25 *wăyyăkkû ᵓæt-gᵉdălyahû wăyyamot*[211]

Although these combinations differ from each other regarding the proximity of the two verbs, they are obviously used together to express the act of slaying. This also holds true for 2 Sam 11,21 and 20,10, although there are several phrases inserted between the two verbs. For comparison, we could take 2 Sam 2,31 with the verbs *hikkû* ... *metû,* where the connection is still looser, and *metû* should perhaps[212] be omitted. This synthetic use of *nkh* (hif.) and *mût* (qal) can hardly be said to have any specific function, other than that death was in fact the result. But it can best be understood as an idiomatic expression for "slaying" or "killing" as such.

6.10.2. hikkā ... hemît

Turning next to combinations of both verbs in hif 'il forms, we may point out that they occur exclusively in narrative texts:

Jos 10,26   *wǎyyǎkkem* ... *wǎymîtem* (Joshua – Canaanite kings);
Jos 11,17   ... *wǎyyǎkkem wǎymîtem* (»   »   );
1 Sam 17,35 *wᵉhikkitîw* ... *wᵉhikkitîw wǎhᵃmîtîw* (David – the beasts);
1 Sam 17,50 *wǎyyǎk* ... *wǎymîtehû* (David – Goliath);
2 Sam 4,7   *wǎyyǎkkuhû wǎymituhû* (Rechab & Baanah – Ishbosheth);
2 Sam 14,6   *wǎyyǎkkô* ... *wǎyyamœt ᵓotô* (the sons of the woman
              from Tekoah);
2 Sam 18,15 *wǎyyǎkkû* ... *wǎymîtuhû* (Joab's armourbearers – Absa-
              lom);
2 Sam 21,17 *wǎyyǎk* ... *wǎymîtehû* (Abishai – Benob); similarly 2
              Kings 15,14: Menahem – Shallum);
1 Kings 16,10 *wǎyyǎkkehû wǎymîtehû* (Zimri – Ela; also 2 Kings 15,10:
              Shallum – Zechariah and 2 Kings
              15,30: Hoshea – Pekah);
2 Kings 15,25 *wǎyyǎkkehû* ... *wǎymîtehû* (Pekah – Pekahjah);
Jer 41,2   *wǎyyǎkkû* ... *wǎyyamœt ᵓotô* (Ishmael and his men –
              Gedaljah);
Jer 52,27   *wǎyyǎkkǣ ᵓôtam* ... *wǎymîtem* (the king of Babylon –
              high officials from Judah).

Here, too, we can distinguish between those expressions where both verbs are immediately connected (Jos 11,17; 2 Sam 4,7; 1 Kings 16,10; 2 Kings 15,10.30) and other cases where the name of the victim and/or other phrases are inserted between them. In 1 Kings 16,10; 2 Kings 15,10.14.25.30 we have larger patterns about conspiration, assassination and succession (cf. above 4.4.2. and 2 Kings 14,19). Although the phrases quoted above show a rather firm wording, one cannot say that they have *one* specific function. They are used about killing in war, assassination and execution and occur in narrative contexts. In this they are similar to *hikkā . . . mût* and can, in my opinion, best be regarded as another idiom for "slaying" or "killing".

Combinations of *hrg* and *mût* are few in number and do not constitute formulas or idioms in the way of *nkh* (hif.) and *mût*. Some cases, however, are worth mentioning. Thus 2 Chron 24,25 has a sequence similar to the pattern found especially in 2 Kings 15: *hitqáš šᵉrû ꜥalâw ... wᵃyyᵃhᵃrguhû ... wᵃyyamot wᵃyyiqbᵉruhû ...* Here *hrg* is used in the same way as *nkh* (hif) or *mût* (hif.) or both together. In Jer 18,21 we have the parallel constructions *hᵃrugê mawæt* and *mukkê-ḥæræb,* which can be divided into two word pairs, namely *hrg/nkh* (hof.) and *mawæt/ḥæræb* (cf. above 5.3.2.). Prov 24,11 gives another word pair *mawæt/ḥæræg,* but since none of them is repeated, they are not strictly speaking word pairs. In addition to this we may point to the combination of *hrg* and the *môt yûmatû* formula in Lev 20,16 and the paronomastic expression *harog tᵃhᵃrgænnû* followed by the infinitive *lähᵃmîtô* in Deut 13,10. Consequently, we can conclude that *hrg* is sometimes used like *nkh* in combination with *mût,* sometimes in parallel forming word pairs with both of them, sometimes independently like *hemît.*[213]

6.11. Repeated expressions

In 6.3. I have dealt with negated qal imperfect forms, which were many in number and showed a variety a formulaic uses. In turning to the corresponding qal perfect forms, we shall see that they are few and best understood as repetitions about actual avoidance of death. In Ex 9,6.7. we have an almost word for word repetition relating how the Israelite cattle were spared during the great plague (cf. above 2.6.). Nothing has, however, to be done on the Israelite side to avoid death: God's intention to make this distinction is the miracle he

134

alone performs to persuade the Egyptians to let his people go, unfortunately without effect. The paradoxality of this distinction is expressed by way of repetition.[214] In 1 Sam 5,12 we are told that even those men of Ekron "who did not die" (ᵃšær loʾ metû) "were plagued with tumours". This statement is preceded by indications that the God of Israel really threatened them with death (lăhᵃmîtenî wᵉʾæt-ʿămmî, v. 10), something that must be avoided (wᵉloʾ -yamît ʾotî wᵉʾæt-ʿămmî, v. 11) and that there already existed the terror of death (mᵉhûmăt-mawæt, v. 11). Here, too, we have a repetitious style to describe the terror and seriousness of the threat,[215] and those who avoided death did not escape unmarked.

In 1 Sam 14,45 the people save Jonathan from death: wàyyipdû haʿam ʾæt-yônatan wᵉloʾ-met. This follows after Saul's oath not to spare Jonathan if he was guilty of failing to receive an answer from God (v. 39 and repeated in v. 44, cf. above 6.2.3.). Jonathan himself had already realized that he was bound to die (hinnî amût v. 43, cf. 2.1.1.). Through the people's intercession, however, he was spared: "Shall Jonathan die (hᵃyônatan yamût), Jonathan who has won this great victory in Israel? God forbid! ..." (v. 45). Again the threat is repeated: this time in the form of a surprised question and finally we hear about the way of avoiding death as a happy end[216] for the hero of this battle story.

In Numb 26,11 we learn, that the Korachites did not die (ûbᵉnê-korah loʾ -metû) when "the earth opened its mouth and swallowed them up with Korah", that is, when God punished Korah, Dathan and Abiram and their followers for "defying the Lord" (v. 10 cf. Numb 16,32.35.). The Korachites are mentioned here because they would later form an important guild of temple singers.[217]

Summing up these instances of having avoided death we may again point to the fact that the threats and following killings were not legal procedures but spontaneous acts of God or, in one instance, the king. It is God who is instrumental in avoiding death since he spared certain individuals or animals. In 1 Sam 14 it is a person threatened by the king and he is saved through the intervention of the people. Here, however, it was within the king's capacity to pass judgement (cf. 1 Kings 2,37.42.).

In two previous paragraphs of this chapter (6.1. and 6.6.) we have encountered the stoning formulas sql baʾᵃbanîm and rgm baʾᵃbanîm in connection with *wamet* and *môt yûmat*. Both of them occur in cases of actual stoning. In 1 Kings 21 Naboth is accused of "cursing God and the king" (v. 10). The repetitive style follows the course of Jezebel's scheme in all its facets: *wᵉsiqluhû wᵉyamot* (v. 10) ... *wăyyisqᵉluhû ba⁻ᵃbanîm wăyyamot* (v.13)... *suqqăl nabôt wăyyamot* (v. 14) ... *kî-suqqăl nabôt wăyyamot* (v. 15). The full expression occurs only once (v. 13), while the instrument *ba⁻ᵃbanîm* is left out in the other repetitions.

We may again point out that this chapter is formulated in a highly repetitive style (cf. v. 15.16.20.21.24.25). The description[218] of the stoning of Naboth is clearly dependent upon the legal formulations of Deut, i.e., it is Deuteronomistic. They may therefore be regarded as "geprägte Wendungen" in the sense of W. Richter. The verb *sql* without *mût* as the expressly mentioned consequence occurs several times, which also holds true for the variant formula with *rgm*. Actual stoning with the combination of *rgm* and *mût* we have in 1 Kings 12,18 with its parallel and with a minor variation in 2 Chron 10,18: *wăyyirgᵉmû kăl-yiśra⁾el bô ⁻œbœn wăyyamot / wăyyirgᵉmû-bô bᵉnê-yiśra⁾el ⁻œbœn wăyyamot*. This formulation is clearly dependent upon the legal formulations, but the offence is a political one and the stoning does not occur as part of a legal procedure but as a popular rebellion against Solomon's son, Rehabeam.[219] Formally it comes close to Numb 35,36, which is formulated in qal imperfect consecutive forms although it is a legal provision and therefore hypothetical.

Although these historical accounts about actual stoning are repetitive rather than formulaic, they nevertheless use legal formulations about stoning, which are formulaic. H. Schüngel-Straumann[220] has pointed out that stoning applies to cases where blood vengeance does not. In both cases the killing does not result in blood guilt. This would explain, too, why stoning as a capital punishment was preferred to killing by the sword.

Still another repetition concerns trampling to death, combining the verbs *rms* and *mût*:

2 Kings 7,17   *wăyyirmᵉsuhû ha'am băśśă'ăr wăyyamot* (the *śaliś* of King
2 Kings 7,20   *wăyyirmᵉsû ⁾otô ha'am băśśă'ăr wăyyamot*   Jehoram of
                                                            Samaria).

The trampling to death of the "lieutenant" in the gate of Samaria is repeated as a demonstration of the fulfilment of what the prophet Elisha had told before (v. 18-20).[221] Another way of expressing "accidental death" is expressed through the combination *pgˁ -bô* plus *mût/hemît*, "to kill upon encounter". This combination occurs three times in 1 Kings 2, two of which have the form *wăyyipgăˁ-bô wăyyamot* (v. 25.46) and the third *wăyyipgăˁ-bô wăymitehû* (v. 34). All of them occur in descriptions about King Solomon's vengeance on his adversaries Adonijah, Joab and Shimei, who are all put to death through Benajah. The correspondence of form and function allow these to be regarded as formulaic. We may point to the oaths pronounced by Solomon himself regarding Adonijah (v. 24), Ebjathar (v. 26) and Shimei (v. 37.42) and the order regarding Joab (v. 29). This chapter is generally formulated in a highly formulaic style. Outside the chapter we have in Numb 35,19 the legal statement about the function of the avenger of blood: *bᵉpigˁô-bô hûᵓ yᵉmîtœnnû*, which formally resembles the statements about Benajah in 1 Kings 2. In this connection we have another phrase, namely *goᵓel hăddam hûᵓ yamît ᵓœt-haroṣeăh* (Numb 35,19) which is the enactment of the death penalty laid down in the preceding verse: *roṣeah hûᵓ môt-yûmat*. In the cities of refuge this is not allowed to happen: *wᵉloᵓ yamût haroṣeăh ˁăd-ˁâmdô lipnê haˁedā lămmišpaṭ* (v. 12). Although these statements are not repeated in exactly the same way, they are formulaic phrases within a given context[222] here, too. Formulas proper involving combinations of *pgˁ* and *mût*, or *mût* and *roṣeăh* do not occur, however.

Finally, we may point to the thrice repeated phrase about God's dislike of the sons of Judah and their evil ways, which led to their destruction:

Gen 38,7	*wăyhi ˁer . . . raˁ bᵉˁênê yhwh wăymitehû yhwh*
38,10	*wăyyeraˁ bᵉˁênê yhwh ᵓăšer ˁasā wăyyamœt găm ᵓotô*
1 Chron 2,3	*wăyhî ˁer . . . raˁ bᵉˁenê yhwh wăymîtehû*

While Gen 38,7 is repeated almost word for word in 1 Chron 2,3, Gen 38,10 has a similar phrase about Onan. It should be pointed out that *raˁ bᵉˁênê (yhwh)* and *ˁasā raˁ bᵉˁênê yhwh*, etc. are very usual phrases which as such can be considered as idioms. The combination of *hemît* and *yhwh* as subject is found only here and should therefore be considered a repeated phrase, employed in this special context.[223]

The repetitions discussed here can be divided in two groups:

1) formulations dependent upon certain legal provisions; the stoning cases in 1 Kings 12,18 (= 2 Chron 10,18) and 1 Kings 21 and the killings upon encounter in 1 Kings 2,25.34.46;

2) *ad hoc* formulations in Ex 9,4.6.7; 1 Sam 5,10-12; 1 Sam 14,39.44. 45; 2 Kings 7,17 and Gen 38,7.10 (1 Chron 2,3).

It is not easy to say whether some of these repetitions are due to the importance of the case described or simply to the repetitious style employed by the author. There does not seem to be any indication that the repetitions resulted from the combination of two or more different sources. We simply do not have other criteria for deciding what kind of repetitions they are.[224] Perhaps we should be content, at least in the cases discussed above, to point out the fact of repetitions even if we cannot explain this fact any further.

6.12. Summary

The material discussed here was much more extensive than that of the preceding chapters. Starting with the qal forms, we have seen, that a perfect consecutive as well as an imperfect form sometimes expressed the consequence of the deed as such ('Tatfolge') and sometimes the punishment prescribed for this deed ('Strafankündigung'). A qal form could be used for spontaneous threats as well as for death sentences. In historical texts the usual forms, then, were the paronomasias *môt tamût* or *môt yamût(û)*. In legal codes, however, the usual way to express a death sentence was the corresponding hof'al paronomasia *môt yûmat(û)*. The simple *yûmat* or *yûm^etû* was used in legal as well as in historical contexts to express capital punishment or to threaten such. In several cases its syntactical position indicated that the simple form was equivalent with the paronomasia and that a legal pattern had influenced the formulation of a historical case. The hif'il forms were used about legal killings performed by the avenger of blood, but usually they express 'spontaneous' killings by God, a king or the like. A special use of the hif'il imperfect was found in the oath formula or pattern.

Avoiding death was expressed through the negated qal, hif'il and – in a few cases – hof'al forms.

In addition to the absolute use of *mût* we found several types of combinations of *mût* and another verb. Sometimes they expressed different actions, but often such combinations (*mût-npl, nkh-mût* both in hif'il) were 'synthetical' and expressed together 'dying' or 'killing'. Then there were the combinations of verbs to express intention (*bqš l^{e}hamît*) or 'wishing' to kill (*ḥpṣ l^{e}hamît*) or denying such an intention. Finally we noted repetitions about actual killings, some of them formulated according to certain laws and some formulated *ad hoc*.

Death as a consequence was thus expressed in a manifold way as was also the avoidance of death through negated forms. In both cases the use of *waw consecutivum* or *copulativum* respectively was a kind of visible mark indicating a consequence. However, there were cases when a form with *waw* did not express the consequence as such but rather the second link of a synthetic expression: such were combinations of *mût* and *ḥyh* (to be discussed below) and *nkh* and *mût* (both in hif'il). On the other hand, there were also cases when the *waw* was not used and we nevertheless viewed the form of *mût* as a consequence due to the context. Distinguishing between legal prescriptions, threats and actual killings was usually not difficult: legal formulations introduced the death sentence at the end of a formulaic pattern describing the criminal act and its result and/or the conditions under which it took place; threats were often connected with a conditional 'if' or 'if not'; and, finally, actual killing was expressed through a perfect or an imperfect consecutive form indicating the past tense. However, these characteristics were not always decisive. There was one case, for example, when the imperfect consecutive was hypothetically used in a legal formulation (6.10.). Death sentences were also pronounced in narrative contexts and threats were made without any conditions mentioned. This means that we have no certain formal criterion by which we could decide which formulations should be regarded as laws, threats or actual killings. One might say, however, that legal formulations probably influenced death sentences, threats and perhaps also the descriptions of actual killings found in the narrative texts. In our opinion it is much easier to regard the legal formulaic use as primary and the narrative formulations as secondary. This is not to say that there is no such thing as formulas originating in everyday speech (according to Lande), but rather that these cases are relatively few in our material and consist of what I have called idiomatic expressions about 'slaying' or 'killing' (6.10.). As for the repetitions (6.11.) I have pointed out that we have repetitions which go back to legal formulations (about stoning to death and killing upon encounter) on the one hand and *ad hoc* formulations on the other. The essence of repetition is thereby the same: the same or a similar formulation is repeated within the same context for various reasons. Although it can have a distinctive function, it cannot be called a formula proper. One result of this chapter might therefore be the possibility of distinguishing between formulas, idioms and repetitions when the material is rich enough.

7. DEATH AND THE NETHER WORLD

In this chapter I shall discuss expressions about "death", "the dead" and "the nether world". They are thereby almost entirely figurative expressions, except in some legal phrases about avoiding contact with corpses and the like. Our question will be to what extent such things as the fate of the dead or the realm of death are expressed in a formulaic way. The occurrence of the stem *mût/mawæt* will again limit our material considerably from the totality of more or less apparent references to the same themes in other expressions.

7.1. Delivery and rescue

In Ps 118,18 the psalmist exclaims: "The Lord punished me severely, but did not hand me over to death" (*wᵉlămmawæt lo nᵉtanenî*). In Ez 31,14 we have a similar expression about "water trees" and "water drinkers": "for all have been given over to death (*kî kullam nittᵉnû lămmawæt)*". Although we obviously have variations of the same phrase, *ntn lămmawæt*, there is no such thing as a common function, which would qualify it as a formula. Therefore one should rather speak of an idiom, once used in a negated form about not being abandoned (by God) to death and once about the powerful men of this world[223] whose fate nevertheless will be the same as that of other men, namely to go down to the nether world (*ʾæræṣ tăḥtît*, cf. v. 14.16.18, etc.).

For comparison I wish to point to another two cases where *ntn* is combined with a verbal form of *mût*. In 1 Sam 11,12 the people demand that Samuel deliver up some of King Saul's opponents: "hand the men over to us to be put to death" (*tᵉnû haʾᵃnašîm ûnᵉmîtem*), cf. above 6.5. In 1 Kings 18,9 Obadiah, the comptroller of Ahab's household (v. 3), asks Elijah, why the prophet should hand him over to the king to be killed (*kî-ʾăttā noten ʾæt-*

ᶜăbdᵉka bᵉyăd-ʾăḥʾab lăhᵃmîtenî). Here the difference is considerable even on formal grounds. But one can nevertheless speak of an idiomatic combination of ntn and mût to express handing over someone to be killed (cf. 6,9.).

Turning to the opposite combination of hiṣṣîl mimmawcet, "rescue from death", we have three instances with similar formulations: Ps 56,14 (= Ps 116,8): kî hiṣṣălta năpšî mimmawcet, "for you have rescued me from death"; Ps 33,19: lᵉhăṣṣîl mimmawcet năpšam, "to save them from death" and Prov 10,2 (= Prov 11,4): ûṣᵉdaqă tăṣṣîl mimmawcet, "uprightness is a safeguard against death" (NEB).

Common to all three cases (five if we count duplications or repetitions) are thus the hif'il form of nṣl and mimmawcet (cf. the opposite lămmawcet above). In addition to this there is the object ncepceš with suffix in the Psalm cases. Substituting miššᵉôl tăḥtiyyă for mimmawcet,[226] "from the depths of Sheol" we have still another case (Ps 86,13), which Culley[227] regards as a formulaic phrase and a variation of Ps 56,14 (= Ps 116,8). In addition to this I would include Ps 33,19 as a variation of this formula since it contains all the main elements of the formula. The common function may be described as a reason for thanksgiving in each of the psalms, which of course differ from each other regarding Gattung.[228] In Prov 10,2 (= 11,4) the subject is no longer God but 'righteousness' seen as a saving force and the function is obviously different too: it is introduced as the opposite of "illgotten wealth" which "brings no profit" (10,2) or "is worth nothing in the day of wrath" (11,4). These chapters are largely built apon antithetic parallels contrasting the ways of the 'righteous' and the 'wicked', the 'wise' and the 'foolish'.[229] Thus I would look upon Prov 10,2 (= 11,4) as a repeated phrase.

7.2. The dead

In this section I shall consider some combinations of the participle met on the one hand and corresponding participles or nouns on the other.

7.2.1. Parallels to met

I shall first briefly point to some expressions which are used in parallelisms or otherwise syntactically combined with met. In Is 22,2 we have the already

142

quoted (5.3.1.) parallel between ḥǎllê-ḥærœb, "slain of the sword" and metê milḥamā, "dead in battle", which are obviously equivalent. In Ps 88,6 again the expression bǎmmetîm, "among the dead", is compared with ḥᵃlalîm šokᵉbê qæbœr, "the slain who sleep in the grave". In Ez 28,8 we have another type of combination, namely mᵉmôtê ḥalal, i.e. the polel participle of mût as a construct to ḥalal. The expression designates a shameful death, "the death of the slain" (NJV) or "a death of disgrace" (NEB), which will be the fate of the "prince of Tyre" (v. 2). It obviously means the same as môtê ᶜᵃrelîm, "the death of the uncircumcised" (v. 10).[230] It should be noted, however, that although expressions like ḥᵃlalîm and ḥǎllê-ḥærœb are rather common themselves, they are not syntactically combined with metîm, except for the few cases mentioned here and Numb 19,16.18 (cf. below 7.2.2.).

In the Book of the Covenant we have a repeated combination of met and nišbar concerning animals to be guarded or borrowed by another person other than the owner. Ex 22,9, for example, has the form ûmet ᵓô-nišbǎr, while v. 13 has the inverted word order wᵉnišbǎr ᵓô-met. Here we obviously do not have equivalents, but instead two related degrees, one higher and one lower: "dies or is injured" (NEB) or one leading over to the other: "dies of injuries" (NJV).[231]

Although rᵉpaᵓîm is rather frequently used about the dead as inhabitants of the nether world, it is only a few times used formally as a parallel to metîm. In Ps 88,11 we have a rather clear parallelism between them: "Do You work wonders for the dead (metîm)? / Do the shades (rᵉpaᵓîm) rise to praise You?" (NJV). In Is 26,14 too, both are used in parallel lines, as a word pair in the sense of Watters. Proceeding to v. 19 we have at the beginning a parallel between metêka, "your dead" and nᵉbelatî (MT), which is textually uncertain. At the end we have once more rᵉpaᵓîm but not in formal parallelism with them nor with šokᵉnê ᶜapar, "(you) who dwell in dust", which looks more like another parallel to metêka. Perhaps this is the original counterpart and nᵉbelatî should be left out.[232] If the parallelism metîm/rᵉpaᵓîm should not be regarded as a repeated word pair in Is 26 alone,[233] it is nevertheless established as such if we regard Ps 88,11 as another instance, as we obviously should.

In Lam 3,6 and Ps 143,3 we have two almost identical expressions, both ending with kᵉmetê ᶜôlam, "like those long dead". The only difference lies in the order of the two preceding words. It has on metric grounds been assumed that $k^e met\hat{e}$ ⟨ôlam is an addition to Ps 143,3.[234] If so, then it would not be a case of a formula but a repetition. Having the phrase "he has made me dwell in darkness" in common with Lam 3,6 it would be easy to understand why its continuation was later adopted, although it did not fit the metric pattern of Ps 143. Another explanation would be, of course, that the psalmist quoted Lam 3,6 in extenso from the outset. In both cases we would not have two independent formulations and thus not a formula here according to Richter. In Culley's sense it is a formula. However, I regard it as a repetition.

7.2.2. Touching the dead

There are certain legal formulations about the need to avoid touching (ng⟨) the dead or other objects related to corpses. Any contact with such will make the subject unclean (ṭmʾ). Beginning with Numb 19 we have a series of similar phrases:

v. 11: hănnogeă⟨ b^emet l^ekăl-næpæš ʾadam w^etameʾ šib⟨ăt yamîm
v. 13: kăl-hănnogeă⟨ b^emet b^enæpæšʾadam ʾªšær-yamût ... ṭimmeʾ ...
v. 16: w^ekălʾªšær-yiggă⟨ ... băhªlăl-hæræb ʾô b^emet ʾô-bʰ⟨æšæm ʾadam ʾô b^eqæbær yiṭmaʾ šib⟨ăt yamîm

We have the basic form in v. 11, which is then slightly expanded in v. 13. In v. 16, however, the objects not to be touched are four: "a person who was killed (by the sword), or who died (naturally), or a human bone, or a grave". These four objects are again mentioned in v. 18, when the prescription for cleaning with hyssop is given. So we have on the one hand laws built upon a form of ng⟨, the objects and the result of which are themselves formulaic, and on the other hand the objects formulated similarly in v. 11 and 13. These may be contrasted with v. 16, repeated in v. 18, where they must be regarded as repeated phrases.

We can compare the laws with another series found in Lev 11:

v. 31: kăl-hănnogeă⟨ bahæm b^emotam yiṭmaʾ ⟨ăd-ha⟨aræb
v. 32: w^ekol ʾªšær-yippol-⟨alâw mehæm b^emotam yiṭmaʾ ...
v. 39: w^ekî yamût min-hăbb^ehemā ... hănnogeă⟨ b^eniblatah yiṭmaʾ ...

We observe certain deviations from the pattern in Numb 19 but also considerable differences between themselves: *yippol* instead of *yiggд̆* in v. 32 and the casuistic formulation in v. 39. The main difference between Numb 19 and Lev 11, however, concerns the objects: there it was human corpses, here it is dead animals, both unclean and clean.

When we leave aside formulations with *ngᶜ* we have variously formulated prohibitions of contact with the dead. It may again be useful to quote the key phrases in the original:

Lev 21,11	*wᵉᶜ ă̆l kȧl-nă̆pšot met loɔ yaboɔ . . . loɔ yiṭṭȧmma ɔ*
Numb 6,6	*ᶜ ă̆l-næpæš met loɔ yaboɔ*
6,7	*loɔ-yiṭṭȧmma lahæm bᵉmotam*
6,9	*wᵉkî-yamût met ᶜalȧw . . . wᵉṭimmeɔ roɔš nizrô*
Ez 44,25	*wᵉɔæl-met ɔadam loɔ yabôɔ lᵉṭȧmɔā*

The verb expressing contact is *bôɔ* (Lev 21,11; Numb 6,6; Ez 44,25). Lev 21,11 concerns the high priest, Ez 44,15 the 'levitical priests', while Numb 6,6ff. concerns the Nazirites. It is interesting to note a qualification about the closest relatives: "not even for his father or his mother" (Lev 21,11); "not even when his father or mother, brother or sister dies" (Numb 6,7); but "except father or mother, son or daughter, brother or unmarried sister" (Ez 44,25). However, formally we can consider Lev 21,11; Numb 6,6 and Ez 44,25 as variations of the same legal prohibition although used in different ways and casuistically elaborated in Numb 6,7.9.[235]

In conclusion we can say that, basically, we have two different patterns, one built upon *ngᶜ - met - ṭmɔ* (Numb 19,11.13.16; Lev 11,31) and one with *loɔ yaboɔ – met – ṭmɔ* (Lev 21,11; Numb 6,6/7; Ez 44,25). Both are varied and expanded or casuistically reformulated, but all the quoted instances can be assigned to one or the other of these two formulaic patterns. The object element always includes the participle *met,* but in addition to this there are various determinations, or conversely *met* being an attribute[236] or other objects are used parallel with *met.* These variations do not, however, obscure the fact, that the formulations about contact with dead corpses are formulated in a highly formulaic style, obviously due to their legal function.

7.2.3. Excursus: 'the dead dog'

The expression *kælæb met* is used once in its simple form, when David rhetorically asks Saul why he is pursuing him: after two questions introduced by *ʾăḥᵃrê mî,* David himself answers with two parallel degrading metaphors: *ʾăḥᵃrê kælæb met ʾăḥᵃrê părʿoš ʾæḥad,* "after a dead dog, after a flea" (1 Sam 24,15). In the definite form the expression occurs twice. In 2 Sam 9,8 it is the only remaining son of Saul, Mephibosheth, who invited to the court of King David, again rhetorically asks: *mæ ʿăbdæka kî panîta ʾæl-häkkælæb hămmet ᵃšær kamônî,* "Who am I that you spare a thought for a dead dog like me". Finally, in 2 Sam 16,9 Abishai asks King David: "Why let this dead dog curse your majesty?". Although he does not refer to himself but to Shimei, the question is again rhetorical. Interestingly enough this expression is used exclusively in comparisons between the king and a supposed adversary. It may be asked, however, whether it is not ironically meant in 1 Sam 24,15, where King Saul is spared only thanks to David's magnanimity. In his relations with Mephibosheth and Shimei King David is again magnanimous, and this is perhaps what the narrator is trying to say by using the same phrase turned somewhat differently according to the demands of the various contexts. The expression *kælæb met* is perhaps the most deprecatory metaphor that could be imagined. About the preference of "a living dog" (*kælæb hăy*) to "a dead lion" (*ʾăryē met*) (Eccl 9,4), se below (8.2.). In a more forceful way the preference for life could not have been stated, since the attribute *hăy* to the most despised of animals is enough to rise it above the king of all animals, when this is dead. However, Koheleth has perhaps chosen this 'overstatement' to show how questionable such a life may be, i.e. by using figurative language intending it to be ironically understood.

7.3. The Nether World

In this section I shall deal with genitive phrases where *mawæt* forms the absolute and a variety of substantives the construct elements. I shall also discuss word pairs containing *mawæt*. I shall begin with those combinations which are repeated and can be considered formulas proper, and then proceed to single phrases of similar types.

146

7.3.1. *The gates of death*

First we shall consider three occurrences of the phrase *šǎ⁽ᵃ⁾rê mawæt,* namely:

Ps 9,14	*. . . mᵉrômᵉmî miššǎ⁽ᵃ⁾rê mawæt,*	"(you) who lift me from the gates of death";
107,18	*. . . wǎyyǎggî⁽ᶜû ⁽ǎd-šǎ⁽ᵃ⁾rê mawæt,*	"they reached the gates of death";
Job 38,17	*hᵃniglû lᵉ ka šǎ⁽ᵃ⁾rê-mawæt /* *wᵉšǎ⁽ᵃ⁾rê ṣǎlmawæt tirᵓ ǣ*	"Have the gates of death been revealed to you / have you seen the gates of the nether world".²³⁷

The gates of death in Ps 9,14 represent "the sphere of death", i.e. to be far away from God, as against the *šǎ⁽ᵃ⁾rê bǎt-ṣiyyôn,* "the gates of Daughter Zion" (v. 15) referring to the city (and temple) of God.²³⁸ This same idea is found also in Ps 107: the sick man belongs to the sphere of death, from which he can be rescued only to God; we have a reference to this in v. 20, although the reading is uncertain. In Job 38 we have the double reference and in the preceding verse (16) another two parallel expressions, namely *nibkê-yam,* "the bed of the Sea"²³⁹ and *ḥeqær tᵉhôm,* "the recesses of the Deep". Although these are the very limits of the cosmos, v. 17 imagines the nether world as being located still deeper.²⁴⁰ An equivalent expression found in Is 38,10 is *bᵉšǎ⁽ᵃ⁾rê šᵉᵓôl,* "in the gates of Sheol". That the nether world has gates like an earthly city is a concept commonly shared at least in Mesopotamia, Egypt and Israel.²⁴¹ In the Hebrew Bible it is expressed through a formula three times repeated and once varied. Its function is not very specific, however: it refers to the entrance to the nether world in poetical texts. It could therefore also be regarded as an idiom.

7.3.2. *The snares and the toils of death*

2 Sam 22,5-6 and Ps 18,5-6 are almost identical, containing several parallel phrases about the nether world. The deviations are perhaps the results of

scribal errors or secondary changes. If we take the first version to be the better preserved,[242] we have:

kî ᵓᵃpapunî mišbᵉrê-mawæt	"For the breakers of Death encompassed me,
năhᵃlê bᵉliyyăᵓl yᵉbăᵃtunî	the torrents of Belial terrified me;
hæblê šᵉᵓôl săbbunî	The snares of Sheol encircled me,
qiddᵉmunî moqᵉšê-mawæt	the toils of Death engulfed me". (NJV)

Ps 18,5 has in the first line *hæblê-mawæt* (like Ps 116,3) instead of *mišbᵉrê-mawæt*. In these contexts *mawæt* and *bᵉliyyă·ăl* can be viewed as the powers of Sheol, their weapons being the 'breakers' and 'torrents' (2 Sam 22,5 = Ps 18,5 if thus reconstructed) and the 'snares' and 'toils' (2 Sam 22,6 = Ps 18,6). In the same way Death/Belial and Sheol/Death are parallels. According to Kraus[243] they represent two parallel traditions, Ps 18 thus being closer to the original than 2 Sam 22. This would mean that we do not have to consider one of them as quoting the other, but as both going back to an independent original. The repeated expressions would thus qualify as formulas. Another question, however, is whether we should count them as word pairs or as repeated phrases. If we take the pregenitives as phrases we have the following formulas: *mišbᵉrê-mawæt, năhᵃlê bᵉliyyă·ăl, hæblê šᵉᵓ ôl* and *moqᵉšê-mawæt*. Then there is the variant *hæblê-mawæt* (Ps 116,3 and 18,5).[244]

However we look at them, they are clearly metaphors from the Tiamat mythology, known also from other psalms (e.g. 42,8; 69,2.15; 88,8; 93,4) and Lam 3,54 as well as Jon 2,4.6.[245] These powers are the enemies of God and the psalmist sings his thanksgiving psalm for deliverance from the "sphere of death". There is another expression for the weapon (*kᵉlê mawæt*, Ps 7,14), which, although occurring in a context with several other hunting metaphors, is not, however, repeated. The immediate nearness of death in Ps 22,16 is expressed by *lăᵃpăr-mawæt*, "to the dust of death". But this is singular, too.

Turning to Prov 13,14 and 14,27 we meet the 'snares of death', again twice repeated: "A wise man's teaching is a fountain of life/ for one who would escape the snares of death (*lasûr mimmoqᵉšê mawæt*)" and "The fear of the Lord is the fountain of life". The expression *mᵉqôr hăyyîm*, "fountain of life", is used about God in Ps 36,10, about "the mouth of the righteous" in Prov 10,11 and finally about 'intelligence' (*śekæl*) Prov 16,22 in addition to the cases quoted above (Prov 13,14; 14,27). But here it is once more a question of the opposites *mût - ḥyh* to be discussed in the next chapter. Still another repeated combination is *dǎrkê-mawæt*, "the way to (of) death" as opposed to *dæræk yašar*, "the straightforward way" (Prov 14,12; 16,25). A further occurrence of *môqᵉšê-mawæt* may be reconstructed from MT's²⁴⁶ *mᵉbǎqqᵉšê-mawæt*, "the seekers of death" (Prov 21,6), if we rely on LXX instead.

It is worth noting that although 'life' here may be interpreted in its specific sapiental meaning, 'success' or 'happiness',²⁴⁷ we nevertheless have the phrase "snares of death" as a typical metaphor of the nether world as found in the Psalms. In this connection we may point to two other expressions *ḥǎdrê-mawæt*, "the halls of death" used parallel to *dǎrkê šᵉʾôl* in Prov 7,27 and *mǎlʾǎkê-mawæt*, "messengers of death" used as a metaphor for "a king's anger" in Prov 16,14. None of these, however, are repeated.

In conclusion we may regard *môqᵉšê-mawæt* as a formula used independently in various contexts as a metaphor for the power of Death. In the Psalms it is a counterpart to *ḥæblê mawæt* or *ḥæblê šᵉʾôl*. In the Proverbs it is used as the opposite of *mᵉqôr ḥǎyyîm* also found elsewhere. Other pregenitive phrases which are repeated are *mišbᵉrê-mawæt*, *dǎrkê-mawæt* and phrases not repeated are *ḥǎdrê-mawæt* and *mǎlʾǎkê-mawæt*. From a purely formal point of view it is questionable whether any of these – except perhaps *mišbᵉrê-mawæt* – can be regarded as formulas, since they are confined to a single literary work. On the other hand, we could include them in the same group of metaphors referring to the sphere of death, to which *šǎᵃrê mawæt* (above 7.3.1.) also referred. Apart from these special pregenitive constructions there are many others, such as *mišbarîm*, used in an absolute way, especially in the Psalms but elsewhere too used as metaphors for chaos or the nether world. Thus one can say that they all belong to a certain kind of formulaic language created under the impact of the rich Near Eastern mythology. It is also possible to speak of a similar function regarding Ps 18,5-6 (= 2 Sam 22, 5-6) and Ps 116,3, while other instances differ,²⁴⁸ so that this criterion does not apply to the use of the same or similar phrases in Lam, for example.

149

7.3.3. Word pairs with mawœt

Word pairs, in Watter's sense, containing the substantive mawœt are not very frequent. In fact I have found only one combination which is repeated, namely mawœt/šᵉʾôl. Since the parallelism is extended to other words in the line, I shall quote them in full here:

Is 28,15 karắtnû bᵉrît ʾæt-mawœt "We have made a covenant with
wᵉᶜim-šᵉʾôl ᶜaśînû hozǣ Death/ concluded a pact with
Sheol";

Is 28,18 wᵉkuppắr bᵉrîtᵉkœm ʾæt-mawœt "Your covenant with Death
wᵉhazûtᵉkœm ʾæt-šᵉʾôl loʾ taqûm shall be annulled,/ your pact
with Sheol shall not endure";

Is 38,18 kî loʾ šᵉʾôl tôdœka "Fot it is not Sheol that praises
mawœt yᵉhắllᵉlœka you/ not Death that extolls you";

Ps 18,6 hœblê šᵉʾôl sᵉbabûnî "The snares of Sheol encircled me,
(2 Sam 22,6)qiddᵉmûnî môqᵉšê mawœt the toils of Death engulfed me";

Ps 49,15 kắs̩s̩oʾn-lišʾôl šắttû "Sheeplike they head for Sheol,
mawœt yirᶜem . .²⁴⁹ with Death as their Shepherd . . .";

Ps 55,16 yắššî(ʾ) mawœt ᶜalêmô "Let him incite Death against them;
yerᵉdû šᵉʾôl hăyyîm may they go down alive into Sheol";

Ps 89,49 mî gœbœr yihyǣ wᵉloʾ yirʾǣ-mawœt "What man can live and
yᵉmắllet̩ năpšô miyyăd-šᵉʾôl not see Death/ can save
himself from the clutches
of Death";

Ps 116,3 ʾᵃpapûnî hœblê-mawœt "The bonds of Death encompassed me,
ûmᵉs̩arê šᵉʾôl mᵉs̩aʾûnî the torments of Sheol overtook me";

Prov 5,5 răglˊha yorᵉdôt mawœt "Her feet go downwards on the path to
šᵉʾôl s̩ᵉᶜadˊha yitmokû Death/ her course is set for Sheol";

Prov 7,27 dắrke šᵉʾôl bêtah "Her house is the entrance to Sheol,/
yorᵉdôt ʾœl-hădrê-mawœt which leads down to the halls of
Death";

Song 8,6 ki-ᶜăzzā kămmawœt ʾăhᵃbā "for love is strong as death,
qašā kišʾôl qinʾā passion cruel as Sheol".

As can easily be seen the parallelism is not confined to the word pair *mawæt/šᵉʾôl* alone but comprises the whole lines as such. Thus one could pick out two or three other word pairs in every instance. It ought therefore to be asked whether the word pair really constitutes the basic unit upon which the parallel lines are built, or whether it is the line (stanza) as such which is to be considered the basic unit. There are certain groups which have more in common than the word pair *mawæt/šᵉʾôl*:

1) Ps 18,6 (= 2 Sam 22,6); Ps 116,3 (cf. above 7.3.2.), which can be said to constitute formulaic systems in the sense of Culley. They can also be said to have a common motif: "Threats of the nether world";

2) Is 28,15.18 about making and breaking "the covenant with Death" and "the pact with *šᵉʾôl*".[250] Here the word pairs are repeated because the author wishes to show the futility of such a pact.

3) Prov 5,5; 7,27 and Ps 55,16 all employing the verb *yrd* to express the *descensio ad inferas*[251] but with different motifs: Prov warning "beware of the whore" and Ps 55,16 hoping for the enemy to "go down alive to Sheol" (cf. Numb 16,33).

In addition to these motifs we have other found in only one instance each: "the fate of the wealthy" (Ps 49,15); "the transience of life" (Ps 89,49), "no praise in Sheol" (Is 38,18) and "the strongness of love and passion" (Song 8,6). However, all these motifs — except the unique "covenant with Death" — can be found elsewhere in contexts where this specific word pair or formula is not used.[252] It is obvious then that the word pair does not itself express any distinct idea or motif but can be used in very different contexts. Motifs, again, are expressed through whole phrases or larger units, e.g. through formulas and formulaic systems like those analyzed by Culley and Ljung. The word pair is the smallest unit in the parallel lines, but it is always combined with other word pairs in phrases from which they take their meaning.

I have found no other repeated word pairs with *mawæt* except of course the opposites *mawæt/ḥǎyyîm* to be discussed below. In this connection I wish, however, to point to the use of other combinations expressing what we have called "the sphere of death". Examples of this are the parallel use of *qæbær* and *mawæt* in Is 53,9 and the word combinations *ᵃbǎddôn wamawæt* in Job 28,22. By way of comparison I would like to mention the parallel use of šᵉʾôl and ᵃbăddôn in Job 26,6. Thus there is a certain affinity between not only šᵉʾôl and mawæt, but also between them and words like qœbær and ᴬbăddôn, which is by no means surprising, since they all refer to this same sphere.[253]

7.4. The transience of life

There are some phrases about dying expressing the transience of life. Although partly repeated they cannot be considered formulas proper. In the preceding paragraph we have already noted Ps 89,49 and others which express the same motif (cf. above n. 251). Here I shall compare two which have in common the expression kᵉmôt . . . In Numb 16,29 Moses addresses the community about the impending death of Korah, Dathan and Abiram: ʾim-kᵉmôt kâl-haʾadam yᵉmutûn ʾellæ . . . , "if these men die as all men do . . .". The description of their actual death follows in v. 33, which has three elements in common with Ps 55,16 (cf. above 7.3.3.), namely (wăy)yerᵉdû . . . ḥăyyîm šᵉʾolā, "they went . . . alive down to Sheol". It is difficult to decide, whether this is to be considered a quotation or an allusion;[254] however, it is not important in this connection. A formulation similar to that of v. 29 is found, however, in Eccl 3,19: kᵉmôt zæ ken môt zæ, "death comes to both alike", that is the common fate of man and beast. The difference in formulation and context, however, does not permit us to regard these expressions as formulaic, but only similar to a certain extent.

There are another two phrases, where the similarity is perhaps greater, although the contexts again differ considerably:

Prov 11,7a bᵉmôt ʾadam rašaᶜ toʾ băd tiqwā   "when an evil man dies, his hope is gone";

Ps 41,6b matăy yamût wᵉʾabăd šᵉmô   "when will he die and his name perish".

Although Prov 11,7a is open to different interpretations, involving leaving out the attribute rašaᶜ, it is beyond doubt that it expresses the transience of life.[255] Similarly the wish for the departure of the enemy in Ps 41,6 presupposes that with his death everything connected with him is removed.[256]

In spite of the similarity in expression, however, these phrases are not formulaic either. But a common motif is expressed in the verbs combined, 'die' and 'perish'. It is open to question, whether it refers to an evil man who is thus punished by God. This interpretation is possible in both cases.

7.5. Conclusions

Although the expressions examined in this chapter share a considerable number of similar phrases, it is difficult to establish common functions in context. This criterion for regarding certain phrases as formulas was satisfied only in a few cases: 1) rescue from death (Ps 56,14 = Ps 116,8 and Ps 33,19); 2) touching the dead (Numb 19; Lev 11 etc.); 3) snares and toils of death (Ps 18,5-6 = 2 Sam 22,5-6 and Ps 116,3). In addition to these there were several cases of repetition, especially in Prov. There were also a bulk of expressions referring to the "sphere of death" although these formally did not qualify as formulas. Finally, there were the word pairs *mawæt/š^{e}ʾôl* and *metîm/r^{e}paʾîm.* In this connection I raised the question, whether such a word pair in itself is to be regarded as the basic unit in parallel lines, as Watters would have it, or whether we should regard the lines as such as the basic unit. It is evident that the parallelism generates whole series of word pairs, usually three or four in every stanza. If we pick one of them at random, we find that it can be used in very different contexts, and does not convey any common function or meaning. If we take the formula in Culley's meaning, we have to consider whole phrases and the possibility of repetition is drastically reduced. On the other hand, we can here detect common functions and motifs. Thus the word pair is a rather technical way of combining two synonyms or antonyms, and we have to turn to the context with its combinations of other word pairs to be able to speak about functions. In this chapter, however, word pairs and formulas were rather sparse and what we found were mostly to be regarded as repeated phrases, idioms and the like. It is in a way slightly surprising, since there is no lack of expressions about the dead and the nether world in the Hebrew Bible. Our restriction to phrases and word pairs containing the stem *mût* was of course one major discriminating factor. Biblical poetry excels here more in variety than in repetition. Moreover, the criteria set forth by Culley for variation and myself for function also contributed to reduce the number of formulas to a minimum. This pertained particularly to the word pairs, which although astonishingly few in themselves, did not stand the test of function. It may be concluded therefore, that the material of this chapter tended to demonstrate the "varieties of repetition" rather than the "formulaic language" about death and the nether world.

8. DEATH AND LIFE

We have already met both stems *mût* and *ḥyh* in several different connections. But we have not yet discussed them as a pair of opposites, which is reserved for this chapter. They occur in different combinations over a hundred times and therefore we cannot discuss every one of these. I shall, however, try to divide the material according to the types of combination and to find out whether there are determinable functions that qualify any specific use as formulaic. It would be an interesting task to compare such a use with that of other opposites, such as 'light' and 'darkness', 'good' and 'evil' etc. However, I shall keep within the scope of my larger theme, i.e. formulas and repeated phrases containing the stem *mût*. There are, of course, other possible words as opposites to 'death'. One which immediately comes to mind is 'birth', but strangely enough this is syntactically combined with 'death' only a few times and it will suffice to show this in a short note (8.8.).

8.1. "Live and not die"

Proceeding from the simplest combinations to the more complex I shall here discuss cases where *ḥyh* is stated in a positive form while *mût* is negated. The opposites thus combined can express the same content, but they can also represent the opposite alternatives.

Common to the phrases in this group is the fact that the negated form complements the positive opposite:

Gen 42,2
    43,8   }   *wᵉniḥyǣ wᵉloʾ namût*   "so that we may live and not die";
    47,19

Numb 4,19   *wᵉḥayû wᵉloʾ yamutû*   "if they are to live and not to die";

Deut 33,6   *y^{e}ḥî r^{e}ʾûben w^{e}ʾăl-yamot* "May Reuben live and not die";

2 Kings 18,32 *wiḥyû w^{e}lōʾ tamutû* "that you may live and not die";

Ez 18,21.28;   *ḥayō yiḥyæ lōʾ yamût* "he shall live; he shall not die";

33,15;

Ps 118,17   *lōʾ ʾamût kî-ʾæḥyæ* "I shall not die but live".

The function of the negated forms is quite clearly to emphazise the positive opposite. There are of course variations due to form and function within the specific contexts. I would accordingly distinguish following subgroups:

1) Gen 42,2; 43,8; 47,19; 2 Kings 18,32. The Gen examples express a conditional avoiding of death (cf. 6.3.3.) which underscores the necessity of getting bread from Egypt. This again is expressed through preceding imperatives: "go down and buy ..." (42,2); "send the boy with me ..." (43,8) and "take us and our land in payment ..." (47,19). Similarly, Numb 4,19 states that certain precautions must be taken: "Do this with them ...", i.e. in order that the Kohathites should not "witness the dismantling of the sanctuary" (NJV) or "cast even a passing glance on the sanctuary" (NEB), which would have fatal consequences (cf. 6.3.5.).[257] Finally, the life-saving consequence of 2 Kings 18,32 follows after a series of negated jussive forms (v. 29-31) not to let King Hezekiah deceive the people of Jerusalem but instead listen to the message of the Assyrian king. Thus we may conclude that this what we may call "save-your-life" formula underscores in all cases an exhortation to do or not to do something.

2) Ez 18,21.28; 33,15. This phrase promises life to "the wicked man who repents ... and does what is just and right" (18,21); "because he took heed and turned back from all the transgressions that he had committed" (18,28) and "if the wicked man restores a pledge, makes good what he has taken by robbery, follows the laws of life, and does not commit iniquity" (33,15 NJV). This assurance probably has its origins in the temple liturgy as known to Ez and here proclaimed anew. Thus it can be considered a formula.[258]

Finally, we have two cases in Deut 33,6 (a blessing, cf. 6.3.2.) and Ps 118, 17 (expression of confidence, cf. 6.3.1.), which are not conditioned in any way.

If we ask whether there are similar expressions negating *ḥyh* and stating *mût*, the answer is that there are a few but they differ considerably from the preceding group as well as from each other. Isaiah's message to Hezekiah (2 Kings 20,1 = Is 38,1) has the form *kî met ʾåttā wᵉloʾ tiḥyǣ*, "for you are dying and will not recover", thus combining participle and imperfect of the opposite verbs. Ps 89,49 asks rhetorically: *mî gæbær yiḥyǣ wᵉloʾ yirʾǣ-mawæt*, "What man can live and not see death?" (cf. above 7.3.3.) and thereby poetically substitutes "not see death" for "not die". Job, finally, puts the question in this way: *ʾim-yamût gæbær hᵃyiḥyǣ*, "if a man dies, can he live again?" (Job 14,14). The questions should obviously be negated, but the imperfect of *ḥyh* is not preceded by a negation but by the interrogative particle. If the formal differences are considerable, the same can be said about function and meaning. Isaiah's message is a divine decision that the king's illness will lead to his death and that he should prepare for his final departure. The psalmist is anguished because God has hidden himself: he cannot wait for ever since his life will inevitably end with his death. Job takes this for granted, although his wish is that he should be left alone (v. 6), while he is enjoying his short life. Thus we can conclude that these examples do not form any counterpart to those about saving one's life. In this respect they are even closer to the singular expressions of Deut 33,6 and Ps 118,17. However, those descriptions of the conditioned avoidance of death or saving one's life do constitute formulas.

8.2. 'Live' or 'die'

When Elisha in 2 Kings 8,10 answers Ben-Hadad about his illness, he first promises recovery (*ḥayō tiḥyǣ*), but then confides to the king's messenger Hazael: "but the Lord has revealed to me that in fact he will die" (*môt yamût*). Both statements flatly contradict each other, but they cannot be understood as alternatives, either (cf. 4.4.1. and 6.2.3.). The king can do nothing about the outcome. Very often, however, the opposites are used to express alternatives and the subject can, and is expected to, do something in order to live.

We shall next consider Gen 19,19-20, where Lot pleads with the "angels" (v. 15) or the "men" (v. 16): "Please, if you favour your servant, having

already shown me so much kindness by saving my life ($l^e h \breve{a} h^a y \hat{o} t$ ²*æt-n*ă*pš*î̂) –
I cannot flee to the hills, lest disaster overtake me and I die (*wamắttî*). See,
that town there is near enough to flee to; it is such a little place! Let me flee
there – it is such a little place – and let my life be saved (*ût^e hî năpšî*)". Lot
may refer to a previous saving act, in order to plead for another chance. The
alternatives before him are expressed through the opposites.

In Gen 20,7 God puts the alternatives before Abimelech of Gerar: "Send
back the man's wife now ... and you shall live (*wæhyē*). But if you do not
send her back, know that you shall surely die (*môt tamût*)". In Gen 42,18.20
Joseph tells his brothers: "Do this and you shall live (*wihyû*) ... but you
must bring me your youngest brother, that your words may be verified and
you may not die ($w^e lo$² *tamûtû*)". The main formal similarity is the imperative form of *hyh* following another imperative.[259] However, the opposites are
expressed quite differently: in Gen 20,7 we have a threat of death (cf. 6.2.2.),
while the undesirable consequence in Gen 42,20 is expressed by negating
mût, which reminds us of the above examples (8.1.); choosing life means
avoiding death.[260]

In Deut 5,24-26 the Israelites plead with Moses for mediation: "today we
have seen that God may speak with men and they may still live (*wahay*). Why
should we now risk death? (*lammā namût*) ... If we hear the voice of the
Lord our God again, we shall die (*wamatnû*). Is there any mortal man who
has heard the voice of the living God ($²^æ lohîm$ *hăyyîm*) ... as we have, and
lived? (*wăyyæhî*)." This is a chiastic composition with two rhetorical
questions; in spite of the paradoxical experience referred to in v. 24 and
again in v. 26, the Israelites should not expose themselves to the same danger
again (v. 25).

In Jer 27,12-13 the prophet relates his message to King Zedekiah in the
following way: "Put your necks under the yoke of the king of Babylon;
serve him and his people, and live! (*wihyû*) Why should you and your people
die (*lammā tamûtû*) by sword, famine and pestilence ...". Here *hyh* takes an
imperative form following two others, whereas *mût* occurs in another rhetorical question, which should again be negated (cf. above 5.1.).

In this connection I wish to draw attention to a case where a threat of
death is uttered and then followed by a comment about those who actually
died and those who were spared. In Numb 14,35 God speaks to Moses about
the men who had plotted against him: "There shall be an end of them here in

158

this wilderness; here they shall die (w^ešam yamutû)". And in v. 36-38 their fate is considered: "But the men whom Moses had sent to explore the land, and who came back and by their report set all the community complaining against him, died of the plague (wắyyamutû ... bắmmăggepă) before the Lord ... Of those who went to explore the land, Joshua son of Nun and Caleb son of Jephunneh alone remained alive (ḥayû)". It is clear that the syntactical connection is rather loose and that there can be no question about formulaic speech, except for the expression about death in the wilderness (cf. above 3.5.1. and 3.5.2.).

Another group of examples is represented in Ez 18,23.32; 33,11. It is denied that God would wish the death of the wicked (cf. 6.9.). Instead it is stressed that he should repent, better his ways and live:

18,23 hœḥapos ˀœḥpoṣ môt raša^c ...   "Is it my desire that a wicked
                                                  man shall die? . . . It is rather
h^alô˃ b^ešûbô midd^erakâw w^eḥayā that he shall turn back from his
                                                  ways and live";
18,32 kî lo˃ ˀœḥpoṣ b^emôt hămmet ...   "For it is not my desire that
                                                  anyone shall die . . .
w^ehašîbû wiḥyû   repent therefore, and live!";
33,11 hăy-ˀanî ... ˉim-ˀœḥpoṣ b^emôt haraša^c "As I live . . . it is not
                                                  my desire that the wicked
kî ˃im-b^esûb raša^c middărkô w^eḥayā shall die, but that the
                                                  wicked turn from his ways
                                                  and live".

Although there were similar formulations about wishing the death of someone (Judg 13,23; 1 Sam 2,25), I regarded these as repeated phrases typical of Ez. This impression is strengthened when we take into account the alternative, which has no real counterpart outside Ez. The combination is peculiar to Ez, which is what counts here.²⁶¹

Also Jer uses the opposites to express alternatives, although both cases are somewhat uncertain from a text critical point of view:²⁶²

21,9 hăyyošeb ba^cîr hăzzo˃t yamût ...   "Whoever remains in this city
                                                  shall die . . . but whoever
w^ehăyyôṣe˃ ... yiḥyœ   leaves . . . shall live";

38,2 *hăyyoŠeb ba'îr hăzzo'ṭ yamût* . . . "Whoever remains in this city
shall die . . . but whoever sur-
w^ehăyyoṣe' . . . *yihyæ* . . . *waḥay* renders . . . shall live . . . and
shall live".

The differences are small: 21,9 is slightly more extensive in the first part,
but 38,2 adds another form of *ḥyh* at the end. If the *ketib* reading of the
consonants *yḥyh* is correct, then both opposites take the qal imperfect form.
The subjects are expressed through participles, as was the case in many of the
legal formulations discussed above (6.6.).
We shall compare these with an example found in Ex 19,12-13:

kål-hănnogeă< bahar môt yûmat   "Whoever touches the mountain shall
be put to death . . .
. . . *'im-b^ehemā 'im-'îŠ lo' yihyæ*   beast or man, he shall not live".

Here the legal formulation has certain casuistic qualifications, although
man and beast are treated similarly. The death sentence formula *môt yûmat*
is here taken up through the negated opposite (*lo' yihyæ*) so that no
alternatives are presented.[263] The subject participle is strengthened through
kål- which is also a characteristic of participial style.

It is possible that Jer draws on formulations connected with the holy
war[264] but in doing so he uses them in a very free manner, e.g. by introducing
the triple formula "by the sword, by famine, and by pestilence" so typical
of him (cf. above 5.3.5.).

If we try to draw conclusions about the examples discussed here, we may
say that all have one formal feature in common, namely that they syntactically combine forms of *mût* and *ḥyh*. This connection is, however, much
looser than was the case in 8.1. In two cases one of the opposites is negated,
so that it virtually repeats the other: Gen 42,20 negating *mût* and Ex 19,13
negating *ḥyh*.

It is doubtful if it is correct to speak of alternatives in these two cases. In
another two cases, however, the second alternative is expressed through a
question which comes close to a negation, but nevertheless can be said to
present an alternative: Jer 27,13 and Deut 5,24. In the other cases the
alternative character of the opposites seems to be beyond doubt. One

common feature lies in the contexts: choosing the right alternative, either avoiding death and choosing life, or being liable to capital punishment, always presupposes that something is done or left undone. This something, however, can be rather different things and the alternatives, although given divine authority in all cases except Gen 42,18.20, are very differently presented, so that one can hardly speak of any common function.

8.3. "The living and the dead"

Turning to the participles *ḥǎy* and *met* I have found only one example, which formally corresponds to the above (8.1.) formulas, namely 1 Kings 21,15: *kî ᵓên nabôt ḥǎy kî-met*, "for Naboth is no longer alive, he is dead". Here the already established fact of Naboth's death is expressed by the participle *met* as well as through the negated *ᵓên ḥǎy*. The function of this combination is again to stress the statement about his death. The use of participles as attributes is not very frequent, either. The largest group is the absolute use of the participles as nouns. Since there is no sharp distinction between these both groups, I shall list the examples together:

Ex 21,35	*ûmak^erû ᵓæt-haššôr hǎḥǎy*	"They shall sell the live ox ... and also share
	... w^egǎm ᵓæt-hǎmmet yœh^æṣûn	the dead beast";
Numb 17,13	*wǎyyǎ^ᵃmod bên-hǎmmetîm ûbên hǎḥǎyyîm*	"He stood between the dead and the living";
2 Sam 12,18	*... kî-met hǎyyœlæd ...*	"that the child was dead ...
	bihyôt hǎyyœlæd hǎy ...	when the child was alive ...
2 Sam 12,21	*bǎ^ᵃbûr hǎyyœlæd hǎy ...*	while the child was alive ...
	w^ekǎᵒᵃšær met hǎyyœlæd ...	but now that the child is dead ...";
2 Sam 19,7	*kî luᵓ ᵓǎbšalôm hǎy*	"if Abshalom were alive today
	w^ekullanû hǎyyôm metîm	and the rest of us dead";
1 Kings 3,22	*loᵓ kî b^enî hǎḥǎy ûb^enek hǎmmet*	"No, the live one is my son and the dead one is
	loᵓ kî b^enek hǎmmet ûb^enî hœḥay	yours ... No, the dead boy is yours: mine is the

1 Kings 3,23	zæ-b^enî hăhăy ûb^enek hămmet	live one . . . this is my son, and the dead one is
	lo^ᵓ kî b^enek hămmet ûb^enî hæhay	yours . . . No, the dead boy is yours, mine is the live one";
Is 8,19	. . . yidroš b^eᶜăd hăhăyyîm ᵓæl-hămmetîm	". . . may inquire of the dead on behalf of the living";
Ruth 2,20	. . . ᵓᵃšær lo^ᵓ-ᶜazăb hăsdô ᵓæt-hăhăyyîm w^eᵓæt-hămmetîm	"who has not failed in his faith with the living or with the dead";
Eccl 4,2	w^ešăbbeăh ᵓᵃnî ᵓæt-hămmetîm šæk^ebar metû min-hăhăyyîm ᵃšær hemmā hăyyîm^{ᶜᵈ}dænā	"Then I counted those who died long ago happier than those who are still living";
Eccl 9,4	kî-l^ekælæb hăy hû^ᵓ tôb min-ha^ᵓăryē hămmet	"even a live dog is better than a dead lion";
Eccl 9,5	kî hăhăyyîm yôd^{eᶜ}îm šæyamutû w^ehămmetîm ᵓênam yôd^{eᶜ}îm m^ᵓûmā	"since the living know they will die, but the dead know nothing".

It is obvious at first glance that the contraposition of the 'living' and the 'dead' is carried out in rather different ways. What shall be done when one ox butts another to death? (cf. above 6.1.). Aaron stands between the living and the dead when he tries to stop a plague (Numb 17,13). David's court wonders about his behaviour before and after his son's death and he explains by way of repetition (2 Sam 12,18.21). Another concrete situation is the argument between the two mothers about whose the living child and whose the dead one is and Solomon as the judge repeats what they have said (1 Kings 3,22-23). Concrete but hypothetical is again 2 Sam 19,7: Joab reproaches King David for his crying over Absalom, for it seems that he would prefer his people dead instead of his rebellious son. In Is 8,19 the opposites are men and divine beings, the latter being identified as ᵓobôt and yidd^eᶜonîm, i.e. as spirits of the dead, which could be asked about the living.[265] In Ruth 2,20 the opposites are used to state that God keeps faith with "all men". Here there remains the concrete meaning of actually 'dead' and 'living'.

Proceeding to Koheleth it certainly seems like a contradiction when he first (4,2) praises the dead saying that they are happier than the living but later (9,5) regards the living as more fortunate, although they know that they will die, whereas the dead know nothing at all. Perhaps this proverb (9,4) is to be regarded as a gross overstatement, which would mean that this seeming preference for life is to be understood ironically.[265]

Looking for formulaic use of the opposite participles, one may again distinguish between word pairs and phrases. In Eccl 4,2 and 9,5 we have argument about whose the live and whose the dead boy is repeats the opposites In the other cases contraposition is used within the same phrases. Beginning with the cases where the participles are used as adjective attributes, the differences in structure between Ex 21,35; 1 Kings 3,22-23 and Eccl 9,4 are so large that the only common feature is the contraposition itself. The argument about whose the live and whose the dead boy is repeats the opposites no less than four times. Turning to participles used in the plural about human beings, we have to distinguish between concrete and abstract use: the contraposition is undoubtedly concrete in Numb 17,13, but already Is 8,19 is questionable. Is it not rather the general possibility of asking the dead about the living which the prophet refers to? Ruth 2,20 again uses the opposites to express "all men", i.e. in an inclusive rather than a contrasting way. None of these three examples can be said to use the opposites in the same meaning. Thus we are left with Eccl 4,2 and 9,5, where the opposites occur in antithetical parallelism comparing the living and the dead. This means that in each of them there are also other corresponding expressions. In 4,2 both opposites are each followed by a relative clause which is antithetical: "who died long ago" / "who are still living". In 9,5 the participles are subjects in two antithetical clauses: "the living know they will die" / "the dead know nothing". This means that Eccl does not contain any formula, formulaic phrase or system with *mût* in Culley's sense, but instead a word pair in Watter's sense. This is, however, repeated in only a single work, and would not therefore qualify as a formula according to Richter but would do so according to Watters. However, Richter does not discuss word pairs at all, but phrases, so that this criterion should therefore not be applied here.

I will now turn to a few combinations of qal ipf forms with participles. They differ from each other quite substantially. However, we shall see that there are certain similarities which justify their being discussed together. Turning first to Is 26,14.19 the ipf and participles are used about the same individuals:

14	*metîm bål-yiḥyû*	"they are dead, they can never live;
	rᵉpaʾîm bål-yaqumû	shades, they can never rise";
19	*yiḥyû metᵉ̂ka*	"Oh, let your dead revive!
	nᵉbelatî yᵉqûmûn	Let my corpses arise! Awake and
	haqîṣû wᵉrånnᵉnû šokᵉnê ʿapar	shout for joy, you who dwell in
		the dust!".²⁶⁷

In v. 14 we have two synonymous word pairs: *metîm/rᵉpaʾîm* and *bål-yiḥyû/bål-yaqumû*. They are at the same time the opposites of each other and the logic is the same as in Job 14,14: "if a man dies, can he live again?". If *mût* is affirmative, *ḥyh* must be negative (cf. 8.1.1.). In v. 19, however, this negation is cancelled: the dead will indeed become alive again. This is expressed so that three parallel words for the dead – *metᵉ̂ka* / *nᵉbelatî* / *šokᵉnê ʿapar* take as predicates another three parallel verbs: *yiḥyû* / *yᵉqûmûn* / *haqîṣû*. An interesting parallel to this sequence is that of Hos 6,2: *yᵉḥåyyenû* / *yᵉqimenû* / *wᵉniḥyǣ*, while the verb *yaqîṣû* occurs in Dan 12,2. However, none of these cases uses the stem *mût*, which shows that these so-called resurrection texts do not really conform to each other. Each of them represents a 'new' statement, which is not yet cast in formulaic diction. As for the seeming contradiction between Is 26,14 and 19, one has to take into account the fact that they affect two different categories of men: the universal truth of v. 14 will still apply to the enemies of God (v. 10-11), whereas v. 19 applies to the righteous (v. 7), also called "your people" (v. 11), "your dead", "my corpses" (v. 19) and "my people" (v. 20).²⁶⁸

In Gen 45,28 and 46,30 we have a repeated combination of the participle *ḥåy* with the imperfect *ʾamût(å)*, the first referring to Joseph and the second to his father Jacob:

45,28:	*ʿôd yôsep bᵉnî ḥåy*	"My son Joseph is still alive! I must go and
	ʾelᵉkā wᵉʾærænnû bᵉṭæræm ʾamût	see him before I die";
46,30:	*ʾamûtā håppaʿåm ʾåḥᵃrê rᵉʾôtî*	"Now I can die having seen for myself that you
	ʾæt-panᵉ̂ka kî ʿôdᵉka ḥay	are still alive".

Also repeated are the adverb ⁽ôd and the verb raʾā. The first statement expresses the intention, the second the realization of this intention. The repetition is in no way mechanical, but there is a chiastic composition:⁽ôd ... hǎy
– bᵉṭærœm ʾamût – ʾamûtā hǎppaⁿⁱám – •ôdᵉka ḥay. It is not a question of
formulaic language here but of an artistic use of repetition.²⁶⁹

These repetitions of the pair of opposites mût/ḥyh are not formulaic,
unless we consider mere repetition as a sufficient condition for calling them
so. But here it is clearly an intended tension created by the authors themselves: the normal way of combining mût and ḥyh in Is 26,14 is replaced by a
new way in v. 19. And Jacob's fear that he might die before seeing Joseph
again is replaced by his relief in the end.

Summing up our findings in this paragraph, I wish to point out that the
combinations of the participles met and hǎy cannot easily be explained as
formulaic, since they differ greatly from each other in form as well as in
function. The contraposition of the two opposites is in itself a most natural
form of expression, which lends itself to many different uses. One might say
that it lies, so to speak, in human thought structure to use opposites of
different kinds and that this sometimes results in formulaic expressions,
sometimes not.

8.4. 'Kill' and 'make'/'keep alive'

In this section I will first and foremost consider cases where mût has taken
the causative (hif'il) meaning and its opposite ḥyh has either the meaning
'make alive' or 'spare', which can be expressed through pi'el, hif'il or sometimes even qal forms. Let us first look at a few cases where God is the
subject:

Deut 32,39	ᵃnîʾamît waᵃhǎyyœ	"I put to death and keep alive,
	maḥǎstî wǎᵃnîʾærpā	I wound and I heal";
1 Sam 2,6	yhwh memît ûmᵉhǎyyœ	"The Lord kills and he gives life,
	môrîd šᵉôl wǎyyaⁿál	he sends down to Sheol, he can
		bring up again".

A brief look reveals that the two examples are similar to each other: both have the combination of *mût* (hif.) and *ḥyh* (pi.) and both have a parallel line giving another pair of opposites, namely *mḥs* / *rpᵓ* (as qal perf and ipf) and *yrd* / *ᶜlh* (as hif. part and ipf). Whereas the second represents a full synonyme (including the use of *šᵉᵓôl*), the first parallel could be viewed as somewhat weakening the meaning of *mût/ḥyh*. On the other hand, sickness/recovery is often described as a kind of delivery to/ rescue from the sphere of death, especially in poetical texts. For comparison we may mention Ps 33,19, where a synonymous parallelism is used to express God's capability "to deliver from death" (*lᵉhaṣṣîl mimmawæt*) and "to make alive" (*lᵉḥayyôtam*). But here, of course, the opposites are not used in the same way; instead they express one and the same motif, namely that God can keep alive in a time of famine. As for the contexts, Deut 32,39, 1 Sam 2,6 and Ps 33,19 are parts of hymns. The two first cases can therefore be said to represent a formula about God's capacity to kill and bring back to life.

Another question is whether we should regard the ascription of these opposites to YHWH as an expression of his "dual character" as a "high god".[270] In Is 45,6-7 he is described as the creator of 'light' and 'darkness', 'good' and 'evil', which is summed up in the statement: "I the Lord do all these things". He does not then create only the opposites, but everything. Therefore the pairs of opposites here, and I take it to be the meaning of the instances discussed above too, do not have the function of stressing the exact opposites, but rather the use of the extremes as a way of making inclusive statements[271] about 'everything'. For comparison I wish to point to Ruth 2,20 (8.3.) for a similar inclusive use of the opposites *mût/ḥyh*.

We shall now turn to some cases where a similar use of the opposites is applied to human subjects:

2 Sam 8,2 *wǎymǎdded šᵉnê-ḥᵃbalîm lᵉhamît* "he measured out two lengths of cord for those
ûmᵉloᵓ hǎhœbœl lᵉhǎhᵃyôt who were to be put to death and one length for those to be spared";

2 Kings 5,7 *hǎᵓᵉlohîm ᵓanî lᵉhamît ûlᵉhǎhᵃyôt* "Am I a God to kill and to make alive?";

Ez 13,19   *l^ehamît n^epašôt ^ʔšær lo^ʔ-t^emûtænā*   "You bring death to
                                      those who should not
        ûl^eḥăyyôt n^epašôt ^ʔšær lo^ʔ-tiḥyǽnā   die and life to those
                                        who should not live".

Common to all three cases is the hif'il infinitive *l^ehamît*, while the opposite *ḥyh* twice takes the hif'il and once the pi'el infinitive. 2 Kings 5,7 is a rhetorical question expecting a negative answer and thereby testifies that the capacity to "kill and make alive" belongs to God alone. This refers to the curing of Naaman's leprosy, and "make alive" could again refer to rescue from the sphere of death. Turning to the other cases, however, it is obvious that powerful men surely are capable of deciding between who should die and who should be spared. 2 Sam 8,2 describes David's treatment of the defeated Philistines. Ez 13,19 contains a denouncement of the false prophets, who foretell death to innocent people and survival for the guilty. Despite the similarity of form in these three cases, it is obvious that the use in the respective contexts is very different. It can, therefore, only be concluded that the opposites, when used about human subjects, again show a rather wide applicability.

We can for comparison take two other examples where 'killing' is expressed with the usual hif'il of *mût,* whereas 'sparing' takes the qal perf consecutive of *ḥyh.* In Ex 1,16 Pharaoh orders the midwives to make a distinction: "if it is a boy, kill him (*wǎh^amittæn ʔotô*), if it is a girl, let her live (*waḥayā*)".[272] In Esth 4,11 Mordecai is informed about the perils connedtec with entering the king's palace: "if any person, man or woman, enters the king's presence in the inner court without having been summoned, there is but one law for him — that he be put to death (*l^ehamît*). Only if the king extends the golden scepter to him may he live (*w^eḥayā*)". Although there are many parallels in forms and motifs between Ex and Esth,[273] these two cases cannot be said to belong to them since the use of the opposites, although testifying to the king's power, is very different indeed. This only verifies our conclusion about the free use of the opposites as such.

Finally, in 2 Kings 7,4 four lepers are pondering about whether they shall enter the gate of the besieged Samaria with famine in the town or rather desert to the Aramean camp: "if they let us live, we shall live (*ʔim y^eḥǎyyunû niḥyǽ*); and if they put us to death, we shall but die (*w^eʔim y^emîtunû* *wamatnû)*". Here we have a double and paronomastic employing of the opposites, one in pi'el/hif 'il and the other as a consequence in qal/qal. Although alternatives they are beyond the decision of the refugees themselves.

If we turn to cases where the opposites are both used to express 'making'/ 'keeping alive', we may first consider the similarity between Ps 33,19 and Jos 2,13. In the first case we met the synonymous parallel $l^e h \breve{a} ṣ ṣ \hat{\imath} l$ *mimmawæt năpšam / $l^e h ă y y \hat{o} t a m$*. In the second case Rahab asks the Israelite spies to provide her with a reliable sign, "that you will spare the lives ($w^e h ă h^a y i t æ m$) of my father and mother ... and save us from death ($w^e h i ṣ ṣ \breve{a} l t æ m$ ᵓ æt-năpšotênû *mimmawæt)*". Here the synonymous expressions are used about a saving act of men, whereas in Ps 33,19 they were used about God. In the latter case it is prose, in the former poetry.

The repetitive argument in 1 Kings 3,22-23 (cf. 8.3.) is followed by King Solomon's decision, which reverses the proposal of one of the mothers, thereby creating another repetition: "But the woman whose son was the live one ($ᵓ^a šær b^e n a h$ *hăhăy*) pleaded with the king, ... 'please, my lord', she cried, 'give her the live child (ᵓæt-hăyyalûd *hăhăy*); only don't kill it'($w^e h a m e t$ ᵓăl-$t^e m \hat{\imath} t u h \hat{u}$) ... Then the king spoke up. 'Give the live child (ᵓæt-hăyyalûd *hăhăy*) to her', he said, 'and do not put it to death ($w^e h a m e t$ loᵓ $t^e m \hat{\imath} t u h \hat{u}$); she is its mother' " (v. 26-27). Here the discussion focuses on the live child only and what shall be done with it, namely, that it must be spared and given to its mother, since the king had established which of the two was in fact the living child's mother. The argument and the decision are in a heavily repetitive style and there is no need to look for formulaic expressions here since the situation is unique.[274] In 2 Kings 8,5 Elisha's servant Gehazi is telling the king, how Elisha had revived a dead person (ᵓet $ᵓ^a šær-h æ h^{æ} y \bar{a}$ ᵓæt-hămmet). The mother whose son he had revived ($ᵓ^a šær-h æ h^{æ} y \bar{a}$ ᵓæt-$b^e n a h$) came in complaining to the king and Gehazi identified her as the woman whose son Elisha had revived ($b^e n a h$ ᵓ$^a šær-h æ h^{æ} y \bar{a}$ ᵓ$^e l \hat{\imath} š a^c$). The paradoxical – almost unheard of – act of the prophet is thus stressed by means of repetition, the first time by combining $h æ h^{æ} y \bar{a}$ with the object *met,* then by replacing this with $b^e n a h$, "her son".

Comparing the last four cases we have three ways of using the opposites: 1) Ps 33,19 and Jos 2,13 with parallel and synonymous expressions for *keep alive* and *save from death*; 2) 1 Kings 3,26-27 with the order *not to kill* the *living* child and 3) relating an act of *bringing* a *dead* child *to life*. Common to all cases is that life must be safeguarded.

For comparison we may consider one case where the opposite was done: in 2 Sam 1,10 the young Amalekite explains his act to carry out King Saul's order to give him the death-blow (^{a}*mâd-na^ɔ ᶜalǎy ûmot^{e}tenî*, v. 9) by saying: "So I stood over him and gave him the death-blow (*wa^{ɔ}œᶜ^{œ}mod ᶜalâw wǎ^ɔamot^{e}tehû*); for I knew that, broken as he was, he could not live (*kî lo^ɔ yiḥyǣ*)". The order and its enactment are formulated with the same expression, thereby creating a repetition, while the opposite possibility is negated and thus given as a reason. However, David refuses to accept this reason and has the young man killed (v. 15-16).

Summing up our investigation in this paragraph, we may regard Deut 32,39a and 1 Sam 2,6a as examples of a formulaic phrase. Another two cases, namely Ps 33,19 and Jos 2,13, use the opposites in an almost similar way, which with hesitation could be called formulaic due to the difference in style and application. In all other cases we have a rather free use of the opposites, which only shows that the opposites themselves do not create formulaic language, or even idioms, but rather are to be considered characteristic of different modes of expression. These can be found in any language and might therefore be regarded as belonging to the thought structure, i.e. a deeper level than the linguistic expression we are concerned with.

8.5. Choose between 'life' and 'death'!

The two noun opposites, *mawœt* and *ḥǎyyîm*, are sometimes contraposed in a way which urges the choice of the right alternative. I shall begin with the cases where God puts both alternatives to his people:

Deut 30,15 *r^{e}ɔē natǎttî l^{e}panêka hǎyyôm* "Today I offer you the
      ɔœt-hǎhǎyyîm w^{e}ɔœt-hǎṭṭôb choice of life and good,
      w^{e}ɔœt-hǎmmawœt w^{e}ɔœt-haraᶜ or death and evil";

Deut 30,19 *hǎhǎyyîm w^{e}hǎmmawœt natǎttî* "I offer you the choice of
      l^{e}panêka hǎbb^{e}rakā w^{e}hǎqq^{e}lalā life or death, blessing and
      ûbahǎrta bǎhǎyyîm lemǎᶜǎn tihyǣ curse; Choose life and then
      ... you ... will live";

Jer 21,8 *hinnî noten lipnêkœm* "I offer you the choice
      ɔœt-dœrœk hǎhǎyyîm between the way of life
      w^{e}ɔœt-dœrœk hǎmmawœt and the way of death".

Although both options in all three instances are open, the choice is put before the people in order that they may choose life. While Jer speaks of the alternatives as "the way of life" and "the way of death", Deut gives two other pairs of opposites parallel to that of life and death, namely 'good'/'evil' (v. 15) and 'blessing'/'curse'. Notwithstanding the variations in expression and syntax, I would here speak of a formulaic phrase built upon the construction *ntn lipnê*, "put before, offer", followed by the objects *mawæt* and *ḥǎyyîm*. Since Jer here probably is influenced by Deut, the phrase can be regarded as 'deuteronomic' or 'deuteronomistic'.[275] Its origin is to be sought in treaty form and phraseology.[276] In Jer, however, this is no longer discernible, since here it is a question of the right choice of the people in the besieged Jerusalem: to remain in the city means death by the sword, famine or pestilence, while surrender to the Chaldeans means survival. A more desperate situation still is depicted in Jer 8,3: "All the survivors of this wicked race, wherever I have banished them, would rather die than live (*wᵉnibḥǎr mawæt mehǎyyîm*)".[277] This extreme choice can be found in some individual cases too: *kî ṭôb môtî mehǎyyay*, "I should be better dead than alive" (Jon 4,3.8; cf. 1 Kings 19,4). Job 3,20-21 asks: "Why is light given to the sufferer and life (*wᵉḥǎyyîm*) to embittered souls/ who long for death (*lǎmmawæt*) – but it comes not – / and dig for it more than for buried treasure, . . ."[278] While 'life' and 'death' in Jer have a quite literal meaning in concrete situations, this is not the case in Prov, where we have several cases combining the two opposed nouns:

5,5a	*rǎglǽha yorᵉdôt mawæt*	"Her feet go downwards on the path of death . . . She does not watch
5,6a	*ʾorǎḥ ḥǎyyîm pæn-tᵉpǎlles*	for the road that leads to life";
8,35-36	*kî moṣᵉʾî maṣaʾ ḥǎyyîm*	"for he who finds me finds life
	wǎyyapœq raṣôn meyhwh	and wins favour with the Lord,
	wᵉhoṭᵉʾî homes nǎpšô	while he who finds me not, hurts himself
	kâl-mᵉšǎnʾǎy ʾahᵃbû mawæt	and all who hate me are in love with death";
11,19	*ken-ṣᵉdaqā lᵉḥǎyyîm*	"a man set on rightousness finds life,
	ûmᵉrǎpped raʿǎ lᵉmôtô	but the pursuit of evil leads to death";
12,28	*bᵉʾorǎḥ-ṣᵉdaqā ḥǎyyîm*	"the way of honesty leads to life, but
	wᵉdærœk nᵉtîbā ʾœl-mawæt	there is a wellworn path to death";

13,14	*tôrăt ḥakam mᵉqôr ḥằyyîm*	"A wise man's teaching is a fountain
	lasûr mimmoqᵉšê mawæt	of life for one who would escape the
		snares of death";
14,27	*yir•ăt yhwh mᵉqôr ḥằyyîm*	"The fear of the Lord is the fountain
	lasûr mimmoqᵉšê mawæt	of life for the man who would escape
		the snares of death";
16,14a	*ḥᵃmăt-mœlæk mălᵌᵃkê-mawæt*	"A king's anger is a messenger
	. . .	of death . . . In the light of
16,15a	*bᵉᵓôr-pᵉnê-mœlæk ḥằyyîm*	the king's countenance is life";
18,21	*mawæt wᵉḥằyyîm bᵉyăd-lašôn* . . .	"The tongue has power of life
		and death . . .".

Although 5,5a and 6a are devoted to the theme "beware of the seductress", the two ways of 'death' and 'life' are clearly hinted at.[279] Rather complex, too, is 8,35-36 with *ḥằyyîm* and *mawæt* contraposed with the help of other antithetical expressions: "he who finds me" / "he who finds me not", i.e. "he who fails me", and "all who hate me" / "are in love with . . .". In Prov 11,19 and 12,28 we have the two-way doctrine stated in an antithetical parallelism. In 11,19 there is another pair of opposites ('righteousness'/'evil') and perhaps in 12,28, too − but only after emendation.[280] In 13,14 and 14,27 we have the contraposition of "fountain of life" and "snares of death", both mythological terms. The only difference between the verses is at the beginning: 14,27 substituting *yir•ăt yhwh* for *tôrăt ḥakam* in 13,14.[281] If we accept Watters' position that word pairs in parallel lines, if repeated, be called formulas, then at least these four last cases are clearly such. But then so would Prov 16,14-15 be, too, although with quite a different meaning: "A king's anger is a messenger of death (*mălᵌᵃkê-mawæt*) and a wise man will appease it. In the light of the king's countenance is life (*ḥằyyîm*), his favour is like the rain-cloud in spring". Opposite expressions are here also the king's 'anger' on the one hand and the 'light' of his 'countenance' and his 'favour' on the other. When the wise man here chooses life, he appeases the king and tries to find favour with him, since his political career is wholly dependent upon the impression he can make on the ruler.[282] Turning, finally, to 18,21, we see that "life and death" are not contraposed in parallel lines but kept together in a phrase. Their meaning is not antithetical but rather polar; the expression is inclusive, i.e. everything is within the power of the tongue. This combination thus resembles that of God's killing and bringing back to life discussed above (8.4.). By way of comparison we may refer to 2 Sam 15,21, where the body-guard Ittai swears his loyalty to David "wherever you may be, in life or in death (*im-l*ᵉ*mawǽt* *im-l*ᵉ*ḥǎyyîm*), I your servant, will be there". Here the opposites again are used in an all inclusive statement, meaning "everywhere, always".

We can conclude, that the opposites 'life' and 'death' are combined in at least three different ways in Prov, namely a) as a word pair in parallel lines (11,19; 12,28; 13,14; 14,27); b) contraposed but in more complex structures (5,5a/6a; 8,35a/36b; 16,14a/15a) and c) in an inclusive phrase (18,21). The two-way doctrine forms the background for all cases except the last two (16,14a/15a; 18,21), where we have moved into political wisdom. I would regard the combinations as formulaic at least in a) but with some hesitation also in b), since there seems to be abundant extra-biblical material.

Although the expressions about 'life' and 'death' in Deut and Jer differ from a formal point of view considerably from those employed in Prov, one can nevertheless say that there is an accordance between the 'way of life' that man should choose and the two-way doctrine of Prov. The main difference is that in the wisdom literature man is addressed as an individual whereas in Deut he is addressed as a member of the covenant people.[283] The term 'life' has in both cases, however, the same meaning, namely 'happiness', 'the good life', sometimes 'longevity'.[284]

One should note, however, that Deut does not use the opposite *mawǽt* as frequently as Prov, but has instead *ᵓbd*, 'perish', in several instances. This does not mean, however, that there must be any major difference in meaning, since the concept of retribution is common, while the two-way doctrine as such is sapiential.[285]

8.6. The spheres of life and death

In this paragraph I shall consider the use of opposites to express 'local' aspects of life and death. I have above repeatedly referred to 'death' as a sphere, realm or 'space', especially in connection with different expressions about the nether world (ch. 7.). Here I shall turn to cases where *ḥǎyyîm* and *mawǽt* or some other derivation of the opposite stems are used in this way.

First I shall consider some cases of rescue from death (cf. 7.1.):

Ps 56,14   *kî hiṣṣălta năpšî mimmawæt* ...   "For you have rescued me
                                         from death . . . to walk
        lᵉhithăllek lipnê ᵊᶠlohîm bᵉᵓôr hăhăyyîm before God in the
                                               light of life";

Ps 116,8   *kî hiṣṣălta năpšî mimmawæt* ...
                                                   ". . . I shall walk be-

Ps 116,9   *ᵓæthăllek lipnê yhwh bᵉᵓărṣôt hăhăyyîm* fore the Lord in the
                                                lands of the living".

Variations of Ps 56,14a and 116,8a can be found in

Ps 33,19a: *lᵉhăṣṣîl mimmawæt năpšam*, "to save them from death";
Ps 86,13b: *wᵉhiṣṣălta năpšî miššᵉᵓôl tăhtiyyā*, "you have rescued me from
                                                the depths of Sheol".

In the first case we have a counterpart in a synonymous parallel (19b):
lᵉhăyyôtam baraᶜab, "to sustain them in famine" (cf. 8.4.). In Ps 86 there is
no such counterpart. Thus we can conclude that Ps 56,14 and 116,8-9 are
formulas in the sense of Culley, whereas Ps 86,13b and 33,19 have variations
of the first lines only.[286]
If we look for the opposite to rescue, namely abandoning to death, we
can quote Ps. 78,50:

loᵓ-hašăk mimmawæt năpšam "not shielding their lives from death but
wᵉhăyyatam lăddœbær hisgîr abandoning their bodies to the plague".

Here we have a synonymous parallelism, too, with the following word pairs:
loᵓ-hašăk/hisgîr, mimmawæt/ lăddœbær and *năpšam/wᵉhăyyatam*. This means
that the opposites *mût/hyh* are not contraposed here but form word pairs with
other words.[287]
The following examples do not have any common phrases and their
similarity lies in the contraposition of the opposite spheres:

Is 38,18   "For it is not Sheol that praises You,
         Not (the land) of Death (*mawæt*) that extols You;
         Nor do they who descend into the Pit hope for Your grace.

Is 38,19   The living, only the living (*hǎy hǎy*) can give thanks to You."
           (NJV);

Job 30,23   "Yes, I know that You will bring me down to Death (*mawæt*)
           to the meeting place of all the living (*l^ekâl-hǎy*)" (Gordis);

Job 33,22   "He himself draws near the Pit (*lǎššǎhǎt*)
           and his life approaches the emissaries of Death (*w^ehǎyyatô*
           lǎmmitîm)" (Gordis).

In Is 38,18-19 we have three parallel expressions for the sphere of Death,
namely *š^eôl, mawæt, yôr^edê-bôr*,[288] as opposed to the living (*hǎy hǎy*). In
Job 30,23 *mawæt* is parallel to a longer expression in the second line:
ûbêt mô^ced l^ekâl-hǎy, which is then a synonym.[289] In Job 33,22 *nǎpšô*
stands in synonymous parallelism with *hǎyyatô*, whereas *lǎššahat* is parallel
to the obscure *lǎmmitîm*. However, even if we don't adopt another reading
(e.g. *l^emô metîm* or *limqôm metîm*),[290] it is beyond doubt that we have a
participle here, referring to the inhabitants of the nether world. But the
contraposition of the opposite stem *mût/hyh* is also quite different in the
three cases under discussion, and a formulaic use of the opposites is restricted to the few cases discussed above. This supports our previous remark
that a word pair in itself is not to be regarded as a formula since the use of
word pairs, and among those, pairs of opposites is a very common mode of
expression which lends itself to a great variety of uses in form as well as in
function.

8.7. "In life and death"

There are several combinations of the two opposite stems which have in
common that they in one way or another express a time aspect. Here, too,
I can refer to a previous chapter (4), where I also discussed some of these.
I will not repeat what I said about "genealogy and age" (4.5.), but instead
give a brief survey of other combinations within our general theme in this
chapter. I shall again begin with a list of these remaining cases:

Deut 31,27:   "even during my life time (*b^{ec}ôdænnî hǎy*) you have defied
              the Lord; how much more, then, will you do so when I am
              dead (*w^eǎp kî- ǎh^ǎrê môtî*)";

174

Judg 16,30 "So the dead whom he killed at his death (hămmetîm *ªšœr
hemît bᵉmôtô) were more than those he had killed in his
life (meⁱªšœr hemît behăyyâw)";

1 Sam 20,31 "For as long as the son of Jesse lives (kâl-hăyyamîm *ªšœr
bœn-yišăy hăy) on earth, neither you nor your kingship will
be secure. Now then, have him brought to me, for he is
marked for death (bœn-mawœt hûᵓ)";

2 Sam 1,23 "Saul and Jonathan, / beloved and cherished,/ never parted/
in life or in death (bᵉhăyyêhœm ûbᵉmôtam)";

2 Sam 20,3 "They remained in seclusion until the day they died (ᶜăd-
yôm mutan), in living widowhood (ᵓalmᵉnût hăyyût)";

Jer 52,34 "A regular allotment of food was given him by order of the
king of Babylon, an allotment for each day, to the day of
his death (ᶜăd-yôm môtô) – all the days of his life (kol
yᵉmê hăyyâw)";

Ps 49,18-19 "for when he dies (bᵉmôtô) he can take none of it along;
his goods cannot follow him down./ Though he congratu-
lates himself in his lifetime (bᵉhăyyâw) . . . / yet he must
join the company of his ancestors";

Job 36,14 "They die in their youth (tamot bănnoᶜăr năpšam), and
their life (wᵉhăyyatam) ends in shame";

Eccl 9,3 "The hearts of men are full of evil; madness fills their
hearts all through their lives (bᵉhăyyêhœm) and after that
they go down to join the dead (ᵓœl-hămmetîm)".

If we try to discern certain sub-groups in this material, we might find the
following: 1) still alive – when dead: Deut 31,27 and 1 Sam 20,31, both
using ᵓim/bᵉᶜôdœnnî hăy but with different expressions for death (cf. above
4.3.4.); 2) during life – in death: Judg 16,30; 2 Sam 1,23 and Ps 49,18-19 all
of them using the nouns mawœt - hăyyîm with the prefix bᵉ and the
appropriate suffixes (cf. above 4.2.2.). The differences lie in the syntactic
combinations: 2 Sam 1,23 has a short inclusive statement, Judg 16,30 makes
a comparison with the help of an impressive paronomasia and Ps 49,18ff.
shows a loose composition with a third link in v. 20: tabôᵓ ᶜăd-dôr ᵓªbôtâw
as an equivalent to mût and opposite to hyh. Eccl 9,3 also has the first link
similarly constructed (bᵉhăyyêhœm) but the second is quite different (ᵓœl-

hằmmetîm); 3) the rest of life — to the day of death: 2 Sam 20,3 and Jer 52, 34 (cf. above 4.1.2.). The expressions for "the day of his/their death" are similar, but while Jer 52,34 gives an equivalent ("all the days of his life"), 2 Sam 20,3 has an expression for a state ("in living widowhood") rather than for a time, if this interpretation is correct.[291] There remain Job 36,14 which, although not easy to interpret, uses the opposites in synonymous parallelism, but with *nặpšam* as the equivalent of *wᵉḥặyyatam*,[292] and 1 Sam 20,31 which has a temporal clause expressing the fact that David is still alive and then proceeds to the order to have him executed (cf. above 6.7.).

The similarities in certain expressions discussed above, especially in group 2) should not be taken as an indication of formulas but rather of idioms. This is true of *bᵉ+mawæt* + suffix as well as of the opposite *bᵉ + ḥặyyîm* + suffix. Neither is the combination of these idioms to be regarded as formulaic, since the syntax and function in context are rather different. If this can be said about group 2), it is all the more true of the other groups and the remaining odd examples. Thus we can conclude, that the pair of opposites used to express time are not combined in a formulaic way, except for the 'P' patterns for "genealogy and age" discussed in 4.5. In the cases here, however, we have to be content with the observations that 'life' and 'death' has found their way into Hebrew idioms expressing time much as in other languages. This is due to the fact that the use of opposites is not a linguistic feature alone, but a feature of human thought structure. But since it is not my intention nor within my competence to enter into structural grammar, it may suffice to point to this borderline as an explanation why I do not regard the use of opposites in itself as formulaic. In addition, of course, there is the fact that my initial distinction between formula and idiom, which is admittedly not easy to sustain throughout, nevertheless seems to be useful in cases like these.

8.8. Two additional notes

There are several cases which combine the oath formula *ḥặy yhwh*, "as the Lord lives" with the expression of a threat of death sentence. Such are 1 Sam 19,6 (*ʾim-yûmat*); 1 Sam 26,16 (*kî bᵉnê-mawæt ʾặttæm*), 2 Sam 12, 5 (*kî bæn-mawæt haʾîš* . . .) and 1 Kings 2,24 (*kî ḥặyyôm yûmắt*). It seems to be clear, that we here have combinations of two distinct formulas (cf. 6.7.). However, this combination is not formulaic in itself since the oath formula is quite independent of any use of the stem *mût*. In this combination *ḥǎy* is attributed to God, and *mût* to a human being, and there is no reason to believe that the combinations is employed to stress the opposite character of these two stems, but is rather to be regarded as quite coincidental.

Finally, I will return to the question, of whether there are other stems used as opposites to *mût* than *ḥyh*. I already mentioned the case of 'birth' (*yld*). As far as I can see, there are three combinations worth mentioning, namely Eccl 3,2; 7,1 and Hos 9,16. The first runs as follows: "a time to be born and a time to die (*ʿet lǎlædæt wᵉʿet lamût*)." It is the first in a series of fourteen pairs of opposites, and one might wonder, why *yld* is chosen exactly here as the opposite to *mût* instead of the — also in Eccl — much more frequent *ḥyh*. However, here we obviously have a case of antithetical moments, rather than the all-embracing 'life' and 'death'.[293] In 7,1a Kohelet introduces a popular sentence: "A good name smells sweeter than the finest ointment" but then continues with his pessimistic view of life: "and the day of death is better than the day of birth (*wᵉyôm hǎmmawæt miyyôm hiwwalᵉdô*)". If life is all vanity, the end of it is preferable to its beginning.[294] In Hos 9,16 the prophet proclaims divine judgement to Ephraim: "Even if they bear children (*yeledûn*), I will slay (*wᵉhemǎttî*) their cherished offspring". This is the pregnant conclusion from the threats about childlessness uttered already in v. 11-13.[295] It goes without saying that these three combinations of *mût/yld* are not to be regarded as formulas. Finally, we may recall the fact that *yld* (hif.) constituted a link in the patterns of genealogy and age (cf. 4.5.1.) but here it is, of course, no opposite to *mût* since it expresses the respective patriarch's fathering of children during his life in the sequence *wǎyḥî ... wǎyyôlæd ... wǎyyamot*.

8.9. Summary

The material discussed in this chapter consisted of syntactical combinations of the opposites *mût/ḥyh*. I distinguished between phrases and word pairs and tried to determine which combinations fulfilled the double criterion of form and function thereby qualifying them as formulas or formulaic phrases. As such I regarded the following:

1) Inclusive combinations of both verbs in qal imperfect, where *mût* was negated ("live and not die", 8.1.);

2) Polar combinations of *mût* (hif.) and *ḥyh* (pi.) with God as subject ("kill and make alive", 8.4.);

3) Antithetical combinations of *ḥǎyyîm* and *mawǣt* as objects to *ntn lipnê* with God as subject ("I offer you the choice between life and death", 8.5.);

4) The word pair *ḥǎyyîm/mawǣt* in antithetical parallelism as an expression for the two-way doctrine in Prov, 8.5.).

Concerning other phrases or word pairs, I regarded the formal or functional differences too great for them to be considered formulas. I argued that the existence of a word pair in itself is not a sufficient criterion for calling it a formula in the way Watters does. Furthermore, the pairs of opposites are in general not always intended poetical devices, but their use stems from what could be called an inherent thought structure, that is from a deeper level than the linguistic expression. This would explain the relative frequency of such combinations on the one hand, but also their great formal variety and free applicability on the other. Accordingly I regard the criterion of 'function' as a useful tool in determining which expressions are formulas, which idioms or perhaps only by coincidence similar in wording.

9. SUMMARY

In my introduction (1) I envisaged a twofold aim to this study. The first was to describe the characteristics of the Hebrew formula from the horizon of the stem *mût*. The other was to find out, whether the formulaic use of this stem is an essential feature to be born in mind in interpreting its meaning. I shall here try to summarize my findings.

Earlier definitions of 'formula' were to my mind either too narrow or too wide. None of them had in fact been applied to all the various types of literature represented in the Hebrew Bible. I suspected, furthermore, that none was entirely applicable, either. Therefore I ventured a definition which combined what I regarded as acceptable criteria from these definitions with a tentative criterion of my own. Proceeding from the very general definition that a formula is 'a repeated word group', I adopted from Culley the limits of flexibility of a formula and used the term 'formulaic phrase', where at least one major element had been substituted by another. In accordance with Richter I used the terms 'pattern' and 'coined phrase'. My own tentative criterion was that a formula should have a distinct function within the larger context, although I was aware that it could have lost this function and therefore be used in a freer manner.

From the outset I was confronted with the task of describing the material. One difficulty was how to determine the different types of formulas and another was what to call those repeated phrases which did not fulfil my criteria. To solve the first problem I distinguished between 'repeated phrases' and 'repeated word pairs' in the sense of Watters. The overwhelming majority of my cases belonged to the first type. In fact word pairs — apart from the pair of opposites (*mût/ḥyh*) — were very sparely represented. Moreover, the opposites mostly formed combinations which were word pairs in Watters' sense only to a small extent. Equally meagre was the material consisting of formulas in Culley's sense. The explanation in both cases is the same:

they have restricted the term 'formula' to poetry alone, while the major part of my material was prose.

As for the material which did not fit my criteria, I applied the terms 'idiom' and 'repetition'. The first generally failed to fulfil the criterion of function within context. Positively stated, an 'idiom' is the natural, simple, but at the same time characteristic, Hebrew way of expression. Thus it was easy to understand why it could be used very freely in different contexts. It was not always easy to distinguish it from a formula which had lost its original function. As a rule, however, I regarded as formulas expressions which occurred in otherwise formulaic language or where the influence of such language could be assumed. A 'repetition' again, occurs within a limited context and it stems generally from the same author. Here I found it necessary to make a distinction between 'repetition' and 'coined phrase'. The latter is borrowed by another author or redactor by way of quotation or direct influence. However, I had often to admit that the biblical material was too scant to permit any far-reaching or definite conclusions regarding difference between these categories. This holds true in respect of the criterion of function, too. Nevertheless, I cannot help feeling strengthened in my opinion that this criterion has proven at least to some degree to be a useful one indeed.

Turning to the most important of my findings I shall begin with the 'patterns'. As such I regarded the regular combinations of series of formulaic elements. The most characteristic patterns were those about 'death and burial' (3.1.), 'transition' (4.3.1.), 'succession' (4.4.), 'genealogy and age' (4.5.) and 'die by the sword, famine and pestilence' (5.3.5.). When forms of the stem *mût* were repeated within the apodictic and casuistic legal patterns I regarded them as formulaic. Otherwise, I did not pay much attention to genres, but looked instead for the context in general.

Outside the patterns the chief characteristic of a formula was the fixed combination of *mût* with another stem, certain prepositions and suffixes, etc. Here, however, idioms were rather frequent, too. In my attempts to determine the function, I did not enter into any detailed analysis, but was content with what could be easily detected or not detected. I am quite aware of the possibility that this point perhaps left much to be desired. But on the one hand I could not easily afford the space and time such an undertaking would gave required. On the other hand, I suspected that a very rigorous analysis of function within genres or the like would prove to be counterproductive, because literature remains literature and does not easily conform to theoretical criteria. However, even a cursory treatment like this left me with fairly many cases, which could reasonably be called formulas, as well as with others, where the label 'idiom' definitely seemed preferable. Of course, there were cases where I simply was not able to decide – be it for lack of material or of methodological tools (e.g. 2.3.3. – 2.5.1. – 2.5.2. – 2.5.3.). It may be said that, by applying the criterion of function, I drastically reduced the number of formulas from what a general definition like Richter's would have produced. In so doing, however, I tried to save the term from what I regard as a misuse. On the other hand, I actually applied my criteria to all kinds of word combinations where the stem *mût* occurred. I thereby demonstrated that there are a great variety of formulas which can and, in my opinion, should be recognized as such. The fact that there has been no attempt, as far as I can see, to make this distinction between 'formula' and 'idiom' before is to my mind due to the restricted application of the term formula, be it to poetry (Culley, Watters), certain prose texts (Richter) or legal formulations (Knierim, Schüngel-Straumann and others). The limits set by my own restriction to the stem *mût* is something which can be easily transcended by chosing other horizons for new investigations.

Comparing legal formulations with others found in narrative texts, I concluded that the expressions of threats and death sentences were probably formulated under the influence of legal patterns, e.g. by using apodictic or casuistic forms. Such an influence could also be found in prophetic diction in manner of the 'preached law' of Deut. Here I was able to refer to other investigations. In this connection I had to consider the fact that a legal formula, although preserved almost intact, had assumed a new function or *Sitz im Leben*. To be careful meant in such cases to speak about 'formulaic with reservation' (*bedingt formelhaft*) or simply to concede that a formula may lose its original function.

Regarding word pairs I distinguished between 'synonymous', 'polar' and 'antithetical' word pairs. Thereby the opposites *mût/ḥyh* actually appeared in the two last mentioned relations. But only a few were really formulaic. The same was also the case with other combinations of Watters' type (7.5. – 8.6. – 8.7. – 8.9.). On the one hand they differed formally too much from each other and on the other they seldom showed a common function. Thus it appeared that Watters' word pair was a rather technical and unsatisfactory way of viewing the Hebrew formula. To use word pairs and opposites does not yet mean to express oneself in formulaic language. Here Culley's poetical phrases come closer to the essence of the Hebrew formula. But we have to transcend his limitations of the formula to poetry and, as Watters pointed out, to 'oral tradition'. Unsatisfactory is also Lande's use of the term formula for expression used in 'every-day speech' (*Umgangssprache*). The application of the criterion of function would to my mind show that in these cases it is in fact often a question of 'idioms'.

Turning briefly to the second aim of my study, I shall try to summarize my views about what formulaic language does and does not say about 'death'. Although the stem *mût* in its various forms and derivations occurs no less than a thousand times in the Hebrew Bible, one cannot conclude that 'biblical man' was preoccupied with death because many, if not most, of the cases do not say anything at all about death as such. This can be seen in Ch. 4, where most of the cases use the word in chronological remarks. This is to some extent also the case with expressions about impending death (2.1. – 2.2.), which have the function of introducing last words, testaments, blessings and the like. In a similar way the death-burial pattern has a compositional function in the patriarchal narratives or in the history of the both kingdoms (3.1. – 3.2. – 3.3.). Even the death penalty is only one element in comparatively large patterns which define the nature of the crime, the circumstances under which it was committed, whether there was blood guilt and whether accordingly capital punishment should be meted out or not. In such cases one would not expect to find any 'concepts' about death expressed.

However, a general attitude towards how and where to die can be said to underlie such formulas as those uttered before one's own departure (2.1.2.), those about dying in exile (3.5.1.) or in the wilderness (3.5.2.). Fear of death is of course a quite natural instinct or feeling, which is presupposed in cases of threats and such threats of death are very common indeed (Ch. 6 and 7), be it against a people or an individual, uttered by a king or God. Formulas and patterns were employed throughout, sometimes to stress the seriousness of the threat, sometimes the totality of destruction. In the latter case three or four different ways of death where combined (5.3.).

That men are punished with death for their own sins is a doctrine which, although developed relatively late, found its expression in several formulas

(5.2.) and rhetorical questions (5.1.). 'Life' and 'death' were alternatives for ethical choice and divine retribution (8.3.). On the one hand, we have the alternatives laid before the people by God in their mutual covenant relationship. On the other hand, we have the two-way doctrine put to the individual especially in Prov. Both follow essentially the same line in their exhortations to choose life (8.5.). Against this background one can understand the problems confronting Job, Koheleth and a few psalmists, who realized the discrepancy between doctrine and reality: namely that wickedness and punishment did not correspond to each other in life — and eventually the fate of all was death. But neither the realization of this discrepancy nor its solution found their expression in formulaic language. There were, of course, the old formulas about God's rescuing and not abandoning his faithful to death (7.1.). But the psalmists and the author of Is 26 probably knew that these expressions of confidence did not mean escaping death for good, but rather recovery from illness. They therefore chose to give their paradoxical convictions new expressions which did not become formalized within the Hebrew Bible. It may be concluded, therefore, that formulaic language covers the commonly held views of death as the natural, inevitable and dreaded end of human life. This did not exclude the possibility to interpret the old formulas anew; in fact they invited such an interpretation. Once the conviction that God will destroy Death for ever (Is 25,8) was established, his rescue of the faithful came to be interpreted in this way, too. But this interpretation, however, is another story.[296]

NOTES

1. Cf. A. Bertholet, 1914 (first edition 1899); E. Aurelius, 1907; G. Quell, 1925; L. Dürr, 1926; Chr. Barth, 1947; R. Martin-Achard, 1956; L. Wächter, 1967; N.J. Tromp, 1969; O. Kaiser - E. Lohse, 1977.

2. Wächter, 1967, 7. His work does not claim to be such an exhausting treatment either: "Hier soll nun ein verhältnismässig weiter Bereich aus dem israelitischen Todesverständnis behandelt werden: die gefühlsmässige Einstellung zum Tode einerseits und die religiöse Wertung des Todes andererseits", *op.cit.*, 8.

3. Such special aspects are the themes of most of the monographs mentioned in note 1 and e.g. H. Jahnow, 1923.

4. N.J. Tromp, 1969, 1.

5. H. Schulz, 1969. Cf. also G. Liedke, 1971; H.J. Boecker, 1964.

6. H. Schüngel-Straumann, 1969. Cf. also R. Knierim, 1965.

7. G. Gerleman, 1971, 893.

8. H. Ringgren, 1977, 883f.

9. This is not to say, that e.g. W. Eichrodt, 1933-1939 and G. von Rad, 1960-61, would not have enhanced our understanding of the theme in general, but rather that I am more indebted to the lexical work, which has been done so far.

10. J. Barr, 1961.

11. M. Parry, 1930, 1932.

12. A.B. Lord, 1960, preceded and followed by a series of shorter studies.

13. R.C. Culley, 1967.

14. I. Lande, 1949, IX.

15. W. Richter, 1971, 101.

16. Culley, 1967, 10. The difference between 'formula' and 'theme' is defined as follows: "The formula has to do with formal characteristics of lines and parts of lines such as the patterns of syntax and metre. The theme

184

has to do with the content, i.e., with elements of subject matter, in groups of lines that have no fixed form ... a group of ideas recurring in variable form", *op.cit.*, 17 f.

17. J.B. Hainsworth, 1968, 35.
18. G. Wanke, 1973, 69, distinguished between "synonyme Wortpaare (Berg/ Hügel); polare Ausdrücke, die durch Nennung von zwei Polen eine Ganzheit darstellen wollen (Himmel und Erde; Tag und Nacht); antithetische Wortpaare, die einen Gegensatz herausstellen sollen und darum leicht mit dem polaren Ausdruck verwechselt werden können". I find these distinctions very useful for my purpose. With his "polar structures" J.A. Loader, 1979, 29ff., refers on the one hand to opposite words, mainly 'life' and 'death', and on the other hand the underlying 'thought patterns' found in the contents. He does not make any distinction between 'polar' and 'antithetical' use of the opposites, and his use of the term 'polar' corresponds, as far as I can see, to that of 'antithetical' in the definition of Wanke.
19. W. Whallon, 1969.
20. W. Watters, 1976.
21. Whallon, 1969, 148ff.
22. This has been pointed out by R.C. Clements in his review of Watters' work in VT, XXVIII (1978), 383.
23. Watters, 1976, 122.
24. Culley, 1967, 30, and Watters, 1976, 45, applying the modifications to the word pair. Cf. also I. Ljung, 1978, 18f., who adopts Culley's definitions and applies them to 'formulaic language in the so-called Ebed YHWH-psalms' for a traditio-historical purpose.
25. Richter, 1971, 38, has for his part defined the functions of the coined phrases, formulas, 'patterns' and genres as follows:

"Funktion der geprägten Wendungen:	der literarische Horizont und Sitz in der Literatur
Funktion der Formeln, Schemata:	der Horizont und Sitz im Leben
Funktion der Gattung:	der Sitz im Leben".

I have the impression that application of this terminology would not be fruitful for my purpose, since I am concerned with formulaic language and not with literature in general.

26. Cf. K. Koch, 1967, 12.

27. Cf. Ljung, 1978, 27: "A set phrase can have different functions in different contexts. If the same phrase occurs in different contexts it must be assumed that the formula/system is primary; if there is a set correlation between phrase and context this indicates the 'Sitz im Leben' of the expression" (with reference to Richter, 1971, 101). Although this may in principle be right, I cannot use this criterion for all kinds of literature, where the relations between phrases and context are very different from those in biblical poetry.

28. For other similarly constructed phrases, cf. 2.1.4.

29. G. von Rad, 1961, 366, 376, regards Gen 48,21 and 50,5 as belonging to 'J', whereas 50,24 belongs to an "elohistic" context. E, Speiser, 1964, 359, 377f., does not make any distinction between 'J' and 'E' in Gen 48, but follows von Rad regarding Gen 50. Perhaps we should be content with a common strand 'JE' distinguishable from 'P' and 'D', but seldom, if at all, to be divided into two separate 'sources'.

30. Wächter, 1967, 70, 75.

31. Cf. Jer 38,10: $b^e t\alpha r\alpha m$ yamût, 'before he dies' as a conclusion of the royal order to take Jeremiah out of the pit, where he had been held in custody (v. 6ff.). It goes without saying that this is not a 'testamentarische Verfügung'.

32. In the case of all three phrases seven out of eleven instances are found in the patriarchal narratives, and nine of them occur within the Pentateuch.

33. Speiser, 1964, 378, points out, that the brothers' guilt is an issue only in the 'E'-version, while it is resolved to 'J' long before (Gen 24). On the other hand, the case between Jacob and Esau was reopened exactly when the mourning for their father had passed (Gen 27,41), and thus it was important for Jacob to ask for reconciliation between Joseph and his brothers "before he died", cf. Jacob, 1934, 938f. and von Rad, 1961, 377f.

34. Wächter, 1967, 75.

35. Cf. Noth, 1953, 133; Wächter, 1967, 75, n. 112. T. Veijola, 1975, 27 accounts 1 Kings 2,2 among "andere unverkennbar dtr Ausdrücke".

36. Cf. Tromp, 1969, 167f.; Kraus, 1978, ad loc. and Fohrer, 1963, ad loc.; Pope, 1965, ad loc.

186

37. While Jacob and David lie on their death bed and can 'feel' their end approaching (cf. Jacob, 1934, 862, with reference to Ramban), this is not the case with Moses. But then the death of Moses is quite a peculiar one: he dies at the command of the Lord (Deut 34,5, cf. below 3.2.2.). But also in his case the formula introduces the transfer of power and obligation to the follower. In fact Deut 31,14 is more similar to 1 Kings 2,1 in this respect: the passing away has to do with the dying leader's will, namely that the commandments of God be observed after his death, whereas Jacob's will is of a more private kind. However, this formula belongs to the group of testamentary or last will formulas like the other discussed above.

38. Thus Kaiser, 1973, 317f.

39. Cf. Myers, 1965 B, 192.

40. In the Chronicler's version the phrase about Hezekiah's death could also be said to have a compositional function, but its use here clearly corresponds with his purpose: although God responded favourably to the king's prayer, he first became proud and then later humbled himself so that God's wrath did not come upon Jerusalem in David's time (2 Chron 32,25-26), cf. Myers, 1965 B, 192.

41. About the combination of the opposites *mawæt/ḥåyyîm*, cf. below ch. 8.

42. Cf. Wächter, 1967, 81f.: "Was aber im Falle Elias echtes Nacherlebnis des Erzählers, den wir wohl in Prophetenkreisen zu suchen haben, ist, das eine geschehene oder wenigstens mögliche Krisensituation nachzeichnet, ist im Buche Jona reine schriftstellerische Fiktion. Dadurch wirkt der ganze Vorgang unglaubwürdig. Daran ändert auch nichts die Tatsache, dass der Verfasser des Büchleins sich bis in die Formulierungen hinein an das Vorbild der Elia-Geschichte anschliesst . . .". Now 'unbelievable' or not, our concern is whether there is a clear literal dependence on the side of the Jonah story, which indeed seems to be the case. Cf. also Rudolph, 1971, *ad loc.*

43. Although this formula is again restricted to these two passages only, the verb *lqḥ* with God as subject and man as object points to what A. Schmitt has called a special 'Vorstellungsbereich' in the Old Testament, Schmitt, 1976, 85.

44. Lande, 1949, 90ff.

45. As to the interpretation of Numb 23,10, cf. Wächter, 1967, 88: "Bileam wünscht, zu Israel zu gehören, weil er dann als Glied des Jahwebundes ein Leben in Segen und Fülle leben dürfte, das mit dem Tode als Erfüllung abgeschlossen wird. Von Todessehnsucht kann demnach bei diesen Worten keine Rede sein".

46. The suicidal act of Samson can be compared to those of Abimelech (Judg 9,54) and Saul (1 Sam 31,4). Wächter, 1967, 90f., concludes that the motif of 'honour' is decisive in all cases. It is the honour of the people and its God, not so much the personal honour of the hero that is at stake.

47. Zimmerli, 1969, 396ff., characterizes Ez 18 as having "die Form eines Disputationswortes" and as belonging to the "Bereich einer Schulerörterung" quite as Ez 3,17-21 and 33,1-9. The style is regarded as "sakralrechtlich" and is borrowed from descriptions of the just and the wicked in the temple liturgy.

48. Both cases belong to the narrative core of the so-called 'Retterbuch' according to W. Richter, 1964, 3, 6, and would thus not be redactional at least from the deuteronomistic epoch.

49. This may be illustrated with a few examples: *kî-ʾaḥîw met wᵉhû* ...(Gen 42,38), *kî-bᵉhæṭʾô met* (Numb 27,3), *kî-met ʾᵃdonêkæm šaʾûl* (2 Sam 2,7), *kî ʾᵃmnôn lᵉbǎddô met* (2 Sam 13,32). It is also obvious, that these sentences differ in meaning from each other as well from *kî met* in sentences guided by a cognitive verb, because *kî* has a different syntactical function.

50. MT has only *bæn-šaʾûl*, whereas the fuller reading is found in 3MMS^G and in the old versions, with variations as to the form of the proper name of Saul's son.

51. The reading *wǎyyîrᵉʾû* indicated by Peshitta and Vulgata could on contextual grounds be attractive. On the other hand, the existence of a phrase consisting of *kî met* combined with forms of the verb *raʾā* rather speaks for the correctness of the MT.

52. Cf. Jacob, 1934, *ad loc*. The expressions *gamǔl raʾā* and *hešîb* are the technical terms for the principle of *talion*.

53. Judg 9,56f. belongs to the reworked frame ('Rahmen') of the Abimelech story: v. 56f. is the punishment or revenge of God for the violence and blood shedding committed by Abimelech and encouraged by the Sichemites (cf. v. 23-24), cf. Richter, 1961, 312ff.

54. In addition to the two occurrences of the phrase *kî met*, the perfect form *met* occurs five times in 1 Sam 12,18.19.21.23. In three of these cases the verbal form is directly followed by the substantive *hǎyyǽlǽd*, which was the case in the *kî met* phrase, too. This does not, however, mean that *hǎyyǽlǽd* should be regarded as belonging to the formula since it occurs only in this context and its use here is due to the repetitive style.

55. There are two instances where forms of *yaddǎ‹* are followed by *kî* plus the paronomastic expression *môt tamût* (Gen 20,7 and 1 Kings 2,37). Since this phrase requires a separate treatment below, I shall only note the main difference between it and *kî met*: whereas the latter is a recognition of death which has already taken place (perf), *môt tamût* is a threat of death that will happen (impf) soon.

56. As to this problem, cf. Illman, 1975, 20ff., 37 f.

57. Judg 10,5; 12,7.10.12.17. In 10,2 we have the name "Tola son of Pua" at the beginning of the verse and it is then not repeated.

58. At the end of Judg 12,7 we should perhaps read *b‹îrô b‹gil‹ad*, "in his own city, in Gilead" instead of *b‹arê gil‹ad*, "in the towns of Gilead". We would thus follow the old version against the Masoretic text. Also difficult is the lengthy geographical location at the end of 12,15: ". . . in Pirathon in the land of Ephraim on the hill of the Amalekite", according to the MT.

59. They are *hǎggil‹adî - gil‹ad* (12,7), *hǎzz‹bûlonî - b‹ǝ‹ærǽṣ z‹bûlun* (12,12) and *happir‹atônî - b‹pir‹atôn* (12,15).

60. In Judg 12,15 *bæn-ḥillel* follows after the proper name of the judge, namely Abdon.

61. This is *b‹śêbā ṭôbā*, "at a ripe old age", cf. below 3.3.3.

62. One should here perhaps read *b‹‹ǎprǎt* (cstr) instead of (the abs) *b‹ǎprā*, or leave out the following *‹abî ha‹ǽzrî*, which is anyway rather obscure, cf. the text critical apparatus to BH.

63. Compare Deut 10,6 about the death of Aaron, where *šam* refers to Moserah, where the Israelites had arrived and where his son Eleazar succeeded him in the priesthood.

64. ". . . and he named it Allon-bakuth", that is "Oak of Weeping", which again refers to the ritual weeping connected with burial, to which I shall return below 3.4.

65. Richter, 1964, 12, regards the passages about the minor judges as belonging to "dem Red. vorliegende Tradition", which according to him is also the case with Judg 8,32 (Richter, 1961, 237). This seems to be the case with 2 Sam 17,23, too (cf. Hertzberg, 1956, *ad loc.*). As to Gen 35,8.19 and Numb 20,1 Eissfeldt, 1922, regards them all as belonging to 'E', that is non-redactional.

66. Gray, 1970, 598, suggests that the phrase "and he went down" in 2 Kings 13,14 refers to neither the prophet's home in Samaria (cf. 6,33) nor his ancestral home at Abel-Meholah, but rather to Gilgal by Jericho, where the "prophetic community" was located, which would be in keeping with the account of his death and burial and the mention of Moabite raids in v. 20f.

67. Against the common opinion that 1 Sam 25,1 be regarded as redactional Stoebe, 1973, 452f., points out that an almost identical phrase belongs to the context in 28,3: "Jedenfalls erscheint die Angabe über das Begräbnis in Rama auf der einen Seite so beiläufig erzählt, auf der anderen Seite so akzentuiert und im Kontext verwurzelt, dass man darin nur schwer das versprengte Bruchstück aus biographischen Angaben sehen kann, wie sie für die listenmässige Verzeichnisse der sogenannten 'Kleinen Richter' characteristisch sind". Cf. Licht, 1978, 38.

68. Cf. Myers, 1965 B, 138: "Jehoiada's symbolic age, 130 years . . . indicated that he was favored by Yahweh. That he was honored by the people – the nation – is shown by his burial in the royal cemetery".

69. Regarding Deut 34,5-6 and Jos 24,29-30 (par Judg 2,8-9) we cannot follow Eissfeldt who regards them as "yahwistic" and "elohistic". Here the epithet *ʿæbæd yhwh* seems to point to a Deuteronomist, that is according to Veijola, 1975, 128, DtrG.

70. The sequence *wǎyyigwǎ ̔ wǎyyamât* occurs only in the 'P' strand (Gen 25,8.17; 35,29) and cannot be regarded as formulaic in itself. *wǎyyigwǎ ̔* alone is used about Jacob in Gen 49,33, where the formula *wǎyyeʾasep ʾæl ʿǎmmâw* also occurs. The reason for its combination with *mût* is not clear. It occurs 24 times in the OT, and as its original meaning has been suggested "gasp for breath" or "be at the last gasp", which is something distinct from *mût*, "to be still, silent in death", G.R. Driver, 1962 B, 15f. For another view cf. B. Alfrink, 1948, 123ff.

71. Cf. note 67, and Hertzberg, 1956, *ad loc.* and Stoebe, 1973, *ad loc.*

190

72. For this translation of ʿalắy, cf. Speiser, 1964, *ad loc.*
73. Speiser, 1964, *ad loc.*
74. In Gen 50,5 we have the participle *met* and in 2 Sam 19,38 and Ruth 1,17 the imperfect *ʾamût* indicating future death to be followed by burial. There is considerable similarity of content, but formally these sentences differ from each other to such a degree that there cannot be any talk of formulas or formulaic expressions. The same is all the more true when we consider Job 27,15 and 2 Chron 22,9, which, to be sure, also combine *mût* and *qbr*. However, there is no similarity in form or in content.
75. We may here distinguish between seven different sentences, three of which end with an imperative directed to Abraham: *qᵉbor ʾæt-metæka,* "bury your dead" (Gen 23,6a.11.15 with inverted word order). Two of them express the intention of Abraham to bury his wife: *wᵉʾæqbᵉrā metî millᵉpanay,* "that I may remove my dead for burial" (v. 4, cf. v. 13). Two others are constructed as infinitives and express the view, that there is no obstacle to carrying out the intention pf Abraham (v. 6a and 8).
76. Alfrink, 1948, 118f. and Tromp, 1969, 168f.
77. Alfrink, 1948, 126 and Tromp, 1969, 169.
78. Alfrink, 1948, 120, 126 and Tromp, *ibid.*
79. Alfrink, 1948, 128 and G.R. Driver, 1962 A, 142.
80. Alfrink, 1948, 129f. and Driver, *ibid.*
81. Alfrink, 1948, 119f. and Tromp, *ibid.*
82. Alfrink, 1948, 128, Driver, *ibid.* and Tromp, 1969, 168. Cf. Jacob, 1934, 536: the formula "kann nur die Vereinigung der *Seele,* d.i. der verklärten Persönlichkeit, mit den Seelen der Vorfahren bezeichnen ... Von einer Vereinigung der Schatten im Scheol wird der Ausdruck niemals gebraucht".
83. This formula has been discussed by Alfrink, 1943, 106-118, Driver, 1962 A, 137ff. and Tromp, 1969, 169ff.
84. Tromp, 1969, 170/71 continues: "in Israel an untimely death was considered a certain consequence of bad life. Simple 'to die', applied to kings in Kings and Chronicles, as a rule implies a violent death; said of other persons, however, it does not connote a judgement about the way of death".
85. Wächter, 1967, 72. He sees in Judg 2,10 (to be regarded as Deuteronomistic) a "Übergang zu der in der Priesterschrift üblichen Redeweise".

86. Wächter, 1967, 71, points out that in the patriarchal narratives the transference of the bones to the family grave took place only later, which is already an indication of its secondary use here.

87. Wächter, 1967, 72, refers to 2 Sam 17,23, where we have the original reference to the burial in the family grave. This would also be the meaning of another expression, namely "to go to one's fathers" (Gen 15, 15, cf. 1 Kings 13,22).

88. Quell, 1925, 13: "Denn dies und nichts anderes ist der ursprüngliche Sinn der Frase 'zu seinen Vätern versammelt werden' " and, *ibid.* n. 13 against Lods *et al.:* "Denn die Fälle, wo die Tatsache nicht buchstäblich zutrifft, wie bei Abraham, Mose und Aron, zeigen wohl einen schon abgeschliffenen Sprachgebrauch im Sinn von 'Begrabenwerden' schlechthin, vgl. bes. 2 Kg 22,10".

89. Dürr, 1926, 31, with reference to A. Šanda, *Die Bücher der Könige I,* Münster 1912, 37, and Quell. He interprets both formulas as euphemisms for 'die', also in their original meaning, which reflects "frühere archäologische Vorstellungen".

90. Meyers, 1970, 2.

91. Meyers, 1970, 10.

92. Meyers, 1970, 15.

93. Instead of the absolute *śabeä͏c* in Gen 25,8, we should adopt the fuller reading *śᵉbä͏c yamîm,* cf. the text critical apparatus to BH.

94. Dürr, 1926, 13, who refers to H. Grapow, *Die bildlichen Ausdrücke des Ägyptischen,* Leipzig 1924, 145, and to MV(A)G 1918, 2.

95. Wächter, 1967, 65f.

96. Wächter, 1967, 67. Like Dürr he also refers to Ps 91,16.

97. Cf. also Jacob, 1934, 536 and Gordis, 1978, 499.

98. Cf. Wächter, 1967, 64 and Jacob, 1934, 536.

99. Dürr, 1926, 4, notes that the expressions are used "vor allem von den 'Freunden' und 'Lieblingen Jahwes'."

100. Driver, 1962 A, 143.

101. von Rad, 1963, 257.

102. We no not have to regard either or both of them as redactional. The similarity in expression is best understood as stemming from the same narrator or 'source'.

103. Again the similarity is best understood as a result of the repetitive style of the narrator, cf. Gray, 1970, 335, who holds that 1 Kings 14,1-18 is "possibly the elaboration of a genuine local tradition".

104. Cf. the combination of *spd* and *bkh* in 2 Sam 1,12 (about Saul and his sons) and of *spd* and *qbr* in 1 Kings 13,29: *wǎyyabo͗ ͗œl-ˆîr* (. . . .) *lispod ûl^eqǎbrô*, "and brought it back to (his own) city to mourn over it and bury it" about the old prophet in Bethel and the man of Judah who was killed by a lion.

105. Exhortations to mourn built on series of expressions (*ḥgr śǎqqîm* - *spd* - *helîl*) can be found in 2 Sam 3,31; Jer 4,8; Joel 1,13; Mi 1,8 cf. also Jer 49,3. Whether they are to be regarded as formulas or patterns can be left aside here, because they are not syntactically combined with *mût* or *qbr*. Only in 2 Sam 3,31 are the mourning expressions preceded by a statement about Abner's death (*hrg*) by Joab and Abishai because he had killed (*hemît*) Asael, their brother (v. 30) and followed by a statement about his (Abner's) burial (*wǎyyiqb^erû*) (v. 32). But this syntactical combination is too loose to be considered as representing the death-burial pattern.

106. Cf. below at the end of this paragraph.

107. Cf. von Rad, 1961, 72: "Die Sprecher des Jahweglaubens in Israel haben alle Formen des Totenkults, ja alle Spuren oder Reste, die mit ihm zusammenhingen, mit grosser Schärfe bekämpft. In Tod und Grab trat dem antiken Menschen Göttliches, Numinoses besonders imponierend und Kult fordernd entgegen. Hier entstand also ein *status confessionis*. Israel hat — eine grosse Leistung! — dem Toten und dem Grab jede sakrale Qualität abgesprochen".

108. Cf. Rudolph, 1968, 139.

109. Cf. Rudolph, 1968, 110: "dieses göttliche Verbot an Jer hat Bedeutung für seine Zeitgenossen: sie sollen daraus lernen, was ihrer noch erwartet; Jer bildet im voraus ab, was alle dereinst erleiden müssen, er ist ein Zeichen für Juda, so wie später Ezechiel dadurch dass er beim Tode seiner Frau alle Trauerbräuche unterliess, auf das Schicksal Jerusalems hindeuten sollte . . .".

110. Cf. Zimmerli, 1969, 573f. It should be noted, however, that neither Jeremiah nor Ezechiel says anything about the rites as such, whether they approve of them or not. So the *status confessionis* (cf. note 107) does not occur to them, cf. Rudolph, 1968, 111.

111. Myers, 1965 A, 102, remarks that the Chronicler "wanted to show that Uzza and Ahio were not 'legally' qualified to handle it", i.e. the removal of the Ark from the house of Abinadab.

112. Cf. Noth, 1966, 134. About the burial of Aaron there is not a word, while Moses is said to be buried (by the Lord?, cf. above 3.2.2.), his grave place, however, is unknown. Neither Mount Hor nor Moserah have been located.

113. The prince is King Zedekiah, who made an unsuccessful attempt to escape (cf. 2 Kings 25,3-7; Jer 39,1-7; 52,6-11), was blinded and sent into exile in Babylon. Cf. Zimmerli, 1969, 263ff.

114. A quite 'normal' case is 2 Kings 7,4, where *šam* refers to a city: *w^eharaʿab baʿîr wamåtnû šam*, "then there is famine in the city, and we shall die there".

115. About Nadab and Abihu, cf. Ex 24,1.9 without explicit connection with Aaron, and Lev 10,1-7 as "sons of Aaron" and committing the offence referred to here. Cf. Noth, 1966, 31f.

116. Numb 27,3 points out that Zelophehad did not belong to the faction of Korah, so that his death was the common fate of all Israelites of the first generation. His name should not be erased because he had no son who could inherit his property. The inheritance would instead go to his daughters, which was ruled a valid law among the Israelites (v. 8-11), cf. Noth, 1966, 181f.

117. About the redactional work in Jos 5,2-9, cf. Noth, 1953, 39.

118. Cf Noth, 1961, *ad loc.,* and 1966, *ad loc.* and von Rad, 1964, *ad loc.*

119. Ex 14,11-12 ('E'?) presupposes that the people already in Egypt had warned Moses against this, which could be a reference to a lost ('E') element of the tradition, but also a false claim to such a warning in a difficult situation, cf. Noth, 1961, 89.

120. The formula *ʾæræṣ zabåt ḥalab ûd^ebåš*, "a land flowing of milk and honey", is quite exceptionally here used about Egypt, cf. Noth, 1966, 111.

121. Moses refers to the exodus from Egypt (v. 26), to the Patriarchs (v. 27) and finally to God's own honour (v. 28), when he asks him not to destroy his people, cf. von Rad, 1964, 56.

122. For the historical background to this law, cf. Noth, 1966, 219ff.

123. Cf. Noth, 1953, 123ff.

124. Cf. Gray, 1970, 297f.
125. Cf. Gray, 1970, 618ff.
126. Cf. Rudolph, 1968, 321.
127. Cf. Rudolph, 1968, 325.
128. The difference is, however, not great, cf. Jacob, 1934, 483: "ich will das Sterben des Kindes nicht mitansehen" and von Rad, 1961, 197: "ich kann des Kindes Sterben nicht ansehen", where $b^e m\hat{o}t$ can be interpreted as the object of Hagar's watching, but the simultaneity, 'at the same time', seems to be implied.
129. Cf. Richter, 1964, 34, 75.
130. Cf. Ringgren, 1962, 48: "Beim Tode des Frevlers geht die Hoffnung verloren", where *adam is regarded as uncertain from the point of view of textual criticism.
131. Cf. Gerleman, 1973, *ad loc.*
132. Cf. Brockelmann, 1956, 73, who translates: "um des Kindes willen, da es noch lebte".
133. Cf. NEB: "in his honesty", and Ringgren, 1962, 60, "in seiner 'Unschuld' ".
134. Cf. A. Schmitt, 1976, 206: "Dies ist ebenfalls ein beliebter Topos der Weisheitsliteratur: Jer 17,11; Ijob 1,21; Pred 5,14f.".
135. The reading of $b^e \hat{c}\hat{o}d$ is adopted by KBL and is of course what one would expect here.
136. Cf. von Rad, 1961, 302/3: "Offenbar ist sie als ein sehr altes zuverlässiges Dokument zu beurteilen".
137. MT gives in 2 Sam 10,1 only the name of the son (Hanun), while 1 Chron 19,1 preserves the name of the father (Nahash) instead. Other variations are found in the *versiones.*
138. This translation is taken from Gray, 1970, 529 and the words within brackets from NEB. Whereas the latter interpretation has the king suffocated, Gray's comment is that it is a question of a mosquito-net, which if soaked might serve as "an air-conditioner". He continues: "The point is that one came in and took the netting away as usual to be freshly soaked and hung up again, and, doing so, he noticed that the king had died," Gray, 1970, 532.
139. Cf. Gray, 1970, 531f.
140. So Würthwein, 1977, 198.

141. Cf. Würthwein, *ibid.* and Gray, 1970, 366.
142. This reading from the Lucian recension of LXX is adopted by Gray, 1970, 620 and NEB.
143. In this description of the pattern I follow K. Aalto, 1978, 32.
144. So Speiser, 1964, 41.
145. Cf. Speiser, 1964, 41ff.
146. Cf. Speiser, 1964, *ad loc.*
147. Rendtorff, 1977, 135, regards 47,28b as the beginning and 49,33b as the end of the characteristic but here interrupted 'P' phrase.
148. Although Gen 50,22.26. differ from the 'P' phrases, no reason for assigning it to 'E' has been given, Rendtorff, 1977, 135f.
149. Cf. P. Weimar, 1974, 45ff., where he discusses the form and function of the formula *(wᵉ)ᵓellǣ tôlᵉdôt* . . . , which occurs eleven times in Genesis and once in Numb 3,1.
150. Cf. Ringgren, 1977, 889 and M. Ravndal Hauge, 1976, 210.
151. This reading is according to Peshitta, whereas LXX would read *yamît.* MT is corrupt.
152. Knierim, 1965, 217.
153. Knierim, 1965, 190f.
154. Zimmerli, 1969, 397ff.
155. Knierim, 1965, 48f.
156. Cf. Boecker, 1964, 112.
157. Knierim, 1965, 49: "Die Bedeutung dieser Verlagerung des Sitzes im Leben liegt darin, dass mit dieser traditionellen Form die aktuelle und zum Teil neue Verkündigung legitimiert und als neues Recht gesetzt wird. In diesem Bereich wird man die Wortverbindung als formelhaft ansprechen müssen."
158. Knierim, *ibid.*
159. Watters, 1976, 43.
160. "In peace" means here a natural death and burial in honour like his "fathers" (cf. above 3.3.1.), cf. Rudolph, 1968, 221.
161. Cf. Rudolph, 1971, 259, 277f.
162. Rudolph, 1968, 221.
163. Rudolph, 1955, 271.
164. Gray, 1970, 96.

165. Cf. Liedke, 1971, 151f., with reference to E. Scherer (diss., Berlin 1964), who regards 1 Kings 14,11 (16,4; 21,24) and 1 Kings 19,17 as 'Fluchorakel' with their origin in magic.

166. Although 2 Chron 32,11 is dependent upon 2 Kings 18,32b, cf. Rudolph, 1955, 312, this particular phrase is not used here.

167. Zimmerli, 1969, 820, regards these three ways of death as corresponding to the real conditions in time immediately after the year 587, which could mean that we have an adaptation of the triple formula found elsewhere in Ez.

168. Cf. Wächter, 1967, 138, n. 66 and 69.

169. Zimmerli, 1969, 155f., points out that the pair of opposites, *rahôq* - *qarôb*, would not allow for a third alternative, which however is introduced here in accordance with the triple formula. *wᵉhᵼnniṣᵊar* again is "ein das rechte Verständnis von *wᵉhᵼnnaṣûr* sicherndes Interpretament", *ibid.*, 141. He may be right in his assumption that the third link here is intended as a kind of "surprise effect".

170. Thus Wächter, 1967, 138f., with reference to Fohrer, 1955, 40.

171. Cf. Zimmerli, 1969, 98, 135, about Ez 5,12, where the triple formula is combined with four ways of punishment (pestilence, famine, sword and dispersion).

172. Cf. Boecker, 1964, 53, who holds that this formulation although it "kommt einer Selbstverfluchung nahe", is nevertheless to be regarded as an insistence on regular and ordered investigation.

173. 1 Sam 26,10: "As the Lord lives", David went on, "the Lord will strike him down (*yiggapᾱnnû*); either his time will come and he will die (*wamet*), or he will go down to battle and meet his end (*wᵉnispā*)". Regardless of the way of death intended by the first alternative, it is obviously thought of as a punishment. Cf. Stoebe, 1973, 468f.

174. A. Alt, 1953, 308. Cf. the discussion in G. Liedke, 1971, 101ff.

175. A. Alt, 1953, 287f. Cf. Liedke, 1971, 19ff.

176. Cf. Noth, 1966, 40, with reference to 2 Sam 6,6f. indicating, that the Lord himself would carry out the punishment.

177. Schüngel-Straumann, 1969, 138. Cf. Liedke, 1971, 49f., who points out that *sql* often requires an additional statement about the mortal consequence, whereas *rgm* already includes this consequence. Originally *sql* expressed the expulsion of a criminal from the community.

178. Schüngel-Straumann, 1969, 122, seems to regard only the three first instances as formulaic, but not the expanded form in Deut 22,25, which she discusses within its immediate context, v. 21-25, *op.cit.*, 123f.

179. B. Johnson, 1979, 55.

180. Boecker, 1964, 146, regards 1 Sam 14,44 and 22,16 as a variation of what he calls 'Tatfolgebestimmung'. Usually these are formulated in the hof 'al form *môt yûmat*, but here exceptionally in qal and directed to the guilty person, cf. Liedke, 1971, 128f.

181. This is of course only a preliminary proposal of sentence ('Urteilsvorschlag'), which leads to an official prosecution against the prophet in v. 10ff. At this preliminary stage he is spoken to, but then spoken about in the third person. Cf. Boecker, 1964, 67, 71f. and Liedke, 1971, 88, 129, n. 3; Schulz, 1969, 122f.

182. Cf. Zimmerli, 1969, 802, who characterizes *môt tamût* in the following way: "Es ist die Formel des apodiktisch angesagten (1 S 14,44 22,16 2 Kö 1,4.6.16) oder angedrohten (Jer 26,8) oder dann unter gewissen Bedingungen hypothetisch verhängten (Gen 2,17 (3,4) 20,7 1 Kö 2,37. 42) Todesurteils ... Immer aber ist es die Antwort auf den Ungehorsam gegen ein ganz konkretes Gebot. Gebotsübertretung und Todesurteil gehören zusammen. Und in allen Fällen handelt es sich um ein Urteil gegenüber einem einzelnen".

183. This threat then leads to the 'Tatfolgebestimmung' of v. 44, cf. above 6.2.2. and Boecker, 1964, 146.

184. Ravndal Hauge, 1976, 220, n. 14, seems to understand all three of them in this way. Cf. Liedke, 1971, 129.

185. Mauchline, 1971, 266.

186. Boecker, 1964, 146, regards some cases (1 Sam 14,44; 22,16) as modifications of the 'Tatfolgebestimmung' *môt yûmat*: "An den wenigen Belegstellen, an denen Tatfolgebestimmungen in erzählenden Texten in der Form der direkten Anrede an den Verurteilten erscheinen, liegt nicht die stilreine Formulierung vor, vielmehr ist aus mehr oder minder einsichtigen Gründen eine Abwandlung erfolgt". Cf. Liedke, 1971, 129, who points out that the main difference lies in the distinction between casuistic and apodictic legal formulations: in the first case we have proposals of sentence, in the latter authoritative pronouncements of judgement.

187. Instead of *lo*ᵓ most scholars since Geiger have preferred the vocalization *lu*ᵓ. Cf. Stoebe, 1973, 375, n. 14 a).

188. According to the Tiqqune Sopherim Hab 1,12 should read *lo*ᵓ *tamût* instead of MT's *lo*ᵓ *namût*. This reading is also adopted in the text critical apparatus of BH and BHS and by Robinson-Horst, 1964, 174. If this is correct, it is an assurance about God's immortality and is of course no consequence or avoiding of death.

189. About 2 Sam 19,24 and 12,13, cf. Boecker, 1964, 133, n. 2, who regards *lo*ᵓ *tamût* in these cases as a 'Freispruch': "Neben der deklaratorischen Form der speziellen Freispruchserklärung gibt es auch die Form der direkten Anrede. Das ist jedoch der seltene Ausnahme". The usual forms of such 'Freispruchserklärungen' are held in the 3rd person, i.e., they are uttered *about* and not *to* the accused person, cf. Boecker, *op.cit.*, 123ff. Cf. Schulz, 1969, 31 and Liedke, 1971, 128, n. 5.

190. Jacob, 1934, 761.

191. Cf. Cassuto, 1961, 145f., who does not see here a rebuttal of *môt tamût*, which "is too far away; moreover, in the woman's speech the warning is worded differently . . . and there was thus no point in making the phrasing here correspond to that in 2,17". In addition to this there is the difference of sing. (2,17) and plur. here. The real contradiction Cassuto finds between the serpent's "you shall by no means die" and the woman's "lest you die". This does not mean, however, that the serpent's expression could not formally be a negated form of God's conditional threat in 2,17. Here I agree with Cassuto's rules: "The negative particle comes between the absolute infinitive and the conjugated verb when it is intended to express the antithesis of *another verb* . . . But when the intention is to qualify adversatively a clause containing the *selfsame root,* then the negative particle precedes the absolute infinitive . . .".

192. Knierim, 1965, 190f.

193. Cf. Schüngel-Straumann, 1969, 92.

194. Cf. Jacob, 1934, 776: "Die Worte sollen dem Versprechen und Gelübde den stärksten Ausdruck geben: ich will lieber meine beiden Söhne durch den Tod verlieren".

195. Cf. Gray, 1970, 96.

196. Cf. Schüngel-Straumann, 1969, 117f.: "Man wird aber wohl kaum annehmen dürfen, dass bei *yûmat* an eine konkret von der Gemeinde Israels oder einer weltlichen Instanz zu vollziehende Todesstrafe zu denken ist. Vielmehr handelt es sich hier um eine alte Auffassung, die in eine rhetorische Drohung gekleidet ist, wonach die Begegnung mit dem Heiligen tötet, wenn nicht besondere Vorkehrungen getroffen werden. . . . Insofern fällt der Gebrauch von *yûmat* im Buche Numeri durch seine spezielle kultische Bedeutung aus dem Rahmen der sonst angetroffenen Bedeutungen heraus, nicht nur innerhalb der Gesetze, sondern im AT überhaupt". Liedke, 1971, 112, calls these cases 'Heiligtumstabusätze'. Cf. Haran, 1978, 183.
197. Cf. Schüngel-Straumann, 1969, 111ff. and Liedke, 1971, 117ff.
198. Knierim, 1965, 109.
199. Cf. Schüngel-Straumann, 1969, 97f.; Schulz, 1969, 51ff. and Liedke, 1971, 102, 116f.
200. Christ, 1977, 67f., regards it as a characterization of the apodosis, because it always follows after *môt yûmat*: "Die Blutformel auf einer Linie mit der Mot-jumat- und Ausrottungsformel zu sehen, befriedigt nicht, denn sie ersetzt die Todesdeklaration nirgends, sondern ergänzt sie bloss. Sie begründet offenbar das Todesurteil".
201. Elliger, 1966, 265, cf. Schulz, 1969, 46f.
202. Schüngel-Straumann, 1969, 101, 255, n. 67.
203. Schulz, 1969, 139ff., tries to show the relation between the 'prohibitions' of Lev 18 amd the death penalties of Lev 20 on the basis of formulaic similarities. He regards Lev 18-20 as a "Formular eines kultischen Gerichtsverfahrens", *op.cit.*, 155ff.
204. Schüngel-Straumann, 1969, 104.
205. Schulz, 1969, 51.
206. Schüngel-Straumann, 1969, 105, 108.
207. Cf. Schüngel-Straumann, 1969, 109 and Haran, 1978, 285, n. 18.
208. Schüngel-Straumann has disregarded this case entirely, while Schulz, 1969, 99ff., interprets it as "Todesrecht in der Stammesgemeinschaft" and Liedke, 1971, 120f., also regards it as "very old".
209. Boecker, 1964, 58, points out that 1 Sam 26,15 is "eine geprägte Urteilsformulierung" and compares it with 2 Sam 12,5, *op.cit.*, 150f. But according to him they are 'Tatfolgebestimmungen', which cannot be said about the threats with *ʾîš/ʾănšê mawæt*, cf. Liedke, 1971, 89.

210. About the use and meaning of *nkh* (hif), cf. Schüngel-Straumann, 1969, 55-79. Although she is aware of the fact that this stem is used in "formelhaften Wendungen", she does not pay much attention to combinations with *mût*, except for observations about the "Tatfolge" *wamet* in Ex 21,12; 22,1, *op.cit.*, 62ff.

211. MT's reading *wǎyyamot* has been doubted both on internal grounds and in comparison with the fuller text of Jer 41,2. It should perhaps be omitted, cf. Gray, 1970, 770, c.

212. See the text critical apparatus in BH.

213. About the use and meaning of *hrg* as such, cf. Schüngel-Straumann, 1969, 79-89. Like *nkh* (hif) *hrg* is not a very precise term for slaying, only more so: "Das Verb ist auch denkbar ungeeignet, einen genauen Tatbestand auszudrücken − im Gegensatz etwa zu *rṣh* −, weil es alle Arten gewaltigen Tötens ausdrücken kann", *op.cit.*, 89. Here I may add that, although *rṣh* alone forms very precise formulas about murder and the murderer, it does not do so in combination with *mût*. They can be found, however, in the same larger casuistic patterns, as we have already seen.

214. Although Ex 9,1-7 by Noth, 1961, 60f., is regarded as "einen sekundären Zuwachs zur J-Erzählung", it is not complex in itself. Cassuto, 1967, 112, points to the parallelism between *wǎyyamât* and *met* in v. 6.

215. Cf. Stoebe, 1973, 144, who with reference to Bentzen also points out that in addition to the description of the severe plague or whatever the illness was, there is a stress on the comic aspects of the Philistine disaster.

216. Cf. Stoebe, 1973, 275: "Saul gibt nach, das Volk bekommt seinen Helden frei. Bei aller Unbestimmtheit des Ausdruckes *wǎyyipdû* lässt er doch wohl erkennen, dass die Berechtigung der Entscheidung Sauls grundsätzlich anerkannt bleibt".

217. Wanke, 1966, points out that the expression *bᵉnê qorǎh* occurs, apart from the headings of the Korachite Psalms, only in Ex 6,24 and Numb 26,11.

218. Cf. Gray, 1970, 441: "The punctilio with which the destruction of Naboth was contrived is grimly sadistic. He is condemned by the elders with a show of conservative Israelite democracy on the evidence of the

two witnesses which custom required (cf. Deut 17,6; 19,15; cf. Matt 26,60) and he is stoned by the community (cf. Lev 24,16)." Cf. Schulz, 1969, 115ff., who regards the procedure as cultic.

219. Schüngel-Straumann, 1969, 138f., shows that the majority of the crimes where the death penalty is enacted through stoning are what she calls "theologischer Art" but that there are a minority consisting of sexual transgressions. Outside these two groups fall 1 Kings 12,18 = 2 Chron 10,18; Deut 21,21 and Ex 21,28-32.

220. Schüngel-Straumann, 1969, 140.

221. Gray, 1970, 525.

222. That this encounter is not thought of as accidental but rather planned by the avenger of blood is stressed by Schüngel-Straumann, 1969, 92. She regards verses 19 and 21 as later additions to Numb 35 on several grounds. Be it as it may, it is however remarkable that Numb 35,19,21 uses the same expression as 1 Kings 2,25.34.46 about killing "upon encounter".

223. Cf. Jacob, 1934, 712f.

224. For discussion about repetitions of various kinds, see Richter, 1970, 51ff., Illman, 1975, 20ff., 36ff., 44-94 and Licht, 1978, 51-95.

225. Cf. Zimmerli, 1969, 760: "Die 'Wasserbäume' and 'Wassertrinker' sind demgegenüber, nur leicht in Bildrede verkleidet, diejenigen, welche aus den machtwollen Wassern, die in 4 beschrieben waren, getrunken haben und dadurch in Versuchung stehen, ihre Zugehörigkeit zum sterblichen Menschentum zu vergessen".

226. Regarding this and other comparable expressions, cf. Barth, 1947, 76ff. and Tromp, 1969, 23ff., 182.

227. Culley, 1967, 57. Cf. Ljung, 1978, 98f.

228. Kraus, 1978, 409ff., 566ff.

229. Ringgren, 1962, 45, 49.

230. Cf. Zimmerli, 1969, 669, 785f., and Ez 32,17ff. against Egypt.

231. Cf. Paul, 1970, 94, and n. 6, who concedes that the expression in v. 13 on the basis of an Akkadian phrase *ul-te-eb-ir-šu ù im-tu-ut,* "he injured it so that it died", which is a hendiadys, could also be interpreted in this way. This is not possible, however, in v. 9.

232. Cf. the text critical apparatus to BH and BHS which also note the suggested reading *niblotam,* "their dead bodies".

233. Watters, 1976, 169, example 374, indicates that this case is not clear by placing v. 19 in brackets. Rather many of his examples do indeed suffer from this or similar uncertainty.

234. Kraus, 1978, 1116: "Diese Worte sprengen das Versmass und sind wahrscheinlich eine Hinzufügung (vgl. Thr 3,6)". Cf. Culley. 1967, 89 and Ljung, 1978, 98.

235. Cf. Zimmerli, 1969, 1136, who points out that Ez 44,25 has its exact counterpart in Lev 21,1-3, albeit without *met*, while Lev 21,11 expresses the stricter rule applied to the high priest alone. About Numb 6,6ff., cf. Noth, 1966, 51: "In dieser Hinsicht galten für den Naziräer dieselben Vorschriften wie nach 3. Mos. 21,11 für den obersten Priester ...".

236. There are various opinions concerning the expression *næpæš met* as to its grammatical form as well as to its meaning. The full expression is found only in Numb 6,6 and Lev 21,11, here in the plur. form *năpšot met*. It cannot be understood as an attributive expression, since a) *met* is masc. and *næpæš* is fem. and b) *năpšot* is plur. and *met* sing. It is uncertain, however, whether MT's reading of the plur. is correct or whether one here too should read sing., following LXX and Peshitta. If, with Elliger, 1966, 279, we adopt the latter reading, the question remains of how the sing. form *næpæš met* should be explained; he translates 'Leiche', cf. "any dead body" (NJV) and "any man's dead body" (NEB). Seligson, 1951, 82, argues for the interpretation *vis letalis* as opposed to the *vis vitalis*, namely the Hebrew *næpæš hăyyā*: "it is the power in the dead (body), *met*." Be it as it may, the translation "dead body" would be correct also from this point of view. It is a longer form for *næpæš* and can be expressed through an even longer, *næpæš ʾadam ʾăšer yamût* (Lev 21,1 and 21,13). Grammatically, it is a construct or pregenitive. It has thus the same meaning as *nᵉbelā* and *pægær*, whereas the expression *pᵉgarim metim* is an attributive meaning literally "dead bodies, corpses".

237. Here I follow Gordis, 1978, 447, who finds no reason for changing *šăᵈrê* in the second stich to *šoᶜᵈrê*, "gatekeepers" on the basis of LXX, nor *tirʾæ* (MT) to *raʾûka* or *raʾita*, which has been proposed.

238. Cf. Barth, 1947, 78 and Kraus, *ad loc.*

239. Gordis, 1978, 436 explaining it, *op.cit.*, 447, as " 'the sources of the sea' on the basis of the parallelism".

240. Cf. Fohrer, 1963, 505. His translation of *ṣǎlmawæt* with 'darkness' presupposes its derivation from an Akkadian stem *ṣalamu*, "grow black", which corresponds to the Hebrew *ṣlm* II from which the abstract noun *ṣǎlmût* would be formed. This derivation goes back to Hehn, MV(A)G 22, 1917, 79ff., and has been widely accepted.

241. Cf. Tromp, 1969, 152f., and n. 3.

242. This pertains to the reading *miŝbᵉrê* instead of *ḥæblê* in v. 5a.

243. Kraus, 1978, 284ff.

244. Cf. Culley, 1967, 49, who taking the respective verbs in account regards Ps 18,5a and 116,3a as representing the same formula and Ps 18,6b as belonging to the same 'system', in addition to which there are variant systems, found in Ps 18,6a, 109,3a and 116,3b.

245. Cf. Kraus, 1978, 289. Cf. Ljung, 1978, 61.

246. Ringgren, 1962, 83; cf. McKane, 1970, 467f., 490.

247. Ringgren, 1977, 887.

248. Cf. Ljung, 1978, 60: "Ps 18,5a, 6a, 6b and 116,3a, 3b are seen as having similar functions in the context; from this differs Ps 109,3a."

249. Ps 49,15 is extremely uncertain from a text critical point of view. Kraus, 1978, 517, proposes the following reading: *ŝǎttû kǎṣṣoᵓn mawæt yircem liŝᵓôl ŝahû wᵉyerᵉdû* translating: "wie eine Herde weidet sie der Tod, zur Unterwelt 'sinken sie nieder' ". NJV tries to preserve the MT. Anyway we are able to preserve the parallelism between *mawæt* and *ŝᵉᵓôl*, which is the point here.

250. About the word *ḥozæ* in Is 28,15, its parallelism with *bᵉrît* and its relation to *ḥazût* in v. 18, cf. A. Johnson, 1962, 13, n. 3.

251. Cf. the use of *yrd* with various nouns referring to the nether world, Tromp, 1969, 32ff.

252. When Kraus, 1978, 792 in his comment on Ps 89,48f. writes "An dieser Stelle klingen konventionellen Formeln an, wie sie in Ps 39,6ff.; 90,9; 102,12 u.ö. in Erscheinung treten", he is speaking not about formulas but about a specific motif, namely "the transience of life".

253. Cf. Barth, 1947, 79ff.

254. Cf. Kraus, 1978, 563: "In seiner Not appelliert der Bedrängte also an ein Gottesgericht, das an Numb 16,33 erinnert und wahrscheinlich auch das dort geschilderte Geschehen vor Augen hat".

255. Cf. Ringgren, 1962, 49.

256. Cf. Kraus, 1978, 468.

257. Cf. Haran, 1978, 178: "A non-priest may not even look at any of the articles of furniture within the tabernacle ... The Kohathites are explicitly told not to look at the furniture while it is being covered up lest they die (Num. 4:18-20). This warning can obviously apply only to the inner articles."

258. Concerning these examples, cf. also Ez 18,13: "He shall not live ... he shall die" and v. 17: "he shall not die for the iniquity of his father, but shall live" (above 5.2.1.). About all these formulas cf. Zimmerli, 1969, 406ff. and 411: "So ist denn festzustellen, dass die kasuistische Schilderung des Sünders zwar in ihrem ersten Teil deutlich als Gegenstück zur Schilderung des Gerechten gehalten ist, in ihrem Schlussteil aber den Einfluss eines anderen, zweifellos nicht in der Torliturgie beheimateten Rechtes erkennen lässt. Es ist ja auch von innen her wahrscheinlich, dass am Tor nicht gleichgewichtig nebeneinander Leben und Tod verkündigt wurde. Das Heiligtum ist der Ort des Lebens".

259. Concerning this use of the imperative, cf. Brockelmann, 1956, 2.

260. Concerning the relations between the two imperatives in v. 18 on the one hand and the expression $w^e lo^{\jmath}$ tamûtû in v. 20 on the other, cf. Jacob, 1934, 769f.

261. Cf. Zimmerli, 1969, 413: "Völlig unerwartet, stilistisch überraschend aber bricht 23 mitten in diese sachlich-kasuistische Ordnungsrede ein ganz anderes Genus des Wortes ein: die um den Menschen werbende göttliche Frage. Dass sie an den Fall des Gottlosen, der Busse tut, angeschlossen wird, zeigt, dass Jahwe nicht kühl wägend über den beiden Möglichkeiten steht, sondern den ruft, der gestern gottlos war, dass ihm heute das Tor zur Umkehr aufgetan sei ...", and op.cit., 804f.

262. I choose the ketib reading yihyœ, although $w^e hay\bar{a}$ as qere reads is quite possible, too. Cf. Rudolph, 1968, 136.

263. Perhaps v. 13a is to be regarded as a variant of v. 12b, which would explain the discrepance between what looks like a death sentence (môt yûmat) and a deadly consequence of touching the mountain (lo$^{\jmath}$ yihyœ), cf. Noth, 1961, 127.

264. Cf. Liedke, 1971, 151, who refers to E. Scherer to justify calling Jer 21,9 and 38,2 'Kriegsorakel'. Other examples are Jer 48,44 (Is 24,18) and Am 5,3b.

265. Kaiser, 1963, 97. Although this practice was punished with death (Lev 19,31; 20,6.27; Deut 18,10f.) it was employed in critical situations (1 Sam 28) as here in time of war.

266. Thus Lauha, 1978, 167f.: "Kohelet will ironisch darlegen, welch fragwürdiges Glück das Lebendigsein ist." Cf. *op.cit.*, 82. Cf. Loader, 1979, 103 and above 7.2.3.

267. MT's reading $n^e belat\hat{i}$, literally "my corpse" has puzzled many commentators, many of them preferring *niblotam*, "their corpses". MT's reading has lately been defended by Habets, 1974, 146f., for example. Instead of the imperatives *haqîṣû w^eráñn^enû* of MT, one should, instead, read the future imperfects *yaqîṣû wîráñn^enû* or perhaps the perfect consecutivum *w^eheqîṣû*, cf. BHS, BH, and Habets, *ibid.*

268. So Habets, 1974, 262f.: "In Jes 26,14 wird als eine allgemeine, jedem einsichtige Wahrheit ausgesprochen, dass Tote nicht leben, dass Leichen nicht auferstehen werden (vgl. Ps 88). Diese allgemeine Regel gilt denn auch den Frevlern, von denen besonders die fremden Gewaltherrscher hervorgehoben werden . . . Desto überraschender klingt 26,19 an . . . die feste Regel gilt also nicht für alle Toten. Für 'deine Toten', 'Meine Leichen' wird eine Ausnahme gemacht. Es geht offenbar um Tote, mit denen in einer anderen Weise verfahren wird. Es sind Menschen, die Jahwe in einer besonderen Weise angehören, Jahwetreue, die für ihn in den Tod gegangen sind . . . .".

269. Cf. Jacob, 1934, 824, 839. Cf. the thrice repeated expression (Gen 37, 35; 42,38; 44,29) of going down to Sheol in grief.

270. Thus Ringgren, 1963, 64f. with reference to G. Widengren.

271. Cf. Elliger, 1978, 498f. The word pair is thus not antithetical but polar to use the distinction of Wanke, 1973, 69 (cf. above n. 18). Our investigation shows that the same word pair can sometimes be antithetical and sometimes polar, i.e., it can have different functions and thereby different meanings.

272. Codex Samaritanus reads $w^e hay^e t\bar{a}$, which one should expect. Concerning MT, cf. Schmidt, 1974, 6 with references to other literature.

273. Cf. Gerleman, 1973, 11ff.

274. The theme is well known, however, outside Israel, cf. Würthwein, 1977, 37 with references to Gunkel and Gressmann. Cf. Gray, 1970, 127: "The narrative style, with vivid direct speech and frequent repetition, suggest the folk-tale".

206

275. Cf. Rudolph, 1968, 134 and Weinfeld, 1972, 346.
276. Cf. von Rad, 1964, 132 and Weinfeld, 1972, 62, 64 with reference to the witnesses invoked in Deut 30,19.
277. Cf. Rudolph, 1968, 59.
278. Cf. Gordis, 1978, 38: "Job is not yet voicing a charge against God ... but complaining against life itself".
279. Concerning the interpretation, cf. McKane, 1970, 314f.
280. Concerning the text critical problems, cf. McKane, 1970, 451f.
281. Cf. McKane, 1970, 474.
282. McKane, 1970, 488.
283. Thus Weinfeld, 1972, 307f.
284. Weinfeld, 1972, 308f., cf. Ringgren, 1977, 887.
285. Weinfeld, 1972, 309f. One should be careful, however, to speak about such things as "wisdom vocabulary" in Deut or dtr literature, since few phrases are peculiar to any of the traditions thus compared, but many belong to the common speech of biblical Israel, cf. Whybray, 1974, 121f., n. 191.
286. Cf. Culley, 1967, 57, 95.
287. Cf. my interpretation of this psalm in Illman, 1976, 32f., 36f., under the theme 'judgement'.
288. Cf. Kaiser, 1973, 322: ". . . erscheinen Unterwelt, Scheol, und Tod geradezu personifiziert. Wie sie verhalten sich alle, die ihrem Bereich verfallen sind."
289. Cf. Gordis, 1978, 336: " 'The meeting house of all the living' is a superb description of the land of the dead".
290. Cf. Gordis, 1978, 376f., who defends MT, which according to him "preserves a reference, not to be eliminated, to the ancient mythological belief in special beings connected with death, that is elaborated upon in post-biblical literature . . .". Also Fohrer, 1963, 454, retains MT's reading, interpreting it as "den Todesboten" literally meaning "den Tötenden", cf. his comment, op.cit., 459.
291. Cf. Driver, 1913, 341 and Mauchline, 1971, 295.
292. Cf. Fohrer, 1963, 473, and Gordis, 1978, 415.
293. Cf. Lauha, 1978, 64f. Loader, 1979, 30.
294. Cf. Lauha, 1978, 124. Loader, 1979, 33.
295. Cf. Wolff, 1965, 218.

296. Concerning "overcoming of the fate of death", cf. Kellermann, 1978, 266ff., and Kaiser-Lohse, 1977, 70 ff.

ABBREVIATIONS

AB	The Anchor Bible
ATD	Das Alte Testament Deutsch
BA	*The Biblical Archaeologist*
BBB	Bonner Biblische Beiträge
BH	*Biblia Hebraica,* ed. R. Kittel, 3rd ed., Stuttgart 1937
BHS	*Biblia Hebraica Stuttgartensia,* ed. K. Elliger et W. Rudolph, Stuttgart 1967-77
BKAT	Biblischer Kommentar Altes Testament
BWANT	Beiträge zur Wissenschaft vom Alten und Neuen Testament
BZ	*Biblische Zeitschrift*
BZAW	Beihäfte zur *Zeitschrift für die alttestamentliche Wissenschaft*
CB	Coniectanea Biblica
HAT	Handbuch zum Alten Testament
HSCP	*Harvard Studies in Classical Philology*
JSS	*Journal of Semitic Studies*
KAT	Kommentar zum Alten Testament
KBL	L. Koehler - W. Baumgartner, *Lexicon in Veteris Testamenti Libros,* 2nd ed., Leiden 1958
LXX	The Septuagint
MT	The Massoretic text
MV(A)G	*Mitteilungen der Vorderasiatisch(-Ägyptisch)en Gesellschaft*
NCB	New Century Bible
NEB	The New English Bible, The Old Testament, Oxford - Cambridge 1970
NJV	The New Jewish Version, Philadelphia 1962-
NTT	*Norsk Teologisk Tidskrift*
OTL	Old Testament Library
OTS	Oudtestamentische Studiën
THAT	*Theologisches Handwörterbuch zum Alten Testament,* ed. E. Jenni and C. Westermann, München - Zürich 1971-1976
TWAT	*Theologisches Wörterbuch zum Alten Testament,* ed. G.J. Botterweck and H. Ringgren, Stuttgart ..., 1970-
UTB	Universitätstaschenbücher
VT	*Vetus Testamentum*
VTSuppl	Supplements to *Vetus Testamentum*
WMANT	Wissenschaftliche Monographien zum Alten und Neuen Testament
ZTK	*Zeitschrift für Theologie und Kirche*

BIBLIOGRAPHY

Aalto, K.
1978   *Liv och död. En undersökning av motsatsparet ḥyh/mût
               i Gamla testamentet* (unpublished degree thesis), Åbo.

Alfrink, B.
1943   *L'Expression šakăb 'im ᵃbotâw*, OTS 2, 1943, 106-118.

Alfrink, B.
1948   *L'Expression næᵃ⁾ᵆsăp 'æl-ᶜămmâw*, OTS 5, 1948, 118-
               131.

Alt, A.
1953   *Die Ursprünge des israelitischen Rechts* (1934), *Kleine
               Schriften zur Geschichte des Volkes Israel*, München, I,
               278-332.

Aurelius, E.
1907   *Föreställningar i Israel om de döda och tillståndet efter
               döden. En studie till Gamla testamentets kanoniska
               skrifter* (diss.), Uppsala.

Barr, J.
1961   *The Semantics of Biblical Language*. Oxford.

Barth, Chr.
1947   *Die Errettung vom Tode in den individuellen Klage- und
               Dankliedern des Alten Testaments*. Zollikon.

Bertholet, A.
1914   *Die israelitischen Vorstellungen vom Zustand nach dem
               Tode*, 2nd ed., Freiburg.

Boecker, H.J.
1964   *Redeformen des Rechtslebens im Alten Testament*
               (WMANT 14), Neukirchen - Vluyn.

Brockelmann, C.
1956   *Hebräische Syntax*, Neukirchen.

Cassuto, U.
1961   *A Commentary on the Book of Genesis.* Transl. by I.
               Abrahams. I: *From Adam to Noah,* Jerusalem.
Cassuto, U.
1967   *A Commentary on the Book of Exodus.* Transl. by I.
               Abrahams, Jerusalem.
Christ, H.
1977   *Blutvergiessen im Alten Testament. Der gewaltsame Tod
               des Menschen untersucht am hebräischen Wort dam*
               (diss.), Basel.
Culley, R.C.
1967   *Oral Formulaic Language in the Biblical Psalms.* (Uni-
               versity of Toronto Press: Near and Middle East Series,
               4), Toronto.
Driver, G.R.
1962 A   *Plurima Mortis Imago,* in *Studies and Essays in Honour
               of Abraham A. Neumann,* Philadelphia, 128-143.
Driver, G.R.
1962 B   *The Resurrection of Marine and Terrestial Creatures,*
               JSS 7, 1962, 12-22.
Driver,, S.R.
1913   *Notes on the Hebrew Text and the Topography of the
               Books of Samuel . . . ,* 2nd ed., Oxford.
Dürr, L.
1926   *Die Wertung des Lebens im Alten Testament und im
               antiken Orient. Ein Beitrag zur Erklärung des Segens des
               vierten Gebotes,* Münster.
Eichrodt, W.
1933-1939   *Theologie des Alten Testaments,* I: *Gott und Volk*
               (1933), II: *Gott und Welt* (1935), III: *Gott und Mensch*
               (1939), Leipzig.
Eissfeldt, O.
1922   *Hexateuch-Synopse. Die Erzählungen der fünf Bücher
               Mose und des Buches Josua mit den Anfängen des
               Richterbuches in ihre vier Quellen zerlegt,* Leipzig.

Elliger, K.
1966   *Leviticus* (HAT 4), Tübingen.
Elliger, K.
1978   *Deuterojesaja, I. Jes 40,1-45,7* (BKAT XI, 1), Neu-
                kirchen-Vluyn.
Fohrer, G.
1963   *Das Buch Hiob* (KAT XVI), Gütersloh.
Gerleman, G.
1971   *mūt, sterben,* THAT, München-Zürich, I, 893-897.
Gerleman, G.
1973   *Esther* (BKAT XXI), Neukirchen-Vluyn.
Gordis, R.
1978   *The Book of Job: Commentary, New Translation, and
                Special Studies* (Moreshet. Studies in Jewish History,
                Literature and Thought, 2), New York.
Gray, J.
1970   *I & II Kings. A Commentary* (OTL), 2nd ed., London.
Habets, G.N.M.
1974   *Der grosse Jesaja-Apokalypse* (Jes 24-27). *Ein Beitrag
                zur Theologie des Alten Testaments* (diss.), Bonn.
Hainsworth, J.B.
1968   *The Flexibility of the Homeric Formula,* Oxford.
Haran, M.
1978   *Temples and Temple-Service in Ancient Israel. An Inquiry
                into the Character of Cult Phenomena and the Historical
                Setting of the Priestly School.* Oxford.
Hertzberg, H.W.
1956   *Die Samuelisbücher* (ATD 10), Göttingen.
Illman, K.-J.
1975   *Leitwort – Tendenz – Synthese. Programm und Praxis
                in der Exegese Martin Bubers* (Publications of the Re-
                search Institute of the Åbo Akademi Foundation, 2),
                Åbo.
Illman, K.-J.
1976   *Thema und Tradition in den Asaf-Psalmen* (Publications
                of the Research Institute of the Åbo Akademi Founda-
                tion, 13), Åbo.

212

Jacob, B.
1934   Das erste Buch der Tora. Genesis übersetzt und erklärt,
                Berlin.
Jahnow, H.
1923   Das hebräische Leichenlied im Rahmen der Völkerdich-
                tung (BZAW 36), Giessen.
Johnson, A.
1962   The Cultic Prophet in Ancient Israel, 2nd ed., Cardiff.
Johnson, B.
1979   Hebräisches Perfekt und Imperfekt mit vorangehendem
                w^e (CB, OT series 13), Lund.
Kaiser, O.
1963   Der Prophet Jesaja 1-12 (ATD 17), Göttingen.
Kaiser, O.
1973   Der Prophet Jesaja 13-39 (ATD 18), Göttingen.
Kaiser, O.-Lohse, E.
1977   Tod und Leben (Kohlhammer Taschenbücher: Biblische
                Konfrontationen, 1001), Stuttgart . . .
Kellermann, U.
1976   Überwindung des Todesgeschicks in der alttestament-
                lichen Frömmigkeit vor und neben dem Auferstehungs-
                glauben, ZTK, 73, 1976, 259-282.
Knierim, R.
1965   Die Hauptbegriffe für Sünde im Alten Testament. Gü-
                tersloh.
Koch, K.
1967   Was ist Formgeschichte? Neue Wege der Bibelexegese,
                2nd ed., Neukirchen.
Kraus, H.J.
1978   Psalmen (BKAT XV, 1-2), 5th ed., Neukirchen-Vluyn.
Lande, I.
1949   Formelhafte Wendungen der Umgangssprache im Alten
                Testament (diss.), Leiden.
Lauha, A.
1978   Kohelet (BKAT XIX), Neukirchen-Vluyn.

Licht, J.
1978   *Storytelling in the Bible*, Jerusalem.

Liedke, G.
1971   *Gestalt und Bezeichnung alttestamentlicher Rechtssätze. Eine formgeschichtlich-terminologische Studie* (WMANT 39), Neukirchen.

Ljung, I.
1978   *Tradition and Interpretation. A Study of the Use and Application of Formulaic Language in the So-Called Ebed YHWH-Psalms* (CB, OT Series 12), Lund.

Loader, J.A.
1979   *Polar Structures in the Book of Qohelet* (BZAW 152), Berlin - New York.

Lord, A.B.
1960   *The Singer of Tales* (Harvard Studies in Comparative Literature, 24), Cambridge, Mass.

Martin-Achard, R.
1956   *De la Mort à la Résurrection d'après l'Ancien Testament* (Bibliothèque Théologique), Neuchatel - Paris.

Mauchline, J.
1971   *1 and 2 Samuel* (NCB), London.

McKane, W.
1970   *Proverbs. A New Approach* (OTL), London.

Meyers, E.M.
1970   *Secondary Burials in Palestine*, BA XXXIII, 1970, 2-29.

Myers, J.B.
1965 A   *Chronicles. Introduction, Translation, and Notes.* I (AB 12), Garden City - New York.

Myers, J.B.
1965 B   II (AB 13), Garden City - New York.

Myers, J.B.
1965 C   *Ezra – Nehemia. Introduction, Translation, and Notes.* (AB 14), Garden City - New York.

Noth, M.
1953   *Das Buch Josua* (HAT 7), 2nd ed., Tübingen.

214

Noth, M.
1961   *Das zweite Buch Mose. Exodus* (ATD 5), 2nd ed., Göttingen.

Noth, M
1966   *Das vierte Buch Mose. Numeri* (ATD 7), Göttingen.

Parry, M.
1930, 1932   *Studies in the Epic Technique of Oral Verse-Making.* I: *Homer and Homeric Style,* HSCP, XL, 1930, 73-147, II: *The Homeric Language as a Language of Oral Poetry,* HSCP XLII, 1932, 1-50.

Paul, Sh.
1970   *Studies in the Book of the Covenant in the Light of Cuneiform and Biblical Law* (VT Suppl XVIII), Leiden.

Pope, M.H.
1965   *Job. Introduction, Translation, and Notes* (AB 15), Garden City - New York.

Quell, G.
1925   *Die Auffassung des Todes in Israel,* Leipzig - Erlangen.

von Rad, G.
1957, 1960   *Theologie des Alten Testaments.* I: *Die Theologie der geschichtlichen Überlieferungen Israels* (1957), II: *Die Theologie der prophetischen Überlieferungen Israels* (1960), München.

von Rad, G.
1961   *Das erste Buch Mose. Genesis* (ATD 2-4), 6th ed., Göttingen.

von Rad, G.
1963   *Genesis. A Commentary.* Transl. by J.H. Marks (OTL), 2nd ed., London.

von Rad, G.
1964   *Das fünfte Buch Mose. Deuteronomium* (ATD 8), Göttingen.

Ravndal Hauge, M.
1976   *Fra Dypet til Guds fjell. Til bruken av dødsmotivet i Det gamle testamente,* NTT, 77, 1976, 193-226.

Rendtorff, R.
1977   *Das überlieferungsgeschichtliche Problem des Pentateuch*
               (BZAW 147), Berlin - New York.
Richter, W.
1961   *Traditionsgeschichtliche Untersuchungen zum Richter-
               buch* (BBB 18), Bonn.
Richter, W.
1964   *Die Bearbeitungen des 'Retterbuches' in der deuterono-
               mistischen Epoche* (BBB 21), Bonn.
Richter, W.
1971   *Exegese als Literaturwissenschaft. Entwurf einer alttesta-
               mentlichen Literaturtheorie und Methodologie,* Göttin-
               gen.
Ringgren, H.
1962   *Sprüche* (ATD 16), Göttingen.
Ringgren, H.
1963   *Israelitische Religion* (Die Religionen der Menschheit,
               26), Stuttgart.
Ringgren, H.
1977   *ḥajah,* TWAT II, 1977, 874-898.
Robinson, Th.H. -
Horst, F.
1964   *Die zwölf kleinen Propheten, Hosea bis Micha* (HAT
               14), Tübingen.
Rudolph, W.
1955   *Chronikbücher* (HAT 21), Tübingen.
Rudolph, W.
1968   *Jeremia* (HAT 12), 3rd ed., Tübingen.
Rudolph, W.
1971   *Joel – Amos – Obadja – Jona* (KAT XIII, 2), Gütersloh.
Schmidt, H.W.
1974   *Exodus* (BKAT II, 1), Neukirchen-Vluyn.
Schmitt, A.
1976   *Entrückung – Aufnahme – Himmelfahrt. Untersuch-
               ungen zu einem Vorstellungsbereich im Alten Testament*
               (Forschung zur Bibel, 10), 2nd ed., Stuttgart.

216

Schulz, H.
1969   Das Todesrecht im Alten Testament. Studien zur Rechts-
            form der Mot-Jumat-Sätze (BZAW 114), Berlin.
Schüngel-Straumann, H.
1969   Tod und Leben in der Gesetzesliteratur des Pentateuch
            unter besonderer Berücksichtigung der Terminologie von
            "töten" (diss.), Bonn.
Seligson, M.
1951   The Meaning of næpæš met in the Old Testament,
            Helsinki.
Speiser, E.A.
1964   Genesis. Introduction, Translation, and Notes (AB 1),
            Garden City - New York.
Stoebe, H.J.
1973   Das erste Buch Samuelis (KAT VIII, 1), Gütersloh.
Tromp, N.J.
1969   Primitive Conceptions of Death and the Nether World
            in the Old Testament (Biblica et Orientalia, 21), Rome.
Veijola, T.
1975   Die ewige Dynastie. David und die Entstehung seiner
            Dynastie nach der deuteronomistischen Darstellung
            (Annales Academiae Scientarum Fennicae, B, 193), Hel-
            sinki.
Wanke, G.
1964   Die Zionstheologie der Korachiten in ihrem traditions-
            geschichtlichen Zusammenhang (BZAW 97), Berlin.
Wanke, G.
1974   Exegese des Alten Testaments. Einführung in die Metho-
            dik, hrsg. G. Fohrer ... (UTB 267), Heidelberg.
Watters, W.
1976   Formula Criticism and the Poetry of the Old Testament
            (BZAW 138), Berlin - New York.
Weimar, P.
1974   Die Toledot-Formel in der priesterschriftlichen Ge-
            schichtsdarstellung, BZ, N.F., 18, 1974, 65-93.

Weinfeld, M.
1972   *Deuteronomy and the Deuteronomic School*, Oxford.
Whallon, W.
1969   *Formula, Character, and Context. Studies in Homeric, Old English, and Old Testament Poetry*, Cambridge, Mass.
Whybray, R.N.
1974   *The Intellectual Tradition in the Old Testament* (BZAW 135), Berlin - New York.
Wolff, H.W.
1965   *Dodekapropheton 1, Hosea* (BKAT XIV, 1), 2nd ed., Neukirchen-Vluyn.
Würthwein, E.
1977   *Das erste Buch der Könige. Kap. 1-16* (ATD 11,1), Göttingen.
Wächter, L.
1967   *Der Tod im Alten Testament* (Arbeiten zur Theologie, II, 8), Stuttgart.
Zimmerli, W.
1969   *Exechiel I-II* (BKAT XIII), Neukirchen-Vluyn.

INDEX OF BIBLICAL REFERENCES

Genesis

2,17	104. 105. 106. 197. 198	20,3	22
3,3	113. 114	20,7	104. 105. 157. 188. 197
3,4	113. 114. 116. 197	21,16	63
4,17-24	77	23,1-2	78
5,3	77	23,1	79
5,5	77	23,2	49
5,6-8	77	23,4	190
5,9-11	77	23,6	190
5,12-14	77	23,8	190
5,15-17	77	23,11	190
5,18-20	77	23,13	190
5,22	77	23,15	190
5,23	77	25,7-9	79
5,24	77	25,7-8	78
5,25-27	77	25,7	40. 79
5,28.30-31	77	25,8	43. 45. 46. 47. 189. 191
5,29	77	25,8-9	40. 44
5,32	77	25,11	66. 67
9,28-29	77	25,17	43. 45. 78. 79. 189
9,28	77	25,19-35,29	71
9,29	77	25,32	23
11,32	78f.	26,9	108
15,15	46. 191	26,11	122. 125. 126
19,15	156	26,18	67. 68
19,16	156f.	27,4	21. 34
19,29-20	156	27,7	21
19,19	100. 101	27,10	22. 34
		27,41	185

33,13	100	47,28-29	78. 79
35,8	38. 189	47,28	195
35,9	44	47,29	23. 24. 34. 79
35,19	38. 41. 189	47,30	22. 44
35,22-29	46	48,7	41
35,28-29	78. 79	48,21	20. 21. 34. 185
35,28	40. 78f.	49,29	22f. 43. 44
35,29	40. 43. 45. 47. 189	49,33	43. 44. 189. 195
36,1	71	50,5	20. 34. 185. 190
36,32-39	71	50,15	30. 35
36,32	71	50,16	22. 34
36,39	71	50,22-26	46. 78. 79
37,18	129	50,22	79. 195
37,35	205	50,24	20. 34. 79. 185
38,7	136. 137	50,24f.	34
38,10	136. 137	50,26	195
38,11	111		
38,12	49	*Exodus*	
42,2	112. 115. 154. 155	1,16	116. 117. 166
42,18	157. 160. 204	3,6	106
42,20	113. 114. 157. 159.	4,24	129. 130
	160. 204	6,24	200
42,37	117. 118	8,22	102
42,38	32. 187. 205	9,1-7	200
43,8	112. 115. 154. 155	9,4	32. 33. 110. 111. 115.
44,9	99		137
44,20	32	9,6	32. 33. 133. 137. 200
44,22	100. 101	9,7	32. 33. 133. 137
44,29	205	12,33	22
44,31	100. 101	14,11-12	57. 193
45,28	21. 34. 163	14,11	56
46,30	163	14,12	56
47,15	82. 83	16,3	26. 92. 93
47,19	82. 83. 112. 115. 154.	17,3	92. 93
	155	17,4	102
47,28-50,41	46	19,12-13	159

19,12	204	10,1	33
19,13	102. 159. 204	10,2	33
20,19	112. 113	10,6.7.9.	113. 114
21,12	100. 101. 122. 123.	11,31	143. 144
	125. 131. 200	11,32	143. 144
21,15-17	122	11,39	143. 144
21,15	123	15,31	114
21,16	123	16,1	33. 68
21,17	123. 124	16,2	110. 111
21,18	110. 111. 112. 115	16,12f.	106
21,20	100. 131	16,13	110. 111
21,28-32	102. 201	19,20	122. 126
21,28	100	19,31	205
21,29	116. 117. 120. 121. 126	20,2	102. 123. 124
21,35	100. 160. 162	20,6	205
22,1	100. 131. 200	20,9	123. 124
22,9	142. 201	20,10-16	124
22,13	142. 201	20,10	123. 124
22,18	122. 123	20,11	123. 124
24,1	193	20,12	124
24,9	193	20,13	124
28,35	110. 111	20,15	124
28,42f.	87	20,16	124. 133
28,43	84. 87. 101	20,27	102. 124. 205
30,20-21	114	21,1	202
31,14f.	126	21,1-3	202
31,14	122. 125	21,11	144. 202
31,15	122. 125	21,13	202
33,20	106	24,11	126
33,23	106	24,16	102. 120. 121. 123. 125.
35,2	120. 121. 126		126. 201
		24,17	123. 125
Leviticus		24,21	120
8,35	113. 114	27,29	123. 125
10,1-2	33		
10,1-7	193		

Numbers

1,51	120. 121. 126
3,1	195
3,4	55
3,10	120. 121. 126
3,38	120. 121. 126
4,15	101
4,18-20	204
4,19	114. 154. 155
4,20	101
6,6ff.	144. 202
6,6	144. 202
6,7	144
6,9	144
14,2	55. 56
14,15	116. 117
14,35	53. 54. 55. 157
14,36-38	158
15,32-35	125
15,35	102. 123. 125
16,1ff.	63
16,13	56. 57
16,29	151
16,32	134
16,33	150. 151. 203
16,35	134
17,13	160. 161. 162
17,25	114
18,3	114
18,7	120. 121. 126
18,22	87. 88
18,32	114
19,11	143. 144
19,13	143. 144
19,16	142. 143. 144
19,18	142. 143

20,1	38. 52. 53. 189
20,4	53. 54. 55
20,24	43
20,25	52
20,26	43. 52
20,27	52
20,28	52
21,5	56. 57
23,10	26. 187
26,10	63. 134
26,11	134. 200
26,65	56. 105. 106. 107
27,1ff.	55
27,3	55. 56. 85. 86. 88. 187. 193
27,5ff.	55
27,8-11	193
27,13	43
31,2	43
33,38	52. 53
33,39	64. 66
35,12	110. 111. 136
35,16-21	125
35,16	123. 124. 131
35,17	123. 124. 131
35,18	123. 124. 131
35,19	117. 118. 125. 136. 201
35,21	117. 118. 123. 124. 125. 131. 201
35,25	60
35,28	60f. 67
35,31	123. 124. 125
35,32	60f.
35,36	102. 135

Deuteronomy

4,22	20. 21. 34
5,22	82. 83
5,24-26	157
5,24	157. 159
5,25	157
5,26	157
9,27	193
9,28	56. 57. 193
10,6	52. 53. 188
13,6	120. 126
13,10	133
13,11	102
14,1	50
17,5	102
17,6	120. 126. 201
17,12	102
18,6	112
18,10f.	205
18,16	108. 109
18,20	102
19,6	86. 87
19,11-12	100
19,11	100. 131
19,15	201
20,5-7	89. 111
21,21	102. 201
21,22	86. 87. 88. 121. 126
22,21-25	197
22,21	102
22,24	102
22,25	102. 197
22,26	86. 87. 88
24,7	102
24,16	84. 85. 86. 88. 115. 116 120. 122. 126
30,15	168. 169
30,19	168. 206
31,14	23. 24. 34. 186
31,27	68. 173. 174
31,29	68
32,39	164. 165. 168
32,50	43. 69. 70
33,1	22. 34
33,2ff.7.11.	112
33,6	111. 112. 115. 116. 155. 156
34,1	52
34,5-6	40. 189
34,5	52. 53. 186
34,7	64. 66

Joshua

1,1	66. 67
1,18	120. 121. 126
2,13	167. 168
5,2-9	193
5,4	55. 56
10,26	132
11,17	132. 133
20,2ff.	61
20,6	61
20,9	110. 111
23,14	23
24,29-30	40. 189
24,33	41

Judges

1,1	66. 67
1,7	52. 53

2,8-9	189	*1 Samuel*	
2,10	43. 44. 190	2,6	164. 165. 168
2,19	63. 64. 69	2,25	130. 158
3,25	28. 35	4,11	33
4,22	28. 35	4,17	33
5,18	27	5,10-12	137
6,22	106	5,10	134
6,23	109. 110	5,11	119. 134
6,30	103	5,12	134
6,31	120. 121.	8,1	62
8,32	38. 46. 189	11,12	117. 118. 140
8,33	69. 70	12,18	188
9,23-24	187	12,19	112.115. 188
9,54	91. 187	12,21	188
9,55	30. 35	12,23	188
9,56f.	187	14,39	105. 106. 134. 137
9,56	30	14,41	84. 117
10,1-5	37	14,43	22. 134
10,2	188	14,44	104. 105. 134. 137. 197
10,5	188	14,45f.	105
12,7-15	37	14,45	134. 137
12,7	188	15,35	62
12,10	188	17,35	132
12,12	188	17,50	91. 132
12,15	188	17,51	31. 35. 91
12,17	188	19,2	129. 130
13,7	62	19,6	175
13,22	106	20,2	109
13,23	106. 130. 158	20,8	84. 117
15,13	119	20,14	107
15,18	93	20,31	127. 174. 175
16,16	27	20,32	82. 97. 120. 121
16,30	26. 65. 66. 174	22,16	104. 105. 197
20,13	117. 118	24,15	145
21,5	123. 126	25,1	39. 41. 48. 62. 189
		25,39	29. 30. 35

26,10	99. 196
26,15	199
26,16	127. 175
28,3	41. 48. 62. 189
30,15	118
31,4	128. 187
31,5	31. 128. 129
31,7	31

2 Samuel

1,1	66. 67
1,4	128. 129
1,5	31. 32. 35
1,9	168
1,10	168
1,12	192
1,15-16	168
1,15	131
1,23	174
2,7	187
2,23	128. 129
2,31	132
3,30	192
3,31	192
3,32	192
4,1	29. 35
4,7	132. 133
4,10	27. 28. 31. 32. 35
6,6f.	196
6,6	52
6,7	52. 53
6,20	62
6,23	62. 80
8,2	165. 166
9,8	145
10,1	71. 194

10,18	131
11,15	100. 131
11,21	131. 132
11,26	29. 35. 49
12,5	127. 175. 199
12,13	88. 109. 198
12,14	105. 106
12,18-19	35
12,18	31. 160. 161
12,21	69. 70. 160. 161
13,28	116. 117
13,32	187
13,39	49
14,6	132
14,14	106. 107
14,32	84. 116. 117
15,21	171
16,9	145
17,23	38. 189. 191
18,15	132
19,1	26
19,7	22. 160. 161
19,11	89
19,23	120. 121
19,24	109. 198
19,29	127
19,38	190
20,3	174. 175
20,10	131. 132
20,19	129. 130
21,9	122
21,13	44
22,5-6	146. 148. 152
22,5	147
22,6	147. 149. 150

1 Kings

1,51	90. 118
1,52	99
2,1	23. 24. 34. 186
2,2	23. 185
2,8	90. 118
2,24	120. 121. 136. 175
2,25	136. 137. 201
2,26	119. 127. 136
2,29	136
2,34	136. 137. 201
2,37	104. 105. 134. 136. 188. 197
2,42	104. 105. 134. 136. 197
2,46	136. 137. 201
3,21	28. 35
3,22-23	161. 162. 167
3,22	160
3,23	161
3,26-27	167
11,21	29. 35
11,40	61. 129. 130
12,18	102. 135. 137. 201
13,22	191
13,29	192
14,1-18	192
14,11	92. 94. 196
14,12	49
14,13	49
14,17	49
14,18	49
15,27f.	73
15,27	74
15,28	75
16,4	92. 94. 196
16,9-10	76
16,9	74
16,10	73. 75. 132. 133
16,18	76
16,22	72. 76
18,3	140
18,9	140
19,4	25. 169
19,17	91. 118. 196
21,10ff.	102
21,10	103. 135
21,13	135
21,14	135
21,15	135. 160
21,16	30. 35. 135
21,20	135
21,21	135
21,24	92. 94. 135. 196
21,25	135

2 Kings

1,1	68
1,2	71
1,4ff.	105
1,4	104. 105. 197
1,6	104. 105. 197
1,16	71. 104. 105. 197
1,17	79
4,16-17	28
4,32	28. 35
5,7	165. 166
6,33	189
7,4	118. 166. 193
7,17	135. 137
7,18-20	136
7,20	135
8,5	167

8,10	72. 105. 106. 107. 156	25,25	131
8,11f.	72		
8,15	72	*Isaiah*	
8,23	72	6,4	106
11,1	31. 35	8,19	161. 162
11,8	120. 121. 126	11,4	118
11,15	90	14,30	92. 93. 116
11,20	90	22,2	89. 141
12,21f.	72. 76. 131	22,18	53. 54
13,1	73	24,18	204
13,14	24. 25. 39. 189	25,8	182
13,20f.	189	26,7	163
13,20	25. 39	26,10-11	163
13,22ff.	72	26,11	163
13,24	72	26,14	142. 162. 163. 164. 205
14,6	85. 86. 88. 115. 116. 121. 122. 127	26,19	142. 162. 163. 164. 202. 205
14,17	68	26,20	163
14,19	133	28,15	149. 150. 203
15,5	62	28,18	149. 150. 203
15,10	73. 74. 133	37,38	73. 76
15,13	75	38,1	24. 156
15,14	73. 74. 75. 132. 133	38,10	146
15,25	74. 75. 132. 133	38,18-19	173
15,27	75	38,18	149. 150. 172
15,30	74. 75. 133	38,19	173
18,29-31	155	45,6-7	165
18,32	114. 115, 155. 196	51,14	110. 111. 112. 115
19,37	73. 76	53,9	150
20,1	24. 156	53,12	27
20,3	24. 25	57,1	44
20,4-8	24	65,11	117
20,9-20	24	65,15	116
22,10	191		
22,20	43. 44		
25,3-7	193		

Jeremiah

4,8	192
8,2	44
8,3	169
11,21	109. 116
11,22	93. 94
14,12	95
14,15	94
14,16	94
14,18	94
15,2	95
16,4-5	50
16,4	50. 94
16,5	50
16,6-7	50. 51
16,6	50
16,7	51
17,11	194
18,21	95. 133
20,6	53. 54
21,6	93
21,7	95
21,8	168. 169
21,9	95. 158. 159. 204
22,10	50
22,12	53. 54
24,10	95
26,8	104. 105. 197
26,11	86. 87
26,16	86. 87
26,21	129. 130
27,8	95
27,12-13	157
27,12	83
27,13	83. 95. 159
28,16	22

29,17.18	95
31,29f.	122
31,30	84
32,24.26	95
34,2ff.	109
34,4/5	90. 109
34,17	95
37,20	53. 54. 108. 109
38,2	95. 159. 204
38,4	121
38,6ff.	185
38.9	92
38,10	23. 185
38,16	118
38,24	109. 116
38,25	119
38,26	53. 54
39,1-7	193
41.2	91. 132. 200
42,16	53. 54. 94
42,17	95
42,22	95
44,12	94. 128
44,17	95
44,27	94
48,44	204
49,3	192
52,6-11	193
52,11	62
52,27	132
52,33-34	62
52,33	62
52,34	62. 174. 175

Ezechiel

3,17-21	85. 187

3,18	84. 104. 105	31,14	140
3,19	84	31,16	140
3,20	85. 88	31,18	140
5,12	95. 96. 128. 196	32,17ff.	201
6,11	96. 128	33,1-9	85. 187
6,12	95. 96. 128	33,8	84. 104. 105
7,15	95. 96	33,9	84
7,16	84	33,11	63. 83. 130. 158
12,12	54	33,13	85
12,13	53. 54	33,14	104. 105
12,16	54. 96	33,15	110. 155
13,19	166	33,18	85
18,4	86. 88	33,27	94. 128
18,10ff.	85	44,25	144. 202
18,10	86		
18,13	123. 126. 204	*Hosea*	
18,14ff.	85	2,5	116
18,17	84. 204	6,2	163
18,18	28. 35. 84	9,11-13	176
18,20	88	9,16	116. 176
18,21	110. 155		
18,22f.	122	*Joel*	
18,23	130. 158. 204	1,13	192
18,24	85		
18,26	85	*Amos*	
18,28	110. 155	5,3	204
18,31	83	7,9	90
18,32	63. 130. 158	7,11	89. 90
24,16-17	50	7,17	54
24,16	50. 51	9,10	86. 88. 90
24,17	50. 51		
28,2	142	*Jonah*	
28,8	142	2,4.6	147
28,10	54. 142	4,3	169
31,4	201	4,8	25. 169

Micah		88,11	142
1,8	192	89,48f.	203
		89,49	149. 150. 151. 156
Habakkuk		90,9	203
1,12	198	91,16	191
		93,4	147
Psalms		102,12	203
7,14	147	107,18	146
9,14	146	107,20	146
9,15	146	109,3	203
18,5-6	146. 148. 152	116,3	147. 148. 149. 150.
18,5	147. 203		152. 203
18,6	147. 149. 150. 203	116,8-9	172
22,16	147	116,8	141. 152. 172
26,9	44	116,9	172
33,19	141. 152. 165. 167.	118,17	108. 115. 116. 155. 156
	168. 172	118,18	140
36,10	147	143,3	142. 143
37,32	129. 130		
39,6ff.	203	*Job*	
39,14	23	1,19	128. 129
41,6	151	1,21	194
42,8	147	3,20-21	169
49,15	149. 150. 203	5,2	118
49,18ff.	174	5,20	89
49,18-19	174	10,21	23
49,18	65. 66	14,14	156. 163
49,20	174	14,16	156
55,16	149. 150. 151	26,6	151
56,14	141. 152. 172	27,15	190
69,2.15	147	28,22	150
78,50	93. 172	30,23	173
78,51	93	33,22	173
86,13	141. 172	36,14	174. 175
88,6	142	38,16	146
88,8	147	38,17	146

42,16-17	78	*Song of Songs*	
42,16	46	8,6	149. 150
42,17	45. 46. 79		
		Ecclesiastes	
Proverbs		3,2	176
5,5	149. 150. 169. 170. 171	3,19	151
5,6	169. 171	4,2	161. 162
7,27	148. 149. 150	5,14f.	194
8,35-36	169. 170. 171	7,1	63. 176
10,2	141	7,16f.	83
10,11	147	7,17	82
11,4	141	8,8	63
11,7	63. 64. 151	9,3	174
11,19	169. 170. 171	9,4	145. 161. 162
12,28	169. 170. 171	9,5	161. 162
13,14	147. 148. 170. 171		
14,12	148	*Lamentations*	
14,27	147. 148. 170. 171	3,6	142. 143. 202
14,32	65. 66	3,54	147
16,14-15	170	4,19	94
16,14	170. 171		
16,15	170. 171	*Esther*	
16,22	147	2,7	63. 64
16,25	148	4,11	166
18,21	170. 171		
19,16	121	*Daniel*	
21,6	148	12,2	163
23,13	110. 111. 116		
23,14	110	*1 Chronicles*	
24,11	133	1,44-50	71
30,7	21. 34	1,50	71
		2,3	136. 137
Ruth		2,24	67
1,17	190	2,30	80
2,11	68	2,31	80
2,20	161. 162. 165	2,32	80

2,34ff.	80	23,21	90
2,34	80	24,15-16	39
10,5	31. 35. 128	24,15	46. 65. 66
10,7	31	24,16	40
13,9	52	24,17	67
13,10	52. 53	24,25	72. 73. 76. 133
19,1	71. 194	24,26-27	73
22,5	22. 34	24,27	72. 76
23,1	45. 46	25,1	73
23,22	80	25,4	85. 86. 88. 115. 116. 122
29,26-27	71	25,25	68
29,28	46. 47. 71	26,21	62
		32,11	93. 196
2 Chronicles		32,24	24
10,18	102. 135. 137. 201	32,25-26	186
15,13	121. 127	32,33	65. 66
22,4	68	34,28	43
22,9	190		
22,10	31. 35	*Matthew*	
23,7	121. 127	26,60	201
23,14	90. 119. 121. 127		

PUBLICATIONS OF THE RESEARCH INSTITUTE OF THE ÅBO AKADEMI FOUNDATION

1. Nils Erik Enkvist (ed.), Reports on Text Linguistics: Four Papers on Text, Style and Syntax, Åbo 1974 (ISBN-951-648-142-6)

2. Karl-Johan Illman, Leitwort – Tendenz – Synthese, Programm und Praxis in der Exegese Martin Bubers, Åbo 1975. (ISBN-951-648-164-7)

3. Mechelinska senatens förslag till regeringsform, Åbo 1975. (ISBN-951-648-170-1)

4. Krister Ståhlberg, Teori och praxis i kommunal planering, Åbo 1975. (ISBN-951-648-189-2)

5. Aulis Gröndahl, Sociologistudier i smågrupper, Åbo 1976. (ISBN-951-648-208-2)

6. Henrik Schauman, Hugo E. Pippings tryckta skrifter 1955 – 1975, Åbo 1976. (ISBN-951-648-216-3)

7. Auli Hakulinen, Reports on Text Linguistics: Suomen kielen generatiivista lauseoppia 2, Åbo 1976. (ISBN-951-648-213-9)

8. Nils Erik Enkvist and Viljo Kohonen (editors), Reports on Text Linguistics: Approaches to Word Order, Åbo 1976. (ISBN-951-648-214-7)

9. Jan Otto Andersson, Studies in the Theory of Unequal Exchange between Nations, Åbo 1976. (ISBN-951-648-218-X)

10. Börje Ekelund, Fysikaliska modeller. En elementär inledning till fysikalisk epistemologi med några tillämpningar på fysikalisk didaktik, Åbo 1976. (ISBN-951-648-233-3)

11. Gustav Björkstrand, Åkerblom-rörelsen. En finlandssvensk profetrörelses uppkomst, utveckling och sönderfall, Åbo 1976. (ISBN-951-648-251-1)

12. Karl-Gustav Sandelin, Die Auseinandersetzung mit der Weisheit in 1. Korinther 15, Åbo 1976. (ISBN-951-648-252-X)

13. Karl-Johan Illman, Thema und Tradition in den Asaf-Psalmen, Åbo 1976. (ISBN-951-648-259-7)

14. Olle Anckar, Finansiering av den högre utbildningen, Åbo 1976. (ISBN-951-648-267-8)

15. Samhällsforskning kring finlandssvensk framtid. Symposium i Åbo den 2 och 3 oktober 1976, Åbo 1977. (ISBN-951-648-268-6)

16. Dag Anckar, Lagstiftning, transformation, responsivitet. Skisser kring ett forskningsprogram, Åbo 1977. (ISBN-951-648-272-5)

17. Lauri Karvonen, Mellanstatlig intervention: teori-inventering, modellbygge och en tillämpning, Åbo 1977. (ISBN-951-648-255-4)

18. Erik Andersson, Verbfrasens struktur i svenskan. En studie i aspekt, tempus, tidsadverbial och semantisk räckvidd, Åbo 1977. (ISBN-951-648-292-9)

19. Föredrag vid konferensen om kontrastiv lingvistik och felanalys, Stockholm & Åbo, 7–8 Februari 1977, Åbo 1977. (ISBN-951-648-300-3)

20. Krister Ståhlberg, Politik och planering. Några kritiska uppsatser kring planering inom statsförvaltningen, Åbo 1977. (ISBN-951-648-325-9)

21. Aulis Gröndahl och Gunnar Grönblom, Radioförkunnare och deras budskap, Åbo 1977. (ISBN-951-648-326-7)

22. Siv Storå, Olof Lagercrantz tryckta skrifter 1933-1950, Åbo 1977. (ISBN-951-648-323-2)

23. Börje Ekelund, Beschleunigungssatz und Kraftbegriff, Åbo 1977. (ISBN-951-648-331-3)

24. Hans-Olof Kvist, Zum Verhältnis von Wissen und Glauben in der kritischen Philosophie Immanuel Kants, Åbo 1978. (ISBN-951-648-342-9)

25. Politik och förvaltning. Fyrtio år statskunskap vid Åbo Akademi, Åbo 1978. (ISBN-951-648-363-1)

26. Leif Finnäs, Några föräldrakarakteristikas samband med relativ skolprestation, Åbo 1978. (ISBN-951-648-364-X)

27. Fride Hedman, Människosyner och vårdmodeller. En studie i terapi och själavård, Åbo 1978. (ISBN-951-648-365-8)

28. Lars Nyström, On the Steady and Disturbed Flow of Material through Rotary Kilns, Åbo 1978. (ISBN-951-648-366-6)

29. Dag Anckar, Politik som studieobjekt. Nio essäer, Åbo 1978. (ISBN-951-648-367-4)

30. Göran Djupsund och Krister Ståhlberg, Korporativisering och byråkratisering i finländsk politik: Två motresponsiva drag, Åbo 1978. (ISBN-951-648-368-2)

31. Nils G. Holm, Pingströrelsen. En religionsvetenskaplig studie av pingströrelsen i Svenskfinland, Åbo 1978. (ISBN-951-648-380-1)

32. Jouko Martikainen, Das Böse und der Teufel in der Theologie Efraems des Syrers, Åbo 1978. (ISBN-951-648-381-X)

33. Lauri Karvonen och Dag Anckar, Om innovativa lagar. Begreppsanalys, mätapparat, empiriska applikationer, Åbo 1978. (ISBN-951-648-391-7)

34. Rune Ingo, Suomen kielen pluratiivit eli monikkosanat, Turku 1978. (ISBN-951-648-392-5)

35. Henrik Nikula, Kontextuell und lexikalisch bedingte Ellipse, Åbo 1978. (ISBN-951-648-408-5)

36. Sven Lindman (utg.), Karl H. Wiiks dagbok. Från storstrejken till upproret 1917 - 1918, Åbo 1978. (ISBN-951-648-431-X)

37. Erik Andersson (ed.), Working Papers on Computer Processing of Syntactic Data, Åbo 1978. (ISBN-951-648-419-0)

38. Viljo Kohonen, On the Development of English Word Order in Religious Prose around 1000 and 1200 A.D., Åbo 1978. (ISBN-951-648-432-8)

39. Nils Winter, Tillväxtstrategier inom sjöfarten med casefall för Finland, Åbo 1979. (ISBN-951-648-442-5)

40. Dag Anckar, Politik, partier, policy: om modeller för arenaförande, Åbo 1979. (ISBN-951-648-443-3)

41. Jan-Ola Östman (ed.), Reports on Text Linguistics: Semantics and Cohesion, Åbo 1979. (ISBN-951-648-447-6)

42. Bengt-Olof Qvarnström, Formalizations of Trubetzkoy's phonology, Åbo 1979. (ISBN-951-648-469-7)

43. Claes Gustafsson, Om utsagor om makt, Åbo 1979. (ISBN-951-648-484-0)

44. Pegas och snöbollskrig. Litteraturvetenskapliga studier tillägnade Sven Linnér, Åbo 1979. (ISBN-951-648-504-9)

45. Sven Lindman, Presidentens ställning. Fyra uppsatser och en efterskrift, Åbo 1979. (ISBN-951-648-523-5)

46. Hans-Olof Kvist, Två essäer i Moral, Kunskap, Religion, Åbo 1979. (ISBN-951-648-534-0 ISSN-0356-7109)

47. Karl-Johan Illman und Jukka Thurén (hrsg.), Der Herr ist Einer, under gemeinsames Erbe, Åbo 1979. (ISBN-951-648-535-9 ISSN-0356-7109)

48. Karl-Johan Illman, Old Testament Formulas about Death, Åbo 1979. (ISBN-951-648-544-8 ISSN-0356-7109